RELIGION
AND POLITICAL
DEVELOPMENT

The Little, Brown Series

in Comparative Politics

Under the Editorship of

GABRIEL A. ALMOND

JAMES S. COLEMAN

LUCIAN W. PYE

AN ANALYTIC STUDY

RELIGION
AND POLITICAL
DEVELOPMENT

Donald Eugene Smith
University of Pennsylvania

Boston

LITTLE, BROWN AND COMPANY

Published simultaneously in Canada
by Little, Brown & Company (Canada) Limited

PRINTED IN THE UNITED STATES OF AMERICA

For
VIOLET
on our twentieth wedding anniversary

Foreword

THE Little, Brown Series in Comparative Politics has three main objectives. First, it will meet the need of teachers to deal with both Western and non-Western countries in their introductory course offerings. Second, by following a common approach in analyzing individual political systems, it will make it possible for teachers to compare these countries systematically and cumulatively. And third, it will contribute toward re-establishing the classic relationship between comparative politics and political theory, a relationship which has been neglected in recent decades. In brief, the series seeks to be global in scope, genuinely introductory and comparative in character, and concerned with broadening and deepening our understanding of the nature and variety of political systems.

The series has two parts: the Country Studies and the Analytic Studies. The Country Studies deal with problems and processes deriving from a functional, as compared with a purely structural, approach to the study of political systems. We are gratified that the participants, all mature scholars with original insights, were willing to organize their discussions around a common set of functional topics in the interest of furthering comparisons. At the same time, each author has been urged to adapt the common framework to the special problems of the country he is discussing and to express his own theoretical point of view.

An introductory book, *Comparative Politics: A Developmental Approach,* written by Gabriel A. Almond and G. Bingham Powell, provides an analytic supplement to the Country Studies. It also opens our set of Analytic Studies, which will offer basic discussions of such topics as political change in the emerging nations, comparative analyses of interest groups, political socialization, political communication, political culture, and the like. We hope these books will prove to be useful and stimulating supplements to the Country Studies as well as points of departure in more advanced courses.

Donald E. Smith's analysis, *Religion and Political Development,* fills a serious gap in the literature dealing with political development. Students of this process have long argued that the prospects for modernization in the new nations are significantly limited and affected by the characteristics of the pre-existing traditional system. Much of this traditional structure and culture is comprised in the ideas, practices, and institutions of religion. Smith shows how Hinduism, Buddhism, Islam, and Catholicism differ in their influence on the processes of cultural secularization and structural differentiation in the countries of South and Southeast Asia, the Middle East, North Africa, and Latin America. His book is the first sustained comparative analysis of this fundamentally important aspect of political modernization.

Gabriel A. Almond
James S. Coleman
Lucian W. Pye

Preface

RELIGION constitutes the core of the traditional cultures of
South and Southeast Asia, the Middle East, North Africa, and
Latin America, and it is meaningful to use religious designa-
tions in referring to these societies as Hindu, Buddhist, Muslim, or Catholic societies. In this book we will explore the
relationship between traditional religions and political development. It is widely, and correctly, assumed that religion is in
general an obstacle to modernization, and a major part of this
analysis is concerned with the complex phenomenon of secularization. However, different religious systems present obstacles at different points, so that while the secularization of
law creates fundamental religiopolitical conflicts in an Islamic
society, it constitutes no problem at all in a Buddhist society.
Then, too, religious factors have played and continue to play
a positive role in certain aspects of political development,
and these factors are explored in the chapters dealing with
politicization and religious legitimation of change.

After surveying the numerous definitions of political development, Lucian Pye concluded that three major themes were
common to many of them: (1) an emphasis on the differentiation and specialization of political institutions and structures;
(2) an emphasis on equality, in particular the idea that political development involves mass participation in politics; and
(3) an emphasis on the increasing capacity of a political system

xi

to direct social and economic change.[1] In the present study
the purpose will be to relate these three major themes to the
religious factor in developing societies. Starting with the disruption of traditional religiopolitical systems, the secularization of polities is a major aspect of *differentiation,* separating
the political from the religious structures. Religious symbols,
leaders, and organizations have served as vehicles to bring the
masses into the political process, producing *mass participation.*
In traditional societies, religion is a mass phenomenon, politics
is not; but religion can be used to make politics meaningful.
Religious values are also an important influence on political
culture, and predispose individuals and societies toward certain patterns of political life. Last, in the contemporary third
world, religions are being reinterpreted to provide ideological
support for political systems seeking to increase their *capacity*
to direct socioeconomic change.

This is the first systematic attempt to analyze the relationship between religion and political development on a broadly
comparative basis. The neglect of this area of comparative research is truly remarkable, considering the intellectual antecedents. It is somehow overlooked that for Max Weber, that
towering figure whose work has in other areas so profoundly
influenced contemporary social science, the relationship between religion and social change was an intellectual problem
of fundamental importance. Weber's research went far beyond
the Protestant-ethic thesis; he was concerned with "the deter-
mination of what was distinctive for the West by comparison
of the causes and consequences of religious beliefs in different civilizations."[2] He was thus drawn into the intensive
study of society and religion in China, India, and ancient
Palestine.

The achievement of political independence by a large
number of Hindu, Buddhist, and Muslim societies since 1947
has provided a richness of empirical data which Weber could

[1] Lucian W. Pye, *Aspects of Political Development* (Boston: Little,
Brown and Co., 1966), pp. 45–47.

[2] Reinhard Bendix, *Max Weber: An Intellectual Portrait* (Garden City,
N.Y.: Anchor Books, Doubleday, 1962), p. 84.

not have dreamed of. The present study is a result of research and reflection on this general problem over a period of fifteen years and follows in a more broadly comparative perspective scholarly concerns which were expressed in earlier books: *India as a Secular State* (1963), *Religion and Politics in Burma* (1965), and a volume which I edited, *South Asian Politics and Religion* (1966). These volumes followed three years of research work in South and Southeast Asia. My field experience in other parts of the third world has been limited to brief visits in the Middle East and three months spent in Latin America (Mexico, Colombia, and Chile) during the summer of 1968. This is admittedly an inadequate base of firsthand knowledge to attempt the task set forth in this book; I find consolation in the thought that the scholar with true competence in all the subjects treated here probably does not exist.

My earlier research on religion and politics was made possible by a Fulbright senior research grant (India) and a grant from the Carnegie Corporation of New York for a three-year project which I directed under the auspices of the Council on Religion and International Affairs. Directly contributing to the work on this book were a summer research fellowship from the University of Pennsylvania (1966) and a summer research grant from the Joint Committee on Latin American Studies of the Social Science Research Council (1968). I gratefully acknowledge the support of these institutions which made the research possible.

It is also a pleasure to acknowledge the help of three research assistants who contributed to this project: Miss Louella J. Long and Mr. Robert E. Paul, students at the University of Pennsylvania, and my wife, Violet R. Smith, who did most of the bibliographic work.

I have benefited greatly from discussions with several colleagues in both the Political Science Department and South Asia Regional Studies Department at the University of Pennsylvania concerning problems discussed here. A graduate seminar in the spring of 1969 provided the first nineteen friendly critics of the substance of this book. I am very grateful for the criticisms and suggestions made by the members of the seminar and equally so for the puzzled expressions which, on occasion, instantaneously communicated my failure to make a point. In successive revisions I have made every effort to take both into account. Finally, I am deeply indebted to Professor Gabriel A. Almond, co-editor of the Series in Comparative Politics, whose valuable suggestions have led to substantial additions to the original manuscript.

                                        Donald Eugene Smith

Table of Contents

xv

Chapter VIII

Religious Systems and Political Development 246

"Historical accidents" and religious systems. Hinduism: ahistorical-organic system. Buddhism: ahistorical church system. Islam: historical-organic system. Catholicism: historical-church system.

RELIGION
AND POLITICAL
DEVELOPMENT

CHAPTER I

Political and Religious Change

DEFINITIONS of modernization have frequently emphasized the technological and economic aspects of change. However, as Manfred Halpern has reminded us, the revolution of modernization "involves the transformation of all systems by which man organizes his society — the political, social, economic, intellectual, religious, and psychological systems." [1] In this book we are primarily concerned with the complex processes by which the traditional relationships between society, polity, and religion are being radically altered. The process is fundamentally one of differentiation, by which integralist sacral societies governed by religiopolitical systems are being transformed into pluralist desacralized societies directed by greatly expanded secular polities.

The analysis which is presented in this book relates to that large part of the third world in which traditional societies have been integrated by one of four major religious systems: Hinduism, Theravada Buddhism, Islam, Roman Catholicism. The geographic regions thus encompassed are vast: South and Southeast Asia, the Middle East, North Africa, and Latin America. The rationale of the scope of this inquiry is based on four points: (1) the developing societies integrated by major religious traditions face many of the same problems of political develop-

[1] Manfred Halpern, "Toward Further Modernization of the Study of New Nations," *World Politics,* vol. 17 (October 1964), p. 173.

ment; (2) these same basic problems were faced in the modernization of the West; (3) the problems are substantially different in areas of the third world not integrated by major religious
traditions; and (4) the differences among the four religious
traditions constitute key variables in explaining different patterns of political development. A brief elaboration of these
points will be helpful in establishing the considerable significance of the religious factor in development.

All the major extant civilizations, according to Toynbee,
have been predominantly religious in orientation and as such
evolved remarkably similar answers to some of the major questions of social and political organization. Most basic was the
essentially sacral nature of government, a firm belief of Hindus,
Buddhists, Muslims, and Catholics alike at the beginning of
the nineteenth century. *From that time to this, the secularization of the polity has been the most fundamental structural and
ideological change in the process of political development.* Because all traditional polities were religiopolitical systems, many
of the basic societal patterns were similar and the conflicts produced by secularization have assumed similar forms.

Many writers on political development have attempted with
uneasiness to bridge the gulf between Asia-Africa and Latin
America. The historical differences (primarily in the imperial-
ism-nationalism syndrome) have presented serious difficulties
for those seeking to create a conceptual framework for truly
comparative analysis. The question treated in this book considerably strengthens the rationale for analysis which attempts
to deal comparatively with South and Southeast Asia, the
Middle East, North Africa, and Latin America.

Unfortunately, in the past such comparative work was dis-
couraged by the researchers' use of a particular set of static institutional concepts with reference to Latin America: "church,"
"state," and "church-state relations." Strongly biased in favor
of juridical and constitutional considerations, these concepts
did not produce the most meaningful results even for Latin
American studies and were totally useless for cross-cultural
comparisons. Since there was nothing even faintly resembling
a church in the Islamic world, an important comparative question could not even be asked.

The pre-1810 Spanish Empire in America, as a traditional religiopolitical system, had fundamental affinities with the Hindu, Buddhist, and Muslim polities of that time. Many of the processes of change have therefore been similar. If the modernizers have found it necessary to secularize law and judicial structures in Mexico, this has also been a problem in Egypt and India. And, interestingly, in Catholic, Muslim, and Hindu societies alike, family law (especially regarding marriage and divorce) has remained the last bastion of the religious concept of law. The process of state secularization of education has been found in virtually every society encompassed by this study. Above all, the erosion or destruction of the religious legitimation of governments, with or without formal constitutional changes, has been a prominent phenomenon everywhere.

In the conflicts engendered by secularization, Catholic, Buddhist, and Islamic religious functionaries have emerged as powerful political leaders. As the politics of mass participation has increasingly become a reality, Catholic, Hindu, and Islamic political parties have appeared. And as the indigenous religious traditions have attempted to come to terms with the problems of socioeconomic change, the ideological innovations have included Catholic, Hindu, Buddhist, and Islamic versions of socialism. Religious tradition has not only molded the institutions of the *ancien régime* but continued as an existential reality, still the core of third-world man's culture, a vital intellectual resource and psychological support.

The second major point is that political development in the West, stretched over a period of five centuries, was a process very similar to the one just outlined. The contemporary nation-states of the West evolved out of a medieval religiopolitical system of Catholic integralism. The medieval synthesis was cracked open by the Reformation and Renaissance, nationalism challenged the religious basis of political community, and the secularization conflicts of individual states have occupied an important place in Western history right up to the present time. And should the observer be tempted to think that complete secularism characterizes public life in the West today, he must be reminded that Christian Democratic parties have dominated the governments of two major Western democracies, Italy and West Germany, since the end of World War II.

Third, the problems of political development are substantially different in areas of the third world not integrated by major religious traditions. In an incisive essay, Ibrahim Abu-Lughod points to the commonality of the European-Asian experience and its sharp difference from that of sub-Saharan Africa. "The first manifestations of national consciousness and, therefore, the early attempts of the European and Asian civilizations to translate that consciousness into concrete political reality in the form of national states meant, *inter alia,* a rejection of the original premises of the religiously rooted political system, religiously defined political frontiers, and the religiously based membership in the political community." [2] In the absence of powerful integrating religious traditions, sub-Saharan Africans could evolve a national consciousness free from the religious complications that accompanied it elsewhere.[3] On the other hand, of course, without broadly integrative value systems, tribalism continued to constitute a serious obstacle to the development of national consciousness.

In the development of ideology the African leaders were not inhibited by the existence of sophisticated religious belief systems but could proceed directly to choose from among the most advanced patterns of thought offered by modernity. As will be demonstrated in detail in Chapter VII, Hindus, Buddhists, Muslims, and Catholics had to reconcile their respective traditions first with liberalism and then with socialism. In large measure all of this immense intellectual effort, exerted over a period of a century and a quarter, amounted to the rationalization of secularism. Religious ideas had lost their power to direct men's actions or mold their institutions, but it was psychologically necessary to prove that the new ideas were not new, but simply restatements of eternal verities already found in the religious tradition. In sharp contrast was the ideo-

---

[2] Ibrahim Abu-Lughod, "Nationalism in a New Perspective: The African Case," in Herbert J. Spiro, ed., *Patterns of African Development: Five Comparisons* (Englewood Cliffs, N.J.: Prentice-Hall, Inc., 1967), p. 39.

[3] *Ibid.,* p. 42.

logical climate of sub-Saharan African politics: "African leaders, whose religious background, when present, was derivative
in nature, had grown in an atmosphere of almost total acceptance of secular society; for the most part there was no conflict
on this issue when the independent state emerged." [4] The
superiority of rationality and the scientific method was taken
for granted; witchcraft and magic, while widely practiced, already stood discredited intellectually. The African leaders embraced socialism as the modern world's most relevant ideological
guide to development and change. This was done with a direct-
ness which was impossible in other parts of the third world.

The fourth and last point is that the four religious systems
considered here constitute key variables in explaining different
patterns of political development. Each of the four systems is
a distinct complex of belief, ritual, socioreligious institution,
and ecclesiastical organization; and the differences among them
produce very different political consequences. Three comparative statements about political phenomena which point to
major characteristics of the Buddhist religious system serve to
illustrate the differences: (1) Buddhist monks in Burma, Ceylon,
and South Vietnam are powerful political activists, deciding
elections and overthrowing governments, while Hindu priests
and holy men in India are of negligible political importance;
(2) there are Hindu, Muslim, and Catholic political parties,
but no Theravada Buddhist political parties; and (3) major
conflicts have arisen over the secularization of law in Hindu,
Muslim, and Catholic societies, but not in Buddhist societies.
These statements elicit the natural question: Why? A later discussion suggests that the political phenomena are related to
important systemic characteristics of Buddhism. Thus, each of
the four systems has highly significant elements of uniqueness.

TRADITIONAL RELIGIOPOLITICAL SYSTEMS

Religion integrates a traditional society by providing it with
a common framework of meaning and experience. Through
the ordinary processes of socialization, the young acquire a
common set of beliefs and values associated with symbols of

[4] *Ibid.*, p. 46.

the sacred. Participating in the same rituals, celebrating the same festivals, bearing the names of the same gods or saints, shunning the same tabus, members of the society are integrated at a profound affective level. Much of the material and artistic culture of the traditional society — art, architecture, literature, music, dance — is expressive of religious ideas and values, and indeed, much of it originated in the setting of the cult.

The sacred permeates the principal social institutions. Laws are divine commands, based on sacred texts or otherwise revealed to man. Where social classes and orders are ranked hierarchically, this pyramidal social system is divinely ordained. All education is religious in content and transmitted by religious specialists. Divine regulations govern economic behavior and ecclesiastical centers frequently wield extensive economic power. Above all, government is sacral. Religion and government, the two major society-wide institutions of social control, form an integrated religiopolitical system.

The following profile of a traditional religiopolitical system is derived from a wide range of states in South and Southeast Asia, the Middle East, North Africa, and Latin America at the beginning of the nineteenth century. First, the ideological component of the system is provided entirely by religion; there are no secular ideologies. Religious ideas maintain the legitimacy of the system and specifically of the ruler; all traditional monarchs rule by virtue of some theory of the divine right or divinity of kings. In many traditional systems, "temple, altar and deity possess a structure strictly analogous with palace, throne and king, for the state is the embodiment of the cosmic totality." [5]

This vital connection between religion and polity, so widespread as to be almost universal, is rooted, psychologically and doctrinally, in fundamental assumptions about *power*. The exercise of power is at the center of the polity and in virtually all cultures power is an attribute of divinity. In the Semitic (Judaeo-Christian-Islamic) religious stream the deity is the almighty, the omnipotent creator; in the Indic (Hindu-Buddhist) reli-

[5] Arend T. van Leeuwen, *Christianity in World History* (London: Edinburgh House Press, 1965), p. 166.

gions the consorts of the gods are *shakti,* divine creative power, and the Buddha himself becomes deified as the reigning lord of the universe. The equation of power with divinity makes inevitable the assertion that he who wields almost unlimited power, the ruler, is either himself divine or an agent of divinity.

Second, the political community of a traditional religiopolitical system is identical with the religious community in theory and substantially so in fact. Apostasy is dealt with severely in all these societies, no matter how loosely structured the established belief system is, for the worship of new gods is thought to be incompatible with loyalty to the ruler, who is divine, semidivine, or endowed with divine powers. Third, it is the religiously integrated and legitimated social system, not an efficient governmental apparatus, which enables the ruler to maintain stability in the realm over considerable periods of time. Fourth, religious specialists perform essential rituals which legitimize royal power, function as advisers to the king, and inculcate in the people the virtue of obedience to divinely ordained authority. Fifth, the ruler's religious functions are extensive: he is chief patron of the clerical class, appoints their hierarchy, and enforces their discipline; he convenes councils for the restatement of doctrine and suppresses heresy. The ruler is in every sense the defender of the faith. For all these reasons, the only adequate conception of the traditional system is that of an integrated religiopolitical system. No other term adequately suggests the profound interpenetration of the major components.

There are two basic models of the traditional religiopolitical system: the *organic model* and the *church model.*[6] The organic model is characterized by a conception of the fusion of religious and political functions performed by a unitary structure. The ruler exercises both temporal and spiritual authority, and his chief function is to maintain the divine social order according to sacral law and tradition. Whatever ecclesiastical hierarchy

[6] The term "church" is used for want of a better one, despite the Christian history of the word. As will be clear from what follows, we are referring to a particular kind of structure which is found in societies of very different religious traditions.

exists is maintained by the ruler to enforce this sacral law and tradition. The equation of religion with society is maximized.

The church model is characterized by the close alliance of two distinct institutions, government and the ecclesiastical body, with extensive interchanging of political and religious functions. The ecclesiastical structure has its own raison d'être, separate from both society and government. The church is *in* society, but can never be equated with it. Because of its separate structural identity, especially when organized hierarchically, its power relationship to government can take three forms: (1) church over government, (2) government over church, (3) bipolar balance of power.

These two models must be understood as ideal types, and historical religiopolitical systems conform to them only imperfectly. Furthermore, in the evolution of societies it is possible that a system dominated by a theory of one model will nevertheless take on some of the characteristics of the other. Thus, at this point we may simply suggest that two of the major religions considered here, Hinduism and Islam, tend strongly toward the organic model while the other two, Buddhism and Catholicism, tend strongly toward the church model.

The traditional Hindu religiopolitical system was dominated by a theory of the sacral caste order of society. This caste order was defined in precise detail in a comprehensive sacral law, and its maintenance was the prime function of the ruler. The Brahman priestly order was in no sense a separate ecclesiastical structure but part of the sacral caste hierarchy of society.

The traditional Muslim state retained the original Islamic vision of the complete fusion of religious and political authority in the Prophet and his successors. A separate clerical class, the *ulama*, which was chiefly concerned with the interpretation of the comprehensive sacral law, did develop in the early centuries of Islam. In the Ottoman Empire and other traditional Muslim states, however, they were trained, organized hierarchically, and appointed to religious and especially judicial posts by the ruler. As a class their raison d'être was tied to the state's function of enforcing the sacred law. An exception to this generalization was found in Egypt in the eighteenth and nineteenth centuries, where the ulama of the famous mosque-university, al-Azhar, developed a largely autonomous, churchlike structure.

It is interesting to note that the Indian word for the Buddhist order of monks, *sangha*, originally meant "assembly," which was also the primitive meaning of the Greek *ecclesia*, the New Testament word which is translated "church." [7] The definition of religion as an assembly or church denies the possibility of its equation with society. The church concept denotes a structure separate from society in general, no matter how pervasively the church might seek to regulate society or how completely it might become identified with government. The complete destruction of these relationships with society and government still leaves a church largely intact, with its essential identity unimpaired and in fact sharpened.

The Buddhist monastic order has a strong sense of corporate identity, distinct from society — one must leave society in order to enter the Sangha. The monastic order has its own raison d'être, completely distinct from that of government. Nevertheless, in all the Theravada Buddhist countries of South and Southeast Asia, kings played a major role in supporting the order by grants of land, appointing the Sangha hierarchy, and enforcing its internal discipline. Similarly, the monks supported royal authority (sometimes proclaiming the king a future Buddha) and played a major role in maintaining the stability of society.

The structural identity of the Catholic church, separate from both lay society and temporal rulers, was fundamental, despite the extensive interpenetration of religious and political functions in both medieval Europe and colonial Latin America. The church was a powerful factor in the maintenance of the Spanish Empire in America. Through its authoritarian teaching, monopoly of education, and vast economic power, it legitimized and supported the authority of the Spanish crown over a period of three centuries. Despite the hierarchical nature and structure of the church, it had practically no autonomy;

---

[7] Marco Pallis, *Peaks and Lamas* (London: Cassell and Co., 1942), p. 285.

viceroys appointed the bishops, convened church councils, disciplined the clergy, and suppressed heresy.

THE DISRUPTION
OF TRADITIONAL SYSTEMS

Whatever the specific structural arrangements of a given religiopolitical system, the system made sense because the religious ideology satisfactorily explained and legitimized the actual power relationships in society. This is not to suggest that traditional states were not subject to serious disturbances through dynastic conflicts and other internal crises as well as external threats. However, none of these touched the core of the system so long as the religious ideology remained unquestioned.

In various forms and at different times, but roughly from the first decades of the nineteenth century in most of the societies in question, traditional systems came under external attack. The attack was most prominently military and political in those countries overrun by Western imperialism, but the technological, economic, social, intellectual, and religious challenge to tradition was soon apparent. The European domains of the Ottoman Empire contracted rapidly, and the empire soon found itself on the defensive throughout the Middle East and in virtually every sphere of life. The revolt of Spain's colonies in America, precipitated by Napoleon's invasion of the motherland, had been preceded by the intellectual penetration of the ideas of the Enlightenment. For the Spanish Americans, the monarchy and the divine right of kings were gone forever.

The attack on traditional systems took various forms and moved at varying speeds, but everywhere it cracked open the integralist nature of society. Everywhere it separated the major components of the religiopolitical system. Religion could no longer legitimize political power in the convincing way it once had done, nor could governments confidently arrange ecclesiastical affairs in the traditional manner. *The disruption of traditional systems left governments without legitimacy and autonomous religions with no prior experience of autonomy.*

This disruption was the beginning of the secularization of

the polity, which we have already identified as one of the major aspects of political development. For those societies which came under Western-imperialist rule, the question of legitimacy was never fully resolved. According to traditional criteria, European Christians were *ipso facto* illegitimate rulers when governing Hindu, Buddhist, and Muslim subjects. At a fairly early stage some Western-educated Asians suggested that the legitimacy of foreign rule might depend on visible progress in education, public health, economy, and so on, but rising nationalist movements soon insisted that no foreign government could be a legitimate government. After independence, liberal, democratic, and socialist currents of thought, merged with nationalism, produced legitimating ideological formulations which were deemed satisfactory to the political elite, despite their Western origin and their near-unintelligibility to the masses still steeped in traditionalist modes of thought. Ideological bridges were built with such slogans as "Islamic socialism" and "Islamic theodemocracy."

The secularization of the polity is a multifaceted process which is still far from complete. We can only mention here the major facets which will be treated later in Chapter IV. Secularization involves the separation of the polity from religion; legal and constitutional recognition is given to the fact that the political system does not derive its legitimacy from religion, and the symbols and structures which linked the two are destroyed. Secularization involves the expansion of the polity at the expense of religion as major areas of social life (education, law, economy, and so on) pass from religious regulation to the jurisdiction of the state. Secularization involves the transformation of political culture as politically relevant values assume a secular orientation. Nationality and nationalism displace religious notions of political community, and secular ideologies develop a legitimating power of their own. Finally, in a few countries which have undergone violent revolutions, secularization extends to state domination of religion, narrowly defined, with efforts to eradicate or drastically alter its very core.

The secularization of the polity is a major aspect of differentiation in the development of modern political systems. It is part of the general movement of modernizing societies from integralism to pluralism. Functional-valuational pluralism is a basic characteristic of modern societies. Functional pluralism recognizes the religious system as only one of several general spheres of life; among the others are the polity, economy, and society in general. While these spheres are interrelated at innumerable points, a considerable degree of autonomy is recognized. Certainly religion no longer provides the rationale, sets the goals, or prescribes the means for the functioning of the polity or the economy. Valuational pluralism includes the notion that there are value systems other than that of the religion in question — philosophies, ideologies, ethical systems, and styles of life — and that these have a legitimate place in society.

Historically, functional-valuational pluralism in the West was powerfully furthered by the emergence of diverse religions represented by separate organized communities of adherents within the same society. In some parts of the third world, religious pluralism will probably continue to play a positive role in the modernization process, despite the strains and conflicts which it often engenders within societies. In other developing countries, sizable religious minorities have not developed for various reasons and are unlikely to appear in the foreseeable future. But modernization of a traditional integralist society involves the emergence of functional-valuational pluralism, regardless of whether this is accompanied by religious pluralism.[8]

THE RESTRUCTURING OF RELIGION

The secularization of the polity is the political consequence of the disruption of the traditional religiopolitical system. The restructuring of religion is an equally necessary consequence. It is totally erroneous to conceive of religion in this post-traditional era as simply a continuation of the old belief systems and structures. Religion finds itself in as grave a crisis as that which confronts the polity. Throughout this entire area of

8 This basic idea of pluralism is developed in Peter L. Berger, *The Sacred Canopy: Elements of a Sociological Theory of Religion* (Garden City, N.Y.: Doubleday and Co., 1967), pp. 134–137.

consideration, at the beginning of the nineteenth century, rulers exercised not peripheral but central and crucial religious functions, such as the appointment of the ecclesiastical hierarchy, the enforcement of discipline among the clergy, and the financial support of the religious establishment. The breakup of the traditional system leaves religion with an autonomy which was neither sought nor desired. Thus, a largely independent *religious system* is set adrift, as it were, on a stormy sea of rapid change, without charts and with serious structural weaknesses.

The relatively autonomous religious systems retain fundamental characteristics from the traditional religiopolitical systems out of which they have come. In particular, religious systems in the post-traditional era may be classified as *organic* or *church* systems. In the organic religious systems, Hinduism and Islam, the primary collective expression of religion is found in societal structures which regulate the entire society; ecclesiastical organization is relatively undeveloped. In the church systems, Buddhism and Catholicism, an ecclesiastical structure separate from both government and the general society is the primary collective expression of religion; regulation of society by the ecclesiastical authority is an open option, so that it may but need not assume a major regulatory role.

The now separate systems, religious and political, do of course interact (see Figure I.1). Clearly, church systems have certain basic advantages over organic systems in transitional societies. Church systems, after all, have an ecclesiastical organization which may adjust and adapt itself to the decapitation which the removal of a sacred ruler constitutes. As we shall see, the Catholic church in Colombia emerged from the colonial pattern of subservience to the state to become a major political power, developing a church-state relationship best described as a neo-traditionalist bipolar balance of power. The Buddhist Sangha has responded to the new situation with much less success, although the points of organizational strength in the monastic order have enabled it on occasion to become a formidable political force in Burma, Ceylon, and South Vietnam. Within the organic systems, the Muslim ulama have

Figure I.1   *Religion and the Modernization of Polities*

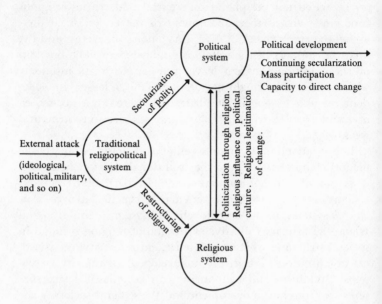

demonstrated little organizational coherence, and the Hindu religious functionaries, practically none.

Professor S. N. Eisenstadt, in his wide-ranging survey of the political relationships of religion in centralized empires (the Ancient Egyptian, Sassanid, Chinese, Roman, Byzantine, Maurya, Mughal, Ottoman, and sixteenth-century European colonial), concluded that "the general *potentialities* for political orientations of the religious groups were rooted in their internal structure and characteristics, even if the actualization of these potentialities was greatly dependent on the 'external' forces." Eisenstadt emphasizes organizational autonomy as a major variable. "Thus the extent to which the religious institutions were organizationally autonomous greatly influenced the degree to which they could participate in the central political struggle of a given society. In general, the smaller the extent of their distinct organization, the smaller was also their ability to participate in the central political struggle. The more closely was the organization identified with that of the state organs and institutions, the more was its political participation confined to the accepted, legitimate level of political activity. Contrariwise, the less were the religious organizations identified with the political institutions, the more could they develop articulated political activities which could go beyond the existing institutional framework." [9]

The organizational capabilities of a clerical group at any given time can be analyzed in order to predict the nature and extent of its possible political involvements or other forms of influence over society. The organizational variables of clerical groups can be outlined as follows:

   I. Corporate Identity (separateness from society)
      A. Formal entrance procedures
      B. Distinctive appearance (clerical garments, shaved heads, and so on)
      C. Corporate life pattern (celibacy, monastic communal residence, and so on)
   II. Corporate Complexity (internal differentiation)
      A. Ecclesiastical hierarchy
      B. Bureaucracy
      C. Communications network
      D. Formal disciplinary procedures
      E. Doctrinal formulation procedures
  III. Corporate Autonomy (independence from government)
      A. Financial independence
      B. Internal selection of hierarchy
      C. Internal assignment of clergy
      D. Internal dicipline of clergy
  IV. Corporate Integration of Laity
      A. Parish organization
      B. Lay organizations under clerical direction
      C. Laity subject to ecclesiastical discipline

This analysis is useful in explaining a number of phenomena.

---

[9] S. N. Eisenstadt, "Religious Organizations and Political Process in Centralized Empires," *Journal of Asian Studies,* vol. 21 (May 1962), p. 292.

The Sangha of Burma, for example, ranks very high in terms of its *corporate identity*. It is clearly and unmistakably separate from society. The monks' yellow robes and shaved heads, as well as their celibacy, set them apart. In the cities and large towns as many as eight hundred monks live together in a cluster of monasteries, and there are many such clusters. This fact, combined with the extremely high prestige of the Sangha, makes the potential for political activism very high. At the same time, since the disruption of the traditional religiopolitical system (under which the king appointed an ecclesiastical hierarchy and enforced discipline), there has been no effective ecclesiastical structure above the level of the individual monastery. This has resulted in low *corporate complexity*. The monks' political activism can therefore only be localized, intermittent, and without effective long-term direction. Low corporate complexity also helps to explain the inability of the Sangha to reformulate Buddhist doctrine to make it more relevant to changing social needs. The effort to produce a new Buddhist social ethic, therefore, is by default largely being made by laymen. The Sangha's low *corporate autonomy* is reflected in numerous attempts by governments since independence to reform the monastic order. The Sangha, ironically, has a high corporate identity and hence sufficient political effectiveness to frustrate government-sponsored reforms, but insufficient corporate complexity and autonomy to reform itself. The order's low *corporate integration of the laity* is reflected in the nature of Sangha political activism — the monks themselves carry out the demonstrations and man the picket lines around the parliament buildings.

This outline of organizational variables permits a rough kind of comparative analysis which is presented in Table I.1. This reveals the vast differences in demonstrated organizational capabilities among the four religions. The four faiths are not competing with each other, but within each society the dominant religious system is competing for influence against a host of secular rivals. For better or for worse, in modern society success in the competition for influence is clearly

TABLE I.1 *Ecclesiastical Organization in Selected Societies (1970)*

Organizational Variables	Brahman Priests in India	Sangha in Burma	Ulama in UAR	Catholic Clergy in Chile
Corporate identity	1	3	1	3
Corporate complexity	0	1	1	3
Corporate autonomy	0	1	0	3
Corporate integration of laity	0	1	1	3
Index of ecclesiastical organization score	1	6	3	12

Code: 3 — high
2 — medium
1 — low
0 — negligible

related to organizational capacity. However much the organizational tendency is decried by critics of contemporary society, the relationship between organization and influence is an undeniable fact.

The religious system thus moves into the modern competition for influence on terms which are not of its choosing. Its capacity for influence, or even survival, may depend, as in the case of Hinduism, on a factor which has been of little importance in its historical evolution and which is even contrary to its essential genius. But the historical process goes on with a certain ruthlessness. From this perspective, Catholicism is singularly fortunate in that its organizational capacity stands out as a major characteristic of the religious system, a characteristic which was evident many centuries before the beginning of the modern period.

RELIGIOUS IDEAS AND VALUES

Structural and ideational factors must be analyzed together at every stage.[10] It was suggested that traditional religiopolitical systems had to be understood in terms of both religious

10 *Ibid.*, pp. 292–294.

ideologies and structural arrangements (organic or church models). The secularization of polities involves drastic changes in both ideology and structure. The restructuring of religion involves the organizational factors analyzed above, but equally important are the doctrinal factors.

The varied religious responses to the challenges of the contemporary world are largely decided by the interaction of structures and ideas. A particular ecclesiastical structure may permit various responses, say, to the secularization of education. However, the religious ideas and values of the leadership largely determine the nature of the response. Historically, the secularization of education has produced intense conflict in Catholic societies, very little conflict in Buddhist societies although the traditional involvement in education has been no less. The difference must be explained largely in terms of differing ideas concerning the religious regulation of the family and society. For the Catholic clergy these considerations made the control of education a crucial issue; for the Buddhist monks this was not the case.

The limitations of organizational factors alone in predicting behavior is even more sharply demonstrated by considering the Catholic clergy in various Latin American countries. Corporate identity and complexity are high in all these societies. The greatest variation is found in corporate autonomy (independence from government), since some republics (Argentina, for example) still continue many of the ecclesiastical prerogatives exercised by the Spanish crown. However, it is quite clear that the predominantly conservative position of the Colombian Catholic hierarchy on most social, economic, and political questions, and the predominantly progressive stance of their Chilean counterparts, cannot be explained in terms of organizational variables. There are basic differences in the ideational and valuational orientations of the two hierarchies. And these are best explained by examining concrete historical situations and, in particular, the ideological influences to which each group has been subjected over the past thirty years.[11]

[11] See the important efforts of Ivan Vallier to analyze these differences: "Religious Elites: Differentiations and Developments in Roman Cathol-

It is of course equally true that the effectiveness of ideas is limited by the structure which must formalize, articulate, and implement them. Thus a carefully formulated doctrine of social change, based on authentically Islamic values of social justice and expounded by a modernist Muslim scholar, can receive no authoritative corporate approval and propagation, for the ecclesiastical machinery does not exist. The declaration of Vatican Council II on the church in the modern world, on the other hand, bears an authority which cannot be so easily ignored. The organizational context of ideological reformulation is examined in Chapter VII.

The ideas and values of four major religions relevant to political development and modernization represent a vast and truly bewildering array of material. One can only suggest here some of the major themes which are clearly relevant. This outline will to some extent be filled out in the following chapter. On one hand, these ideas and values help to explain the possible motivation of individuals and groups functioning politically in contemporary transitional societies. On the other hand, these ideas and values may be viewed as the doctrinal resources (and limitations) of Hindus, Buddhists, Muslims, and Catholics who are seeking to make their respective religious systems relevant in a positive way to the problems of development.

The religious ideas and values relevant to modernization are organized under six major elements of a world view: the world, the individual, the social order, the political order, religious truth and authority, and the ecclesiastical institution. The ideas outlined under these categories in Table I.2 essentially represent the formal doctrinal notions of scriptural religion, not the religion of the illiterate peasantry.

Some of these major ideas and symbols have deeply penetrated the consciousness of the peasant, but others (certainly the more philosophical and theological) obviously have not. The relationship between scriptural religion and popular reli-

---

icism," in S. M. Lipset and A. Solari, eds., *Elites in Latin America* (New York: Oxford University Press, 1967); "Church 'Development' in Latin America: A Five-Country Comparison," *The Journal of Developing Areas* vol. 1 (July 1967), pp. 461–476.

gion (or more broadly, between great tradition and little
tradition) is a matter of considerable complexity, which can
only be touched on at this point. We can note in passing, however, that popular Hinduism, Buddhism, Islam, and Catholicism have far more in common with each other than do the
more sophisticated versions represented by scriptural religion.
Peasant religion in all four traditions is essentially polytheistic
and concerned with the magical manipulation of unseen forces
for the protection and practical benefit of the worshiper. In
many cases peasant religion represents a syncretist amalgam —
Catholic saints merge with Indian gods in Latin America,
Southeast Asian Buddhists and Muslims propitiate the spirits
like their animist ancestors, Indian Hindus and Muslims sometimes worship at the tombs of the same saints, and throughout
the Muslim world, Sufism accommodates a vast variety of local
cults under its sprawling tent.

Why, then, does the normative religion of the scholars and
clergy warrant so much attention? First, despite all of the syncretism, the great-tradition religions have powerfully integrated
the traditional cultures of the third world and their continuing influence is clear and unmistakable. Secondly, as education
comes to the village, the initial change in world view is not
toward secularism but toward a more sophisticated and knowl-
edgeable perception of the dominant religious heritage. Magical
and animistic conceptions are the first victims of modern-type
education. Thirdly, the vast majority of those who are presently educated and politically conscious do in fact identify
with the symbols of scriptural religion, draw psychological and
spiritual sustenance from them, and are at least to some extent influenced by them in behavior. The highly secularized
individuals are of course still a small minority. For the present and for some time to come, therefore, these symbols must
be taken seriously as part of the intellectual and emotional
makeup of political man in the third world.

Turning to Table I.2, one is struck by the ambiguous implications of various components of the religious world views
that are analyzed. Buddhism, for example, provides no divine
pattern of society, no sacred law, no political theory. This es-

TABLE I.2 *Religious Ideas and Values Relevant to Modernization*

Elements of World View	Hinduism	Buddhism	Islam	Catholicism
I. The world				
A. Reality of the world	*Ultimately unreal* Metaphysically unreal in dominant philosophical tradition.	*Ultimately unreal* All existence is impermanent and substanceless.	*Real* World is created by God and is real.	*Real* World is created by God and is real.
B. Religious value of the material	*Ambivalent* Strong emphasis on renunciation of material things, but wealth and pleasure valid at certain stage of life.	*Not valued* Renunciation of material things necessary for serious religious life (in monastic order).	*Valued* Wealth not incompatible with religious goals. The Prophet began as a merchant.	*Not Valued* Strong emphasis on renunciation and asceticism. Rewards in the next life.
C. Significance of history	*Not significant* History is cyclical, without significance, and ultimately unreal.	*Not significant* Metaphysically, similar to Hinduism. In practice, history taken more seriously.	*Decisive* A certain pattern of life must be established on earth.	*Significant* History moves toward divine culmination, but man's highest fulfillment is in heaven.
II. The individual				
A. Reality of individual	*Illusory* Perception of individual existence based on ignorance. Salvation is absorption into Absolute, ending cycle of rebirth.	*Temporary* Cycle of rebirth. Nirvana achieved with extinction of the ego.	*Eternal* Each individual is created an eternal soul.	*Eternal* Each individual is created an eternal soul.
B. Spiritual equality	*Unequal* Individuals are inherently unequal, can progress spiritually through successive existences.	*Equal* Individuals essentially equal, although conditioned by past karma.	*Equal* Spiritual equality of all souls.	*Equal* Spiritual equality of all souls.
C. Freedom – determinism	*Determinism* Individual action strongly conditioned by karma, but some freedom remains.	*Freedom* Strong emphasis on individual decision and self-reliance despite doctrine of karma.	*Determinism* Primary emphasis on predetermination by will of God, but moral striving also urged.	*Freedom* Emphasis on moral responsibility of the individual.
III. The social order				
A. Divine pattern of society	*Divine pattern* Divinely ordained caste order.	*No pattern provided* Absence of detailed social regulations.	*Divine pattern* Total society theoretically regulated by sacred law.	*Divine pattern* Integralist concepts of Catholic society, rooted in medieval period.

TABLE I.2 (cont.)

Elements of World View	Hinduism	Buddhism	Islam	Catholicism
B. Egalitarian — hierarchical	*Hierarchical* Rigidly hierarchical caste system, based on inherent inequality and degrees of ritual purity.	*Egalitarian* Egalitarian assumptions, but not highly developed as positive principle of society.	*Egalitarian* Strong emphasis on equality of believers, although hierarchical concepts in medieval political theory.	*Hierarchical* Hierarchical concepts in papal encyclicals until recently.
C. Concept of social justice	*Caste-determined justice* Man must be treated according to his place in the caste hierarchy.	*Individualistic ethic* Social ethics not a significant doctrinal concern.	*Transcendent justice* Social justice commanded by transcendent and sovereign God.	*Transcendent justice* Prophetic biblical tradition and natural law concepts. Development of modern social ethic from the end of 19th century.
IV. The political order A. Religious and political structures	*Differentiation* Rulers and priests belong to different castes. But ruler is a divinity.	*Differentiation* Roles of ruler and monk very different. But ruler is semidivine (future Buddha).	*Fusion* Concept of fusion of temporal and spiritual authority in Muhammad and caliphs.	*Differentiation* Strong corporate identity of church separate from ruler.
B. Theory of clericalism (clerical domination of polity)	*No clerical theory* No priestly challenge to ruler's power.	*No clerical theory* None in Theravada countries, but such theory does exist in Lamaist Buddhism of Tibet.	*No clerical theory* No theory of rule by ulama; caliphs exercised spiritual and temporal authority.	*Strong clerical theory* Tradition of Papacy as temporal power. Papal states in Italy until 1870.
C. Concept of law	*Religious law* Complete code of religious duty which includes all law. In practice, Hindu criminal law no longer enforced and civil law greatly restricted.	*Secular law* No Buddhist religious law ever developed.	*Religious law* Complete code of religious duty which includes all law. In practice, Islamic criminal law today virtually gone and civil law greatly restricted.	*Religious and secular law* Certain topics of state law relating to sacraments and natural law concepts embodied in canon law. But validity of secular law in other spheres recognized.
D. Judgments regarding modern ideologies	*No fixed position* Only individual attitudes toward nationalism, democracy, socialism.	*No fixed position* Only individual attitudes toward nationalism, democracy, socialism.	*No fixed position* Only individual attitudes toward nationalism, democracy, socialism.	*Formal doctrinal position* Until recently papal encyclicals opposed liberalism, socialism. Basic changes since Pope John XXIII.

V. Religious truth and authority

	Hinduism	Buddhism	Islam	Christianity
A. Scope of religious system	*Ethnic* No conversions to Hinduism. Hindu majority only on Indian subcontinent.	*Universal* Buddha's message for all men. Buddhism spread throughout Asia.	*Universal* Prophet's message for all men. Muslim countries from West Africa to Indonesia.	*Universal* Christ's message for all men. Pope is his representative, head of worldwide church.
B. Nature of knowable truth	*Pluralist, relative* Each worshiper chooses his god. The Absolute is unknowable.	*Unitary but proximate* Buddha professed agnosticism on various major metaphysical questions.	*Absolute* Revealed truth is final and perfect.	*Absolute* Revealed truth is final and perfect, although process of revelation continues.
C. Attitude toward truth	*Experimental, pragmatic* Individual self-realization is the goal.	*Experimental, pragmatic* Individual is invited to experiment with teachings of the Buddha.	*Authoritarian* Tradition of coercion to suppress heretical beliefs.	*Authoritarian* Tradition of coercion to suppress heretical beliefs.
D. Religious authority	*No fixed authority* Scriptures, individual gurus, mystical experience.	*Nondogmatic scriptural authority* Rational inquiry encouraged.	*Revealed dogma* Qur'an is eternal, supplemented by tradition.	*Revealed dogma* Church, through Pope, is infallible teacher. Scriptures and tradition secondary.
E. Doctrinal development	*Unlimited doctrinal change* No creedal norms exist to limit change, but doctrinal innovations produce only new sects.	*Static* Neither theory nor tradition of doctrinal development in Theravada Buddhism.	*Basically static* Little change since medieval times, although principles of private judgment and consensus provide for change in jurisprudence.	*Doctrinal change valid* Since church is the infallible authority, doctrinal development continues through Popes and councils.
VI. The ecclesiastical institution				
A. Internal corporate raison d'être	*No corporate concept* No coherent ecclesiastical organization exists.	*Strong corporate concept* Sangha has a clear and self-contained reason for its existence. Exists to facilitate quest for Nirvana, totally apart from society or its needs.	*Weak corporate concept* Ulama's functions and raison d'être are entirely externally oriented – administration of law and education.	*Strong corporate concept* Church has a clear self-contained raison d'être. The sacramental life of church a religious end in itself, apart from relationship to society.
B. External concept of clergy	*No generalized concept* Some holy men worshiped but many not respected. Temple priests have low prestige.	*Extreme veneration* Sangha venerated and worshiped as one of the Three Gems, along with the Buddha and Dharma (teaching).	*Respect* Ulama respected for their knowledge and piety but not venerated.	*Extreme veneration* Pope is vicar of Christ, and all priests share his supernatural sacramental powers. Church is divine institution, perfect society.

23

sentially secular view of state and society accords well with modern conceptions, and Buddhist societies do not face the intense conflicts generated by secularization in Hindu, Muslim, and Catholic societies. From this point of view, Buddhism does not represent an obstacle to modernization. By the same token, however, Buddhism seems to lack the doctrinal resources necessary for a *positive* ideology of social change and economic development. Its monastic orientation has, in fact, meant a basic indifference to society, and its low valuation of material things makes difficult the formulation of a convincing doctrine of economic development. Thus a Burmese cabinet minister in 1951 could reconcile Buddhism and Marxism by assigning them to completely separate spheres of life. "Marxist theory deals with mundane affairs and seeks to satisfy material needs in life. Buddhist philosophy, however, deals with the solution of spiritual matters with a view to seek spiritual satisfaction in life and liberation from this mundane world." [12] This is of course very different from the assertion that religious values make imperative the striving for man's economic well-being.

Catholicism in Latin America has a tradition of ideas and values which are clearly antagonistic to various aspects of modernization. An integralist concept of a hierarchical society and a pronounced preference for authoritarian rule are prominent components of the Ibero-Catholic heritage. A strong emphasis on the ideals of renunciation, asceticism, and otherworldliness for the individual has also characterized the Catholic value system. From the middle of the nineteenth century until recently, papal encyclicals condemned liberalism, socialism, and in general the values of modern life. Modernization, and especially the secularization of the state and society, has met with fierce hostility from Catholic hierarchies everywhere until very recently.

Other elements of Catholic teaching, however, have permitted a remarkable doctrinal development over the past decade. The traditional Catholic concern for social institutions has been retained, but hierarchical and authoritarian concepts

---

[12] Cited in Donald E. Smith, *Religion and Politics in Burma* (Princeton, N.J.: Princeton University Press, 1965), p. 129.

are being displaced by a social ethic drawing on biblical prophetic perspectives and reformulated natural-law ideas regarding social justice. The Catholic doctrines of continuing revelation through the teaching authority of the church legitimize the internal ideological revolution now taking place. Pope John XXIII in his encyclical *Mater et Magistra* (1961) not only accepted but embraced certain basic principles of the welfare state and socialism. The expanding role of the state, while entailing dangers which must be guarded against, was welcomed for its positive contribution to human welfare.[13] This clear endorsement was theologically grounded in the conception of the inherent worth and dignity of the human being. The teaching of the church "embraces the whole man, namely his soul and body, intellect and will. . . ."

Religious values may thus carry very ambiguous implications for modernization. Buddhism's basic unconcern with social structures make it much less of an obstacle to social change, but provides scant resources for the promotion, direction, and motivation of social change. Traditional Catholic ideas and values clearly obstruct many aspects of development, but the church's historic concern with society provides certain doctrinal resources for a positive reinterpretation. Hinduism's pluralistic and relativistic view of the nature of truth, the absence of a fixed religious authority, and the unlimited possibilities of doctrinal innovation are strikingly "modern," but would seem to provide no universal values and norms which could motivate and guide the process of development. Islam's high valuation of the material, egalitarianism, emphasis on the decisiveness of history, and transcendent justice clearly provide such norms, but these are still largely embedded in notions of static legal and social institutions. Thus creative efforts to extricate these universal Islamic norms do not receive ecclesiastical recognition, legitimation, and support.

It was mentioned earlier that the relationship between organization and ideas is both crucial and complex. The final element of the world view in Table I. 2 is "ecclesiastical insti-

---

[13] *Mater et Magistra,* art. 61, in Anne Fremantle, ed., *The Social Teachings of the Church* (New York: Mentor-Omega Books, 1963), p. 231.

tution" because we have to consider not only organizations on one hand and ideas on the other but *ideas about organizations*. One of the major characteristics of both the Buddhist and the Catholic ecclesiastical institutions is their strong corporate concepts. The concrete organization in a particular place and at a particular time may in fact be extremely weak, but it survives because it is sustained and can be revived by a certain *concept* of the organization. The survival of the Buddhist Sangha, despite its lack of a centralized international structure and despite all the political vicissitudes of South and Southeast Asian states over the past 2,500 years, must be largely attributed to the power of an idea. The Sangha itself is a major value in the Buddhist world view. It is precisely the absence or weakness of such a corporate concept, even more than the organizational weaknesses, among contemporary Hindu and Islamic clerical groups which places their future in such doubt.

The nature of a religious system, the particular complex of structures and ideas, thus explains much of the interaction of religious phenomena with politics and social change. Much, but not all. There are important nonsystemic religious factors, such as the patterns of religious diffusion which have created large religious minorities in some societies but none in others. Social and political conflicts between religious groups frequently have little to do with differences in the character of religious systems; pluralism itself, accentuated by strong religious group identities, is the major fact. Other "historical accidents," such as patterns of Western imperialist expansion, largely account for the nature of certain religiopolitical interactions. The Spanish and the British, for example, pursued very different religious policies in their Asian colonies, and these differences were reflected in the forms of religious nationalism which emerged in the late nineteenth century.

RELIGION AND POLITICAL DEVELOPMENT
IN THE WEST

In order to see the problems discussed in this book in the broadest possible comparative perspective, we must now seek to relate our analysis to political development in the West.

Two points are of fundamental importance: (1) modernization in the West proceeded from a medieval synthesis of church integralism; and (2) the integralist medieval society was shattered by revolutionary pluralization in the religious and intellectual spheres.

So much of the history of the West is so directly related to the existence of a *church* that it is impossible even to speculate about the course of events had Christianity originated and developed as a religion of organic integralism. The centuries of struggle between church and state, including periods of clear-cut church dominance, would obviously not be a part of the history we read today. The church articulated the notion, and incarnated it institutionally, that men must reserve their ultimate loyalty for something higher than the state (God, natural law, Pope, church). This basic idea has an unbroken tradition in Western political thought and, in secularized form, continues to demonstrate great vitality today. The whole concept of constitutional government which developed in Western society has been traced to the Christian notion of transcendent justice.[14]

The existence of a church maintained certain tensions with the political authority which could only be covered over when the equilibrium of the medieval integralism was at a near-perfect state. The church itself was a major fact of differentiation which implied its separability from the political structure, once the integralist religious ideology lost its cohesive power.

Some recent writers have sought to establish the thesis that secularization in the modern world is itself the direct consequence of the impact of biblical ideas.[15] According to Professor

---

[14] See Carl J. Friedrich, *Transcendent Justice — The Religious Foundations of Constitutionalism* (Durham, N.C.: Duke University Press, 1964).

[15] The idea was first put forward by the German theologian Friedrich Gogarten. One of the most influential recent statements of the thesis is found in Harvey Cox, *The Secular City* (New York: Macmillan Co., 1965). The theologians' strained efforts to document the Judaeo-Christian origins of contemporary secularization are somewhat reminiscent of the work of nineteenth-century Hindu and Muslim apologists who found modern science, rationalism, liberalism, democracy, etc., in their respective sacred texts.

van Leeuwen, in the biblical *theocratic* conception God is sharply distinguished from the universe (nature, man, and society) and rules over it. The opposing *ontocratic* view sees all reality as a cosmic totality suffused with divinity; ancient Near Eastern religions, the Indic religions, and many others have shared this ontocratic conception. According to van Leeuwen's argument, secularization has taken place in Christian Western society because of the biblical view that God has placed man in charge of the world; nature and society are desacralized.[16]

This argument is weak. Although the idea of divine transcendence matters, the key consideration is how the divine is understood to relate to human society. In the West, God was believed to be present in society chiefly through the church, a visible structure separate from the temporal order. The church institutionalized the idea of divine transcendence, of separateness. Islam, with an even heightened sense of divine transcendence, lacked this institutionalized duality and hence lacked the basis for the secularization of society. In the absence of a church, some of the most sophisticated modern interpreters (for example, Iqbal) have insisted that it is *impossible* to separate the sacred from the secular in the Islamic world view.

From the sociological standpoint, it makes little difference whether the conception of a divinely ordained social order is decreed by a transcendent God (Islam and medieval Catholicism) or inherent in a sacral cosmos (Hinduism). The medieval Catholic conception, historically, was undermined by a host of factors largely unrelated to the biblical theocratic view of the universe.

And last, the other major church system, Theravada Buddhism, promoted a largely secular society. Because the Sangha is the focal point of the sacred in society ("I take refuge in the Buddha, Dhamma, and Sangha," the layman intones), the distinction between the sacred and secular could approximate that between Sangha and society. An agnostic or possibly atheistic philosophical system was linked to a secular, social-contract theory of kingship, although in practice non-Buddhist Brah-

---

[16] Arend T. van Leeuwen, *op. cit.*

manical ideas and rites legitimized all rulers in the Buddhist countries of South and Southeast Asia. But there never developed a Buddhist law nor a Buddhist system of social hierarchy. Buddhist societies in general were far more secular in structure than their Hindu, Muslim, or Latin American Catholic counterparts at the beginning of the twentieth century. Therefore, the church-organic distinction is more useful than the theocratic-ontocratic distinction in explaining secularization in the West.

The medieval Catholic synthesis was cracked open by revolutionary religious pluralization in the sixteenth century. The Protestant Reformation in the religious sphere, the Renaissance and later Enlightenment in the intellectual sphere, revolutionary movements of *internal* origin, were major steps toward the secularization of Western society. While attempts were made to reconstruct society on the basis of a number of smaller Christendoms instead of one (*cuius regio eius religio*), the logic of the new pluralism was that sooner or later men of differing religions would have to contrive political arrangements by which they could coexist peacefully in the same state and society. The rationalism of the Enlightenment brought all dogmatic creeds into question.

A fundamental concern for securing the right of religious liberty was the basis of Roger Williams's experiment in separation of church and state in seventeenth-century Rhode Island. But the question of religious liberty powerfully affected the whole development of liberalism in the thought of John Locke and others. As Mill noted in his great essay: "It is accordingly on this battlefield, almost solely, that the rights of the individual against society have been asserted on broad grounds of principle, and the claim of society to exercise authority over dissentients openly controverted. The great writers to whom the world owes what religious liberty it possesses, have mostly asserted freedom of conscience as an indefeasible right, and denied absolutely that a human being is accountable to others for his religious belief." [17]

17 John Stuart Mill, *On Liberty and Considerations on Representative Government* (New York: Macmillan Co., 1947), p. 7.

Although Luther was authoritarian and antidemocratic in
many of his ideas and actions, his insistence on the priesthood
of all believers opened up new possibilities of participation for
the laity. The internal democratization of church life was carried further by Calvinists and more extreme Protestant groups
and had a profound impact on the local political institutions
which developed in parts of colonial America. Thus in the
seventeenth century we find Christian churches stressing freedom of conscience, voluntarism in church membership, democratic procedures internally, separation of church and state,
and a remarkably desacralized view of the nature of political
authority. In short, some of the key assumptions made concerning the role of religion in a modern pluralist society can be
found in these sources. Furthermore, as Weber emphasized in
his famous thesis, some of these same churches taught a new
ethic which supported and legitimized the values of a nascent
capitalism.[18]

The Catholic church in Europe assumed a conservative and
defensive posture in the face of the revolutionary ideological
and political changes of the eighteenth and nineteenth centuries. There was a small group of liberal Catholics which
sought a *rapprochement* between Catholicism and liberalism.
The Papacy, however, firmly opposed their ideas, and the *Syllabus of Errors,* published in 1864, condemned propositions
favoring: the withdrawal from church control of state-sup-
ported schools, the separation of church and state, the abolition of the temporal power of the Papacy, and religious
toleration.[19] In nineteenth- and early twentieth-century Catho-

[18] Robert N. Bellah has written: "Protestantism, particularly in its
Calvinist and sectarian forms . . . first worked out in detail a Christian
pattern of life that led directly to the emergence of major features of
modern society." "Epilogue," in Robert N. Bellah, ed., *Religion and
Progress in Modern Asia* (New York: Free Press, 1965), p. 196. See Max
Weber, *The Protestant Ethic and the Spirit of Capitalism* (London:
George Allen & Unwin, Ltd., 1930); and Ernst Troeltsch, *Protestantism
and Progress* (Boston: Beacon Press, 1958).

[19] This last mentioned Error was stated as follows: "In this age of ours
it is no longer expedient that the Catholic religion should be treated as
the sole State religion and that any other forms of religious worship
should be excluded." Sidney Z. Ehler and John B. Morrall, eds., *Church*

lic Europe, anticlericalism was a major aspect of political life. The church staunchly opposed several key ideological orientations which were in the ascendant. Liberalism clashed with traditional church authoritarianism; nationalism with ultramontanism and the temporal power of the church; democracy and republicanism with the church's strong preference for monarchy. For the most part, to be a liberal, a nationalist, and a democrat, was also to be an anticlerical.

By the last quarter of the nineteenth century the rise of Marxist ideology and Marxist political movements was generally perceived by both Catholics and Protestants as the major threat to Christianity. Pope Leo XIII in 1878 condemned "the deadly plague that is creeping into the very fibres of human society," spread by socialists, communists, and nihilists.[20] In 1891, however, he published *Rerum Novarum* ("Rights and Duties of Capital and Labor"), which marked the beginning of modern Catholic social doctrine. Leo rejected the socialist doctrines of class war and the abolition of private property, but approved a larger role for the state in the protection of workers, attempted to define the just wage, and emphasized the legitimacy and necessity of trade unions for the protection of the workers' interests.[21]

The major *aggiornamento* ("updating") of the church was initiated by Pope John XXIII. His encyclicals *Mater et Magistra* and *Pacem in Terris*, and the documents of Vatican Council II (1962 to 1966), breathed a new spirit which seemed free from the dogmatic controversies of the past. Accepting the religious and ideological pluralism of the modern world, John opened the way for cooperation even between Catholics and Marxists in the solution of problems confronting humanity.

Christian Democratic political parties have played a prominent role in the politics of western Europe, especially since the

---

and State Through the Centuries: A Collection of Historic Documents with Commentaries (London: Burns and Oates, 1954), p. 285.

[20] *Quod Apostolici Muneris* [*On Socialism*], in Etienne Gilson, ed., *The Church Speaks to the Modern World: The Social Teachings of Leo XIII* (Garden City, N.Y.: Image Books, 1954), p. 193.

[21] *Ibid.*, pp. 206–207.

end of World War II. While these predominantly Catholic parties had antecedents going back to the nineteenth century, both the *Mouvement Républicain Populaire* (MRP) in France and the *Partito Democratico Cristiano* in Italy were founded in 1944, and the Christian Democratic Union in West Germany in 1946. The Catholic parties have controlled the governments of both Italy and West Germany throughout most of the postwar period; in Bonn the chancellorship was lost to the Social Democrats only in 1969. While the church hierarchies have supported these parties informally, there is no official connection between church and party, and membership in the party is open to non-Catholics.[22]

The role of religion in political development in the West has thus been a highly significant one. It has contributed to the idea of limited government and individual freedom, been deeply involved in the general process of modernization through its internal upheavals, interacted with the major ideologies of modern times, given rise to important political parties, and been an influential factor in the molding of political cultures. The question of the relationship between religion and political development in the third world can be no less significant.

[22] Michael P. Fogarty, *Christian Democracy in Western Europe, 1820–1953* (South Bend: University of Notre Dame Press, 1957).

CHAPTER II

The Religions
of the Third World

IN THIS BOOK we deal with political development in relation to four major religions: Hinduism, Buddhism, Islam, and Catholicism. Some basic information about these four religious systems will be presented before we attempt to analyze their interaction with politics. In the pages which follow, each religion is analyzed in terms of (1) belief and ritual, (2) ecclesiastical organization, (3) mechanisms of societal integration, and (4) movements of reform and modernization. The key variables in the analysis proposed in Chapter I deserving special attention are (1) and (2). The modernizing impulses described in (4) also deserve emphasis, for the case is not simply one of dynamic political processes acting upon static religious traditions.

To analyze and describe four religious systems in a few pages necessitates broad generalizations with their well-known limitations and pitfalls. The perils of generalization, however, are unevenly distributed. Theravada Buddhism is much the same throughout South and Southeast Asia, but the Islam which stretches from Morocco to Indonesia encompasses profound diversity. While Hinduism is the majority religion only on the Indian subcontinent, its innumerable sectarian divisions make generalization difficult. While Roman Catholicism throughout Latin America (and the world) has a fixed, authoritative doctrinal content, the forces of aggiornamento blessed by Vatican Council II have had greatly differing impacts on various countries. Recognizing these difficulties, we shall make the effort in the following pages to take into account both the universal and the particular, the static and the dynamic.

HINDUISM: GODS, DHARMA, AND CASTE

Hinduism contains a bewildering array of beliefs and rituals. Hindu religious diversity is so striking that some scholars have argued that there is little to be gained by regarding Hinduism as one religion; it is rather a congeries of sects, local cults, and regional religious practices which are related to each other by the most tenuous ties. Hindu belief ranges from primitive animism through extravagant polytheism to the philosophical monism of Vedanta. While the Vedas are revered by many Hindus as the ultimate scriptural authority, they are rejected by others who look to sectarian sacred books, and for many modern Hindus the Bhagavad Gita is the highest authority. The worship of a particular god in a temple, pilgrimage to a sacred place, veneration of the cow, and participation in festivals are all important aspects of popular religion, yet all of these are rejected by some devout Hindus. In his interpretation of Hinduism, Gandhi regarded the ethical precept of *ahimsa,* "noninjury to life," as absolutely central, but many Hindu scholars find it necessary to qualify his interpretation very substantially, at least from the historical point of view.

Despite the profusion of mythology and cult, the seemingly unrestrained proliferation of gods and sects, Hindu religion has been partially integrated by certain key concepts which are accepted by virtually all Hindus. The doctrine of the cycle of rebirth asserts that all living beings are involved in the eternal process of birth, death, and rebirth. The "law of cause and effect," *karma,* operates in such a way that a person's next rebirth will constitute the moral consequence (reward or punishment) of deeds performed in this life. So pervasive is the belief in rebirth that even the most westernized and secularized Hindus will in most cases affirm it. Rebirth and karma are the basic assumptions of life in a Hindu culture, and there have been very few serious attempts to challenge them in present-day India.

It is only in recent decades that caste has been repudiated as a Hindu religious value, and only by a small minority which has been rather ineffectual in communicating its version of casteless Hinduism to the masses. For the traditional Hindu, however, the social hierarchy of caste, with the Brahman priest at the apex, is divinely ordained as stated in the scriptures. Caste practices are intimately related to notions of ritual purity and pollution, and the gross social inequalities of the system are perfectly explained and justified by the operation of the law of karma.

The concept of *dharma* in Hinduism includes everything which might be suggested by the English words "religion," "duty," and "law"; it is the sum total of the rules of behavior for all aspects of life. It must be emphasized, however, that dharma was never understood in universalist terms. There is a different dharma for each caste, and according to the Bhagavad Gita, it is far better to perform one's own caste dharma poorly than another's well. There is considerable justification, therefore, for the assertion that caste, along with the notions of rebirth and karma, have provided a basic framework for the integration of traditional Hinduism. Despite its great diversity and modern efforts at radical reformation, there are important unifying elements within Hinduism.

The worship of innumerable gods is perfectly compatible with the dominant Hindu philosophical view of the universe. The Vedic seer proclaimed, "Reality is one; sages speak of it in different ways." [1] The Ultimate Reality or Absolute is without name, form, personality, or qualities. Because of the weakness of men, who long for the worship of gods of love and mercy, theism is necessary, but it is recognized that the Absolute alone ultimately exists, beyond all differentiation. The "doctrine of the chosen deity" (*ishta-devata*) invites the Hindu to worship the particular god who best meets his spiritual, psychological, and intellectual needs. Because of the great differences in

[1] *Rig Veda,* i, 164.46.

men's capacities, it is understood that one worshiper will sacrifice a goat before a sacred image, while another will dispense with theistic concepts altogether and by disciplined meditation seek union with the Absolute. The vast diversity of Hindu belief and ritual is thus accommodated within this philosophical framework.

Just as Hinduism contains no single creedal statement of religious truth, there is no ecclesiastical organization to give it a fixed shape. The many sects within Hinduism are not effectively organized. Many of them consist of a "spiritual guide" (*guru* or *swami*), who is reputed to have achieved a high degree of sanctity, and a large number of unorganized followers, who periodically come to receive his blessing and teachings and make their offerings. Very few sects have developed a coherent centralized institution with hierarchical structure and authority.

There is, in Hinduism, no clearly defined group of religious specialists or clergy. In the traditional system, the Brahman caste provided the priests, and the training of priests was largely a family and caste function. In modern times this system has largely broken down as the Brahmans quickly took to Western education and found jobs in the civil service and professions. Today most Brahmans are not priests, and some priests are not Brahmans. The clerical functions of Hinduism are performed by a variety of religious specialists including temple priests, sect and family gurus, and wandering holy men. Temple priests do not enjoy high prestige in Hindu society, and the wandering holy man is even more suspect in the eyes of many.

Commenting on the absence of Hindu ecclesiastical structure, a British scholar wrote: "Hence Hinduism has never prepared a body of canonical Scriptures or a Common Prayer Book; it has never held a General Council or Convention; never defined the relations of the laity and clergy; never regulated the canonization of saints or their worship; never established a single center of religious life, like Rome or Canterbury; never prescribed a course of training for its priests." Furthermore, the absence of such institutional development cannot be attributed to war, foreign rule, or any other external circumstance, but simply to the fact that "all such action is essentially opposed to its spirit and traditions." [2]

In a remarkable way, Hinduism has combined the absence of coherent ecclesiastical organization with elaborate mechanisms for the regulation and integration of society. Without any kind of centralized authority or direction, the mechanisms of caste and Hindu law, mutually reinforcing, have served to integrate Hindu society. Caste was not a system of predetermined coordination of social groups but was rather the all-pervasive principle on which social life evolved. Each caste had its own dharma, was an endogamous unit, and tended to develop its own subculture. Patterns of regularity in the relations among members of different castes were based on prescriptive custom, notions of ritual purity, and economic interdependence. In the traditional Hindu state one of the major functions of the king was the maintenance of the divinely ordained caste order of society; intercaste marriage and the consequent confusion of castes were regarded as the greatest evils.

Hindu law was a complete body of law, criminal and civil, based on the ancient texts on dharma. Hindu law gave powerful support to the caste system, and the criminal law prescribed different penalties for the same crime depending on caste status. A secular penal code was imposed by the British in India in 1860, but religious law continues to be applied in the courts in cases concerning marriage, divorce, inheritance, adoption, and so on. It was not until 1949, two years after independence, that the marriage law was amended by legislative enactment to permit the marriage of persons of different *varnas* (the four major caste divisions).

It is thus clear that religion was the primary factor in Hindu societal integration. The central Hindu concept of dharma encompassed the whole religious duty of man, and the institutions of caste and traditional law were simply aspects of dharma. In short, Hinduism evolved as a religion of organic integralism.

In order to understand contemporary Hinduism, however,

---

2 W. Crooke, "Hinduism," in James Hastings, ed., *Encyclopedia of Religion and Ethics*, vol. 6 (1925), p. 712.

we must grasp not only the framework of immemorial tradition but the modernizing impulses which have shaken and
gravely weakened the structure at some points. Unquestionably the most serious challenges have been external — the impact of British rule with its radically different assumptions and
principles. The influence of Christian missionaries on the reformulation of Hinduism has also been profound. While it is
clear that external stimuli account for much of the internal
change, it is also true that Hinduism has produced a remarkable line of religious reformers, from Rammohan Roy in the
early nineteenth century to Gandhi, Vinoba Bhave, and Radhakrishnan. Like most reformers, these men discarded major
elements of religious tradition by interpreting them as the unwholesome accretions of the past which had hidden the time-
less spiritual verities.

Broadly speaking, the reformers sought the disengagement
of religion and society. The liberation of Hindu religion from
society would mean that its universal spiritual message could
be taken to the world. Swami Vivekananda declared: "Let foreigners come and flood the land with their armies, never mind.
Up, India, and conquer the world with your spirituality!" [3]
The liberation of society from religion would mean that dis-
approved social institutions (for example, some aspects of caste)
would no longer be protected by divine sanction. Thus the
state could by legislative action undertake the total restructuring of Indian society along egalitarian and democratic lines.

The modernizing impulse within Hinduism led to the emphasis on a new social ethic derived from the metaphysics of
Vedanta, which posits the ultimate unity of all beings in the
Absolute. If all individual souls are part of the same Ultimate
Reality, all are equal. Egalitarianism thus became a prime
value in the reformulated Hinduism. In the realm of practical
action, Vinoba Bhave asserted on his own authority that formerly princes and other wealthy laymen gave land to the deities installed in temples, but that now God wanted the land to
be given to the landless. As the modernization of Hindu reli-

[3] W. Theodore de Bary, ed., *Sources of Indian Tradition* (New York:
Columbia University Press, 1958), p. 652.

gion proceeded, dharma was increasingly divorced from caste practices and ritual taboos. Increasingly it came to mean the free individual's search for truth and morality, epitomized in the title of Gandhi's autobiography, *The Story of My Experiments with Truth.*

While the intellectual reinterpretation of Hindu religion is a significant facet of modernization, the absence of a coherent ecclesiastical structure has greatly limited the implementation of practical reform measures. In the absence of such machinery, the most important reforms (for example, in temple administration) have been brought about by legislation. And it must be said that, despite the strenuous efforts of all the reformers, the religion of the masses is still largely the traditional Hinduism.

BUDDHISM: BUDDHA, DHARMA, AND SANGHA

Siddartha Gautama was a historical figure of the sixth century B.C., a prince in a small kingdom in southern Nepal. The Buddha (Enlightened One) was the title later applied to him by his disciples. Siddartha lived in a Hindu society, derived his most fundamental assumptions from Hindu philosophical teachings, and probably thought of himself as a Hindu throughout his life. The doctrines of the wheel of rebirth and the law of karma constituted for him the statement of the basic problem of human existence. Chained as it is to the wheel of rebirth, the Buddha taught, all existence is impermanent, substanceless, and full of suffering. Man cannot overcome the problem of suffering without extricating himself from the cycle of rebirth, and this cannot be achieved except through the extinction of desire.

The path of salvation therefore lay in the renunciation of the world, in the life of self-discipline and meditation. The search for *Nirvana,* according to the Buddha, was by its very nature a highly individualistic quest. The earliest Buddhist disciples were solitary wandering mendicants who came together only during the rainy seasons. Gradually an organized monastic order, the Sangha, took shape, and evolved its own code of discipline. The Buddhist monks became known by their distinctive appearance (yellow robes and shaved heads) and took up permanent residence in monasteries.

Early Buddhism devoted very little attention to the laity. The layman was taught the elementary morality of the Five Precepts, which forbade him to kill, steal, commit adultery, lie, or drink alcohol. By providing food, clothing, and shelter for the monks who were actively engaged in the quest for *Nirvana*, the layman acquired merit which would improve his chances for salvation in a later existence. Acquiring merit became one of the basic religious activities of the laity and took numerous forms in addition to the primary one of serving the Sangha.

The Buddha rejected Brahmanical ritual and the religious authority of the priestly caste; since these had no power to alter the working of the wheel of rebirth they were useless. However, the first two centuries after his passing witnessed the emergence of a Buddhist cult which included the veneration of relics of the Buddha, the construction of *stupas* in which these relics were kept, and the worship of Buddha images. These activities took place in or near the dwellings of the monks, who also preached the Buddha's dharma or doctrine to the laymen. The Buddhist confession of faith was found in the Three Refuges: "I take refuge in the Buddha, I take refuge in the Dharma, I take refuge in the Sangha."

As Buddhism developed, two major schools emerged. *Theravada* ("Way of the Elders") Buddhism is based on Pali texts and is believed to be closer to the original teachings of the Buddha. Theravada doctrine is professed by the Buddhists of Ceylon, Burma, Thailand, Laos, and Cambodia. *Mahayana* ("Great Vehicle") Buddhism is based on Sanskrit texts and developed most notably in China, Japan, and Korea. Here, and throughout this book, primary attention will be devoted to Theravada Buddhism because of its important relationship to political development in South and Southeast Asia. In considering the politics of South Vietnam, however, we must deal with the Mahayana school, since Buddhism reached that country via China.

The Theravada Buddhist dharma was an austere doctrine which indeed illuminated the path to ultimate salvation but left the layman without divine help to face his earthly trials. The Buddha was not a divine being to whom one could pray when an epidemic struck. He was simply a man who had sought and found the path of deliverance from rebirth. The Buddha, in fact, was an agnostic (or possibly an atheist) with respect to the question of a supreme being. It is not surprising, therefore, that in all the Theravada countries, popular religion includes not only distinctively Buddhist practices but the propitiation of various spirits or gods who exercise some control over the worldly fortunes of men. In Burma these are the indigenous spirits of pre-Buddhist animism, in Ceylon there are gods of Hindu origin, but the basic system is the same. The Buddha's dharma addresses itself to the ultimate questions of existence; the spirits and gods deal with man's day-to-day problems.

The ecclesiastical organization of Buddhism is found in the relatively well-organized monastic order, the Sangha. The Buddha rejected the suggestion that he appoint a successor to lead the monks, and after his death none appeared. The Sangha was held together by common adherence to an elaborate code of monastic discipline, the *Vinaya*. At bimonthly assemblies the monks recite the 227 rules of the Sangha and confess any violations which they have committed. Monastic discipline largely depends on the willingness of the individual monk to comply with the regulations, since entering the Sangha entails no vow of obedience to an ecclesiastical superior. The monk is expected to show deference and respect to his seniors, and especially to his principal teacher and the abbot of his monastery, but the discipline is voluntarily accepted.

The Theravada Buddhist *vihara* is not the secluded and inaccessible dwelling suggested by the word "monastery" in the West. It is, on the contrary, a center of social life, especially in the villages. Not only lay worship on the Buddhist sabbath, but festivals, and sometimes elementary education are centered in the monastery. There is a network of monasteries covering the entirety of a Theravada Buddhist country, with a vihara in virtually every village. In cities such as Rangoon or Mandalay there are clusters of monasteries which occupy entire city blocks, with as many as eight hundred monks in residence in a single complex.

In most of the Theravada countries the Sangha is divided into two or three sects. These divisions sometimes reflect different historical origins; thus the Siam sect in Ceylon was formed when monks were brought from Thailand to restore the pure Theravada doctrine to the island during a period of monastic decline. More important, however, is the fact that monks of the Siam sect are drawn exclusively from the dominant Goyigama caste. This caste basis of Sangha sect divisions is found only in Ceylon. The sects usually differ only in minor points of ritual or practice, not in doctrine.

Despite the fact that there was no successor to the Buddha as head of the entire Sangha, there did evolve in various countries a hierarchical ecclesiastical structure headed by a primate called the *Sangharaja,* literally, "ruler of the Sangha." In Burma, for example, the primate was usually the head of the monastery in which the king had received instruction in the dharma as a youth. The Sangharaja was appointed by the king, held office at his pleasure, and was replaced after a new king ascended the throne. The Sangharaja lived in the capital in a magnificently decorated monastery from which rose a lofty gilded spire.

The Sangha hierarchy roughly paralleled that of the government. The Sangharaja had a council of from eight to twelve learned monks which formed a final court of appeal in ecclesiastical disputes. The country was divided into ecclesiastical districts, each presided over by a senior monk with a title approximating that of bishop. The districts were subdivided into smaller jurisdictions headed by ecclesiastical officials, and finally there were the abbots of the local monasteries. The chief function of the hierarchy was the maintenance of discipline and the settlement of disputes within the Sangha, although there were important political relationships as well, and the support of the Sangha was vital to establishing the legitimacy of the king. It should be noted that this traditional Theravada Buddhist ecclesiastical structure, with some modifications, remains intact in present-day Thailand, while it disintegrated in Burma under the impact of British rule.

With respect to societal integration, we must remember that Buddhism emerged in a complex Hindu society which had already solved the problems of social organization, law, and political theory. Early Buddhism was essentially a new sect of individual salvation; it was voluntaristic, and had no blueprint for the restructuring of society. The Buddha did reject Brahmanical domination and rejected the whole caste basis of society to the extent that members of all castes were welcomed into the Sangha. Caste was made irrelevant within the monastic order, and the general egalitarianism of Buddhist teaching was bound to have some impact on society at large, but social reform per se was not the Buddha's purpose. In terms of his perception of the problem, extrication from the cycle of rebirth is as difficult in an egalitarian society as in a hierarchical caste society.

As Buddhism spread beyond the borders of India, its egalitarian emphasis produced diverse reactions. In Burma and Thailand it reinforced loosely structured societies, but in Ceylon it had to accommodate itself to the caste principle. The caste structure of Buddhist Ceylon has neither Brahmans nor untouchables, and in other ways is less rigid than the Hindu system. However, caste is nonetheless a very important factor in social life, and as noted earlier, the sectarian divisions of the Sangha itself are partly along caste lines.

Buddhism produced no system of law. There is evidence that Buddhist laymen in India continued to be governed by Hindu law in respect to inheritance, civil disputes, and other matters. There was of course the most detailed regulation of life within the Sangha in the Vinaya code, but no Buddhist law which would apply to society in general.

Buddhism did integrate the societies of South and Southeast Asia where it became dominant, but by a very different process of integration than took place in Hindu society. The key integrative mechanism was not caste or law, but the Sangha. The monks, who were found in almost every village, were an agency of social control, custodians of religion and culture, teachers of the young, and communicators of tradition. Until recent times most of the literature produced in the Theravada Buddhist countries in the indigenous languages was religious literature written by the monks. Like all other major religions, Buddhism provided powerful integrative factors such as a common value system, shared social experiences (festivals and pilgrimages), symbols and myths which enriched folklore and the arts. But it was the Sangha which provided the basic structure of this societal integration.

Significant modernizing forces are at work within contemporary Buddhism. The Buddhist reformer has never faced as formidable a task as that which confronts his Hindu counterpart. The Buddha's revolt against the Brahmanical religion of his day was aimed precisely at some of the practices condemned by present-day Hindu reformers.

Buddhist modernism, from the early years of this century, has sought to emphasize the rational and scientific aspects of the Buddha's teaching and to discourage such nonrational elements in popular religion as the veneration of relics. The Buddha instructed his disciples not to accept the doctrine on his authority, but to test the teachings by personal experience. This experimental approach in the search for truth, together with the Buddha's agnosticism, are emphasized by the modernists as evidence that Buddhism, in contrast with other religions, is fully compatible with the age of science. It is recognized, however, that the Buddhism of the masses falls far short of the rational philosophy of the Master.

Modernist interpreters of Buddhism have sought to moderate the doctrinal emphasis on the goal of Nirvana and to stress the importance of material well-being in this life. Not withdrawal and meditation, but energetic activism for the good of society is seen as the ideal for the Buddhist layman and monk alike. These interpretations did not necessitate the formulation of new doctrines, but did involve a shift of emphasis.

Laicization is a definite trend within Theravada Buddhism. Increasingly the intellectual leadership comes from Western-educated laymen who are strongly committed to the vigorous defense of Buddhist doctrines and interests. Laymen are also increasingly concerned about the organizational deficiencies of Buddhism in the context of modern society. They would like to see both Sangha and laity organized into a unitary Buddhist church so that resources and energies could be more effectively coordinated and directed to make Buddhism relevant to its rapidly changing environment.

ISLAM: PROPHET, LAW, AND COMMUNITY

In the seventh century A.D. the Prophet Muhammad set about establishing on earth a divinely ordained Community which encompassed the total life of man. Following the format of the preceding two sections, we shall first direct our attention to belief and ritual, but this is not to imply that these are the central core of Islam. The most fundamental affirmation of Islam as a system of belief and social organization is indeed that no part of man's life can be independent of God's awesome sovereignty.

The Pillars of Islam are the five basic religious duties of the Muslim. The first obligatory observance is the recitation of the Islamic creed, "There is no god but Allah, and Muhammad is the apostle of Allah." By reciting this brief but powerful formula, called the "Word of Witness," a person may become a Muslim. The second pillar is the saying of the stated prayers five times daily. The prayer is preceded by ceremonial ablutions, and the worshiper must always face in the direction of Mecca. The third pillar is observance of the month of fasting, Ramadan, throughout which no food or drink may be taken during the day. Fourth is the giving of alms specified in Islamic law; in traditional Muslim states these were collected like taxes. Finally, the pilgrimage to Mecca is required at least once during the lifetime of every pious Muslim who is physically and financially able to make the trip.

Congregational worship in the mosque, especially on Friday when the sermon is delivered, forms an important part of the corporate religious life of pious Muslims. Various religious festivals are celebrated both in the mosque and at home and, as in other religions, provide the major occasions for joyous social gatherings.

The Qur'an occupies a unique place in the Islamic belief system, and according to Muhammad, it was dictated to him by the angel Gabriel. Orthodox Islamic theologians hold that the Qur'an is eternal, that it existed with Allah before its revelation to the Prophet. Second only to the Qur'an as a source of Islamic law is the Sunnah, the collection of orthodox traditions which record what Muhammad said and did with respect to various religiolegal questions. Islamic theology lays considerable stress on the doctrine of predestination which attributes everything that happens to the unchangeable decrees of Allah. Of great importance also is the teaching concerning the day of judgment, the pleasures of paradise, and the eternal fires of hell.

The predominant motif in Islam has been the concept of Allah as the almighty ruler of the universe whose sovereign transcendence over all creation is absolute. In his relations with man, Allah is above all else the Lawgiver and the Judge. On the centrality of the law, the sublime *shari'ah*, in the total system of traditional Islam, more will be said later. It must be noted here, however, that a very different emphasis was developed by the Sufis or mystics. Sufism emerged during the first century of Islam and emphasized the Muslim's direct personal experience of Allah. Rejecting the temporal power, glory, and luxury which came with the territorial expansion of Islam, the Sufis adopted an ascetic way of life. In the search for personal union with Allah, they sometimes fell into ecstatic trances and lost awareness of their own identity. While the Sufis sometimes combined their mysticism with obedience to the detailed prescriptions of Islamic law, more often they found themselves in conflict with the legalists. The Sufis were the great missionaries of Islam, and the Sufi orders continue to be powerful in various parts of the Muslim world.

There was no question of an "ecclesiastical structure" in primitive Islam, since the Community was a unitary society ruled by the Prophet. Muhammad was the divinely inspired leader who functioned in what we would call the religious, political, administrative, legal, and military spheres of life without conceiving of them as separate compartments. The unity of life was based on the unity and absolute sovereignty of God, and Muhammad was his apostle.

After the death of the Prophet, a successor (*khalifah*, "caliph") was chosen who exercised similar authority. The caliphate's prestige and power declined rapidly under successive caliphs, however, and a deep cleavage developed between the religious and political functionaries of the community. Those learned in Islamic law, the ulama, early acquired the characteristics of a clerical class and in some areas exercised the same kind of religious authority which the Christian clergy had developed. Within the first century after Muhammad, the ulama refused to recognize the claims of the caliphs to spiritual as well as temporal authority. The historic caliphate disappeared with the Mongol destruction of Baghdad in the thirteenth century, was revived by the Ottoman Empire, and was finally abolished by the Turkish Republic in 1924.

The ulama were never organized as an autonomous body, despite the ecclesiastical differentiation early in the history of Islam which gave them a separate identity. The ulama ecclesiastical structure became hierarchical and well integrated but was organized and maintained entirely by the state. In the Ottoman Empire, for example, the ulama were graduates of state-financed colleges of Islamic law and were registered in official ulama ledgers upon appointment as ministers of religion, juris consults, or judges.

The hierarchical organization of the ulama by the state as part of its judicial structure was not the only form of ecclesiastical development. Well-known centers of Islamic learning, such as the mosque-university of al-Azhar in Cairo, acquired great authority in the delineation of orthodox Muslim belief and practice. The Council of Leading Ulama of al-Azhar sometimes issued *fatwas* condemning modernist interpretations of Islam and, at times, has been in open opposition to Egyptian governments. During certain periods of its thousand-year history, al-Azhar has been extremely rich, independent, and politically powerful. More recently the *shaikhs* of the university have found it expedient to issue fatwas upholding the Islamic validity of certain of Nasser's revolutionary policies.

In most Muslim countries today the legal and judicial functions of the ulama have been virtually eliminated. The ulama are therefore poorly organized and maintain a degree of cohesion chiefly through voluntary associations. In India, an organization known as the *Jamiat-ul-Ulama-i-Hind* was founded in 1919 to give guidance to the Indian Muslims in religious and political matters. The Jamiat cooperated with the Indian National Congress in the struggle against British rule and, since independence, has continued to act as spokesman for Muslim interests in relations with the government. The ulama of Pakistan are organized into two associations which reflect different Islamic colleges. Similar ulama organizations exist in most countries of the Muslim world.

The ulama, however, cannot be regarded as the only "clergy" of Islam. A totally different and much more coherent pattern of ecclesiastical organization is found in the Sufi orders. From the twelfth century these mystical brotherhoods began to spread their network over the whole Islamic world. A brotherhood is a group of men who are bound together by strict obedience to the founder of the order or his successor. Each order has a distinctive esoteric doctrine and ritual, its own rules of discipline, and is hierarchically organized. The Shaikh, successor to the founder, is the spiritual and temporal leader who is believed to possess divine power and sanctity. The khalifah is the Shaikh's right hand and second in command; if the order is spread over a large area there are several khalifahs with territorial jurisdictions. The *mokaddem* is head of a local cell of the brotherhood, which may include in its physical assets a meeting house, mosque, school, hostel, and tomb of saints. The mass of followers are organized into these local groups.

A man becomes a member of a brotherhood by making application to the Shaikh, passing various entrance requirements, and presenting a substantial offering to the leader. Various orders are international, and in some cases frequent communication takes place between the Shaikh and his subordinates stationed thousands of miles away. The brotherhoods played a very influential role in the development of Islam in North Africa, but have declined in recent decades; in Africa south of the Sahara, however, they have retained much of their vigor.

In the expansion of Islam, the Sufi orders tended frequently to tolerate and even absorb the non-Islamic religious beliefs and practices of the new converts. Islam has thus come to embrace great diversity in its vast territorial domains stretching from West Africa to China and Indonesia. While the Sufi orders have promoted diversity, the role of the ulama functioning in the same society has been to uphold the unity of Islam through the patient teaching of the fundamentals of the faith and especially through the application of Islamic law.

We must now look more closely at the shari'ah as the primary mechanism for the integration of Muslim society. The law was developed on the bases of the Qur'an, Sunnah (traditions of the Prophet), analogy, and consensus. The last two refer to the interpretations of the ulama which became fixed in the four great schools of traditional jurisprudence.

The shari'ah largely accomplished the monumental task of regulation of virtually all aspects of private and social life. The law is a total system of duties which fails to distinguish what modern jurisprudence would regard as religious, ethical, and legal norms. It includes all branches of civil and criminal law as well as detailed regulations concerning ritual purification before prayers.

The performance of the five Pillars of Islam is regulated in minute detail, and the treatment of this subject always comes first in the books of jurisprudence. Other sections of these books deal with the laws of personal status (marriage, divorce, inheritance, and so on), criminal law, and the political constitution (the institution of the caliphate). This jurisprudence was not the product of Islamic scholarship in medieval times alone. As noted by one author: "Until the nineteenth century A.D. the general tendency of the *ulama* was to expand the practical application of the Law — already in theory eternal and universal — so as to give religious value to every act and aspect of life." [4] As we shall see in a later chapter, the secularization of law in the Muslim countries has produced one of the most serious conflicts of modernization.

Islamic modernism, a broad trend which began in the nine-teenth century, has sought to interpret Islam in radically new terms. This was in no sense an organized movement, but rather the intellectual work of a number of individuals in the Arab world, Turkey, Iran, India, and Indonesia. Most of them were significantly influenced by western liberalism and nationalism. While the emphasis varied considerably among the modernists, they were all consciously or unconsciously responding to the challenge posed by an aggressive, self-confident Christian West to a weak and stagnant Islamic civilization. While their inter-pretations called for drastic reforms in Muslim religion and society, the modernists argued that the values of rationalism, science, material progress, individual freedom, and democracy were already basic to Islam. Direct and explicit acceptance of these values was therefore simply a return to a purer form of Islam.

The most fundamental question concerned the possibility of directed change in the role of the shari'ah in Muslim society. While legal problems concerning the status of women and the institution of polygamy were matters of practical social reform, the basic question was whether Islamic law could be changed by legislatures and still retain its Islamic legitimacy. The mod-ernist answer to this question involved new interpretations of the principles of *ijma* ("consensus") and *ijtihad* ("private judg-ment"), and it usually meant taking these functions from the ulama and vesting them in popularly elected assemblies.

CATHOLICISM:
CHRIST, DOGMA, AND CHURCH

The Roman Catholic view of the universe, like that of other Christians, has emphasized the biblical themes of man in radi-

---

[4] John A. Williams, *Islam* (New York: Washington Square Press, Inc., 1963), p. 118.

cal alienation from God because of sin, Christ as the divine redeemer who by his death on the cross provides forgiveness and reconciliation, and the church as the agency by which God's love is mediated to the world. Catholic theology affirms the doctrines of the Trinity, personal immortality, purgatory, the future resurrection of the body, the intercession of the saints, and the exalted position of the Virgin Mary as the Mother of God. The most distinctive aspects of Catholicism, however, lie in its doctrine of the church as an infallible authority and in the sacramental system by which the church mediates divine grace to man.

All other sources of religious truth, such as the Bible, are secondary to the authority of the church. The scriptures, tradition, liturgy, and other sources all have to be interpreted, but Christ speaks directly in the teaching voice of the church. In the words of a contemporary Catholic writer: "If the Church is no more than a fellowship of men, it can by no means constitute a rule of faith; if, however, it is the Mystical Body of Christ, it constitutes not only the possible, but the only rule of faith. The divine infallibility becomes readily and with relentless logic the infallibility of the Church which is the body of Christ, the God-man present among men." [5] In Catholic thought the infallible teaching authority of the church is made concrete and operational through the pronouncements of the Pope. As the vicar of Christ, his visible representative on earth, the Pope's solemn pronouncements (made *ex cathedra*) on matters of faith and morals are infallible. While this dogma was not proclaimed until the first Vatican Council, it had long been believed by the church.

The sacramental system of Catholicism places the individual believer in a position of extreme dependence upon the clergy. There are seven sacraments: baptism, confirmation, holy eucharist, penance, extreme unction, holy orders, and matrimony. By virtue of the sacramental act itself, totally independent of the spiritual worthiness of the priest, grace is imparted to the soul disposed to receive it. As salvation depends on this sacra-

[5] George Brantl, *Catholicism* (New York: Washington Square Press, Inc., 1962), p. 171.

mentally imparted grace, the clergy who administer the sacraments occupy a central position in the entire religious system.

In the sacrament of penance, the penitent confesses his sins to the priest who then pronounces forgiveness: "I absolve thee from thy sins in the name of the Father and of the Son and of the Holy Ghost." This sacrament has the effect of remitting the eternal punishment which these sins would otherwise cause. In the sacrament of the holy eucharist the priest, endowed with supernatural powers, performs the miracle of transubstantiation by which the bread and wine are literally changed into the body and blood of Christ. "Everyday throughout the world the Sacrifice of Christ is renewed in the Mass, the sacrifice of the Cross offered in an unbloody manner. The same Victim is offered, the same High Priest makes the offering." [6]

The ecclesiastical organization of the Roman Catholic Church is the largest, most widespread, and most differentiated that the world has known. Max Weber included the Catholic church, along with the modern European state, in his short list of "distinctly developed and quantitatively large bureaucracies." [7] The church is organized on a strictly monarchical basis, and supreme authority is vested in the Pope. While there are various consultative and administrative bodies, all derive their authority from the sovereign pontiff, who is the vicar of Christ and the visible head of the church. The entire ecclesiastical structure, from the Pope down to the parish priest, is hierarchical.

The center of the church's ecclesiastical administration is found in the Roman Curia, the constitution, functions and powers of which are set forth in the Code of Canon Law. All of the highest positions in the Curia are held by cardinals. The cardinals, who now number 136, are chosen by the Pope from among the leading ecclesiastics of the church. Collectively, as the College of Cardinals, they have the exclusive right to elect a new Pope upon the demise of the encumbent. Individually, a cardinal is appointed to one or more of the sacred congrega-

6 *Ibid.*, p. 131.

7 H. H. Gerth and C. Wright Mills, eds., *From Max Weber: Essays in Sociology* (New York: Oxford University Press, 1958), p. 204.

tions of the Curia at the time of his elevation to the College. The twelve sacred congregations deal with the major areas of the life of the church; among them are the Sacred Congregation for the Discipline of the Sacraments, the Sacred Congregation for the Propagation of the Faith, and the Sacred Congregation of Seminaries and Universities. Many of the decisions of the sacred congregations have immediate effect, in areas where papal authority has already been conferred on the congregations. Other decisions must be referred to the Pope for his approval before implementation. In addition to the sacred congregations, the Roman Curia contains three judicial tribunals and various offices such as the Apostolic Chancery and the Secretariate of State.

Roman Catholic ecclesiastical organization is thus highly centralized. Outside of Rome, all church administrative authority is vested in the local bishops. Bishops are appointed by the Pope and organize and administer their dioceses in accordance with his directives and the prescriptions of canon law. Each diocese is divided into parishes, and the bishop has direct control over the training, ordination, and assignment of all clergy in his jurisdiction. Bishops must visit Rome periodically to present detailed reports to the Pope.

Catholicism has been a powerful force in the integration of societies at every level, from the family to the state. Catholic teaching, embodied in papal encyclicals and canon law, has given much attention to the regulation of the family. The sacramental nature of marriage and hence the rejection of divorce as an institution, the total prohibition of artificial methods of contraception, the emphasis on the Catholic education of children, the priest's use of the confessional to influence decisions relating to family problems — in all these and other ways the church's regulatory power has been impressive.

But the concept of a Catholic society extends far beyond the family. In the classical theological formulation, one of the three functions of the church is to govern men by laws, and the church has both legislative and judicial powers. By its system of ecclesiastical courts, the church decides matters of moral interpretation and applies penalties, the ultimate penalty being excommunication. Historically the church has frequently succeeded in imposing various forms of censorship of the media of communications. It has maintained a virtual monopoly of education in some countries, and even in contemporary Western societies it operates a complete system of Catholic education, from primary school to university. It has sought to promote, by coercive means when necessary, the Catholic viewpoint on every public issue. Catholic labor unions and Catholic political parties both proceeded from this integralist view of society.

The church's relationship with the state has of course varied greatly from one country to another, but the stated ideal has been the official recognition of Catholicism as the state religion; in return the church teaches the divine origin of temporal power and thus supports the state. The papal encyclical *Immortale Dei,* published in 1885, clearly demonstrated how the intimate connection with the church served to legitimize government: "The ruling powers are invested with a sacredness more than human . . . obedience is not the servitude of man to man, but submission to the will of God, exercising His sovereignty through the medium of men." [8] The encyclical vehemently rejected the notions that the state "is bound to grant equal rights to every creed" and that "everyone is to be free to follow whatever religion he prefers, or none at all if he disapprove of all." The doctrine of the sovereignty of the people was explicitly rejected, on the ground that all power has its origin from God.[9] In another of the encyclicals of Leo XIII, socialism was condemned because of its idea of the equality of all men; the teaching of the church, on the other hand, was that "the inequality of rights and of power proceeds from the very Author of nature." [10]

Modernizing impulses within the Catholic church have been evident at different levels. In the nineteenth century the efforts of Lamennais and Montalembert to reconcile liberalism

[8] *Immortale Dei,* art. 18, in Etienne Gilson, ed., *The Church Speaks to the Modern World: The Social Teachings of Leo XIII* (Garden City, N.Y.: Image Books, Doubleday & Co., 1954), p. 169.

[9] *Ibid.,* pp. 173–174.

[10] *Quod Apostolici Muneris,* art. 5, *ibid.,* p. 193.

and Catholicism were repudiated by Pope Pius IX, but nevertheless had a certain impact. Toward the end of the century the problems of industrial society became so acute that the church could no longer address them in terms of the traditional categories. In 1891, Leo XIII issued his monumental encyclical *Rerum Novarum,* which marked the beginning of the modern social teachings of the church. While rejecting socialist doctrines of class war and the abolition of private property, the encyclical took seriously the plight of the working class: "a small number of very rich men have been able to lay upon the teeming masses of the laboring poor a yoke little better than that of slavery itself." [11] The solutions advocated were: vigorous legislative intervention by the state to protect the worker and the formation of trade unions by which workers could defend their own legitimate interests.

The new social teachings of the church were developed without any fundamentally new theological orientation; they were superimposed on orthodox Catholicism in recognition of changes in society, but these changes had not yet affected theology. It was not until Pope John XXIII initiated his revolutionary aggiornamento ("updating" of the church), which led to Vatican Council II (1962 to 1966), that the church began to come to terms with the modern world theologically. We can here only touch on a few of the major themes found in Pope John's encyclicals *Mater et Magistra* and *Pacem in Terris* and the documents of Vatican II. First, there is the ethical doctrine of religious freedom as a human right, which stands in clear although unacknowledged contradiction to previous Catholic teaching. Secondly, there is a new concept of the basis of church-state relations: "The role and competence of the Church being what it is, she must in no way be confused with the political community, nor bound to any political system." [12] Thirdly, there is acceptance of the basic idea of the welfare state and the necessity of increased governmental intervention

[11] *Rerum Novarum,* art. 3, *ibid.,* pp. 206–207.
[12] "Pastoral Constitution on the Church in the Modern World," art. 76, in Walter M. Abbott, ed., *The Documents of Vatican II* (New York: America Press, 1966), p. 287.

in social and economic affairs. Fourthly, there is acceptance of the ideological and religious pluralism of the modern world; the modest claim put forth is that the church can make its contribution on the basis of *dialogue* with the world.

Seen in historical perspective, and even compared with the Asian religions, the reinterpretation of Catholicism came very late in the day. The leaders of Hindu and Islamic religious reform began, a century ago, the great task of reinterpreting their respective traditions in the light of the modern West. The fact is that before John XXIII, the Popes basically rejected the modern world. The *Syllabus of Errors* (1864) condemned the proposition that "the Roman Pontiff can, and ought to, reconcile himself, and come to terms with progress, liberalism and modern civilization." [13] Even Pius XII, writing in 1939, interpreted the modern world solely in terms of religious, moral, social, and political degeneration consequent to the Protestant revolt of the sixteenth century.[14] Pope John, however, affirmed the good which modernity had brought and identified himself positively with the struggle of humanity to fulfill the possibilities which were thereby opened to it.

In conclusion, Hinduism and Islam lacked the ecclesiastical organization to implement the plans of their respective reformers. Catholicism, on the other hand, was able to advance in a coordinated manner, and there were few dioceses in the world which did not make an almost immediate response, at least superficially, to the modernizing directives of Vatican II.

[13] Anne Fremantle, ed., *The Papal Encyclicals in their Historical Context* (New York: G. P. Putnam's Sons, 1956), p. 152.
[14] See E. E. Y. Hales, *Pope John and His Revolution* (Garden City, N.Y.: Image Books, Doubleday & Co., 1966), pp. 45–50.

CHAPTER III

Traditional Religiopolitical Systems

IN ANALYZING traditional societies it is possible to distinguish two major society-wide sources of social control: religion and government. In the functioning of any such society, however, the two aspects were integrated and fused at so many points that it is more meaningful to speak of a traditional religiopolitical system. The ideological component of this system was provided almost entirely by religion; secular political ideologies did not exist, and the legitimacy of the ruler was based on religious ideas. In a period of very slow communications, the maintenance of law and order was more a function of religious mechanisms of social control than of governmental authority. The religiopolitical system was thus an integrated system in which ruler, clergy, religious ideology, religious norms of behavior, and coercive governmental power were combined in order to maximize the stability of society.

We will point here to some of the most important aspects of this traditional integralist society. Some form of patrimonial kingship has existed in the vast majority of traditional religiopolitical systems. The religious status of the ruler has ranged from that of a god to an agent of a god. Thus King Mahendra of Nepal is today worshiped as an incarnation of the god Vishnu, as have been countless Hindu kings before him. The divinity

of the Dalai Lama of Tibet is taken very seriously by his subjects, although technically he is an incarnation not of a god
but of Avalokiteshvara, the chief Bodhisattva. Even in the
Theravada Buddhist countries, the Hindu notion of the divinity of the king was believed and coalesced with the conviction that he was also a future Buddha. Local Muslim kings
sought legitimacy by claiming to be vice-regents of the caliph,
who was successor to the Prophet and theoretically ruler of the
entire Islamic community. The Muslim ruler was also regarded
as the "shadow of God." Spanish Catholic monarchs functioned as Defenders of the Faith and ruled by divine right. In
all cases, whether the king was regarded as a god or as the human agent of a god, he was also the chief patron of the religious institution and devoted much time, energy, and resources
to promoting the general interests of the faith.

In the intricately woven fabric of traditional systems, the
political functions of the clergy were no less important than
the religious role of the king. The Brahman priest, the Buddhist monk, the Muslim divine, and the Catholic bishop were
in general loyal supporters of royal authority. While there
were, to be sure, different interests which occasionally con-
flicted, by and large the ideological integration of society and
mutual advantage operated to maintain the equilibrium of the
system. Clerics functioned as advisers to the king, performed
rituals deemed essential to the well-being of the state, and
legitimated royal authority. High-ranking clergy functioned as
colonial administrators in eighteenth-century Spanish America;
several archbishops were also viceroys, and at the lower eche-
lons of civil administration, there were many clergy. Above all,
the religious elites in all cases were effective agents of social
control, and their influence greatly reduced the necessity of the
king's resort to coercive methods of rule.

 In traditional systems, law is generally regarded as an expression of the divine will, not as a human contrivance designed to regulate social relations. This is clearest in the cases
of Hindu and Islamic law, which were comprehensive systems
of religious, civil, and criminal law. In some traditionalist
Catholic societies, similar views of law have continued to be

influential, especially in legal questions which touch the sacraments or the church's interpretation of natural law. As we have seen, Theravada Buddhism represents a significant exception to this generalization.

Society is viewed as a divinely ordained order in most traditional systems. The caste system of Hinduism, with its rigid hierarchy of religiosocial groups, is the most extreme case. But in traditional Muslim countries also, despite the theoretical equality of all believers, society is viewed as a hierarchy of different orders ordained by God. Thomist philosophy posited a similar concept of the social hierarchy, and this remains part of the Catholic heritage of Latin America. Again, Buddhism remains an important exception to this generalization.

In all traditional systems, education had no autonomy as a field of human endeavor but was subordinate to the sacred. Religion provided the rationale, objectives, and content of traditional education, as well as the teachers and classrooms. The ruler patronized learning as part of his overall patronage of the faith.

The traditional economy was also subject to various forms of religious control. Church or monastic landlordism dominated the economies of several Catholic and Buddhist societies. Religious ascriptive statuses determined occupations in the Hindu caste hierarchy. In Muslim societies, religious regulations prohibited certain kinds of economic activity such as interest taking. On the whole, traditional religion tended to denigrate the significance of material well-being for human life and to emphasize otherworldly goals.

This general picture of a traditional integralist society may suggest a static, unchanging order, yet this would not be an acceptable generalization without significant qualifications. First, most of the religiopolitical systems which we will describe below are not of ancient origin; for example, the Ottoman Empire dates from the fourteenth century, the Lamaist theocracy in Tibet from the seventeenth, and the Catholic republic of Colombia from the nineteenth century. They came into being, in some cases, through violent upheavals and military invasions. Second, there were bloody dynastic conflicts throughout the history of some of these systems, as in the case of the Burmese kingdom. Third, the religious beliefs which legitimized the system, far from existing from time immemorial, were in some cases the deliberate creations of interested parties; this was true, for example, of the religious ideology elaborated in the reign of the fifth Dalai Lama. Fourth, there were important changes within all four religious traditions, some with significant political implications, in the pre-modern period; *bhakti* devotional cults in medieval Hinduism, reform movements within the Buddhist Sangha, Shiism and later Sufi mystical orders in Islam, and various pre-Reformation reform movements and heresies in Catholicism.

The correct picture, then, is definitely not one of static sacral societies existing unchanged over millennia. What we wish to emphasize, however, is that traditional integralist societies, varying widely over time and space, tended toward similar kinds of internal societal relationships oriented by sacral norms. Thus, as we have seen in the preceding pages, the king was a god or agent of a god, religious functionaries legitimized and supported the king's political authority, law was an expression of divine command, the social structure was sacral, education was the transmission of divine teaching, and important segments of the economy were made to subserve religious ends. From the early decades of the nineteenth century, all of these relationships have come under such powerful external attack that the nature and magnitude of the changes produced are qualitatively and quantitatively without precedent in the history of these societies.

ORGANIC RELIGIOPOLITICAL SYSTEMS

Organic religiopolitical systems are characterized by three essential components: an integralist religious ideology, internal societal mechanisms of religious control, and a dominant political authority.

There is, first, a concept of the total religious community, of the comprehensive religious ordering of society. Second, conformity to the religious norms of social behavior is largely effected by internal mechanisms (custom and small-group sanctions), not imposed by an ecclesiastical establishment which stands over and against society. Third, the maintenance of the socioreligious order is ultimately the responsibility of the political authority, which is dominant in the system. There is relatively little religiopolitical conflict in organic systems because (1) the ruler ordinarily understands his role in terms of the religious ideology, and (2) there is no well-organized ecclesiastical structure capable of challenging him politically.

We shall here examine two organic religiopolitical systems which are based on radically different understandings of man and the universe. In terms of the three components analyzed above, however, nineteenth-century Hindu kingdom and Islamic empire had much in common.

Ruler and Sacral Caste Order: the Hindu Kingdoms. The Hindu kingdoms of ancient, medieval, and modern times have been dominated by a particular integralist concept of society. Hindu political theory has meaning only in relation to this theory of society. "The king is the guardian of something greater than himself, his subjects, and his realm put together — the eternal and holy laws of a society which is itself part of the eternal cosmic order." [1] The divinely ordained social order is highly differentiated yet integrated; caste pluralism is interpreted by a theory which gives each group its appropriate place within the social hierarchy. A sacred elite — the Brahman priestly caste — is at the apex of the hierarchy, but the entire structure, down to the lowest untouchable class, reflects the cosmic order. Each caste has its own dharma — its divinely ordained norms of conduct — and the dharma of each individual within that caste varies according to his stage in life. "The *dharma* of all classes and ages, taken collectively, was known as *varnashrama-dharma,* the dharma of class and stage of life. *Varnashrama-dharma* was in fact the traditional order of Aryan society, a society which by virtue of this very *dharma*

---

[1] A. L. Basham, "Some Fundamental Political Ideas of Ancient India," in C. H. Philips, ed., *Politics and Society in India* (London: George Allen & Unwin Ltd., 1963), p. 16.

formed a unity, though composed of diverse ethnic and social groups and of men and women of all ages and characters." [2]

In its evolution over three millennia, Hindu society has undergone important changes, but this basic concept of the social order has remained dominant and has only recently been seriously challenged. In some of the Hindu kingdoms which came to an end only after Indian independence in 1947 and in the kingdom of Nepal which still survives, the chief function of the monarch has been the preservation of the sacral social order. The role of the king in the maintenance of the caste hierarchy, however, has always been a secondary mechanism of control. The primary mechanisms have been internal. Norms of social conduct, based on scriptural authority and custom, have been enforced chiefly through caste councils concerned with maintaining the ritual purity and status of their respective castes. The detailed and effective regulation of private and social life developed without the supervision of an autonomous ecclesiastical establishment and with only occasional intervention by the king as the upholder of varnashrama-dharma.

The law enforced by the traditional Hindu monarch was that of the texts called *Dharmashastras,* which did not recognize the distinctions suggested by the English words "morality," "religion," and "law." "The distinction drawn by modern jurists between positive law and moral law is not observed in Hindu jurisprudence. According to Hindu conception, law in the modern sense was only a branch of *dharma,* a term of the widest significance. The term *dharma* includes religious, moral, social, and legal duties and can only be defined as the whole duty of man; positive law was therefore regarded as only a branch of *dharma.*" [3] The principle of radical social inequality embodied in the caste hierarchy found its logical reflection in legal inequality. In the law of Manu, all penalties were graded according to the respective castes of the offender and the person against whom the offense was committed. The texts prescribed lighter punishments for Brahmans than for others

[2] *Ibid.,* p. 13.

[3] S. V. Gupte, *Hindu Law in British India* (Bombay: N. M. Tripathi Ltd., 1947), p. 3.

guilty of the same offense, and no Brahman could ever be exe-cuted. Penalties were much more severe for offenses against one's caste superiors.

One-third of India never came under direct British rule but was composed of princely states, most of which were ruled by Hindu *rajas* and *maharajas*. After the 1947 partition of the country, 562 of these states found themselves within the bound-aries of independent India. Many of these states had carried on the traditions of the old Hindu polity without major altera-tions, despite the proximity of the British *raj*. Many of the rajas enforced untouchability in their territories. Until 1911 the state of Jaipur maintained separate courts of law for un-touchables, and in many states children of untouchable castes were denied admission to government schools until after In-dian independence.

One ancient text states: "Let the king, paying attention to all the laws of countries, castes, and families, make the four *varna* [castes] fulfill their particular duties. Let him punish those who stray." [4] In many of the Hindu states, the kings ex-ercised final authority over caste matters, promoting or demot-ing subcastes in the social hierarchy, punishing violations of caste rules, and sanctioning the excommunication of persons found guilty of serious lapses by the caste councils. These ac-tions were taken either by the ruler personally or through special courts such as the *Dharma Sabha* established by the maharaja of Kasmir. Until well into the twentieth century the Hindu kings took seriously their function of upholding *varna-shrama-dharma*.

The preservation of the sacral social order above all meant the prevention of conversion to an alien religion, since this *ipso facto* meant the repudiation of an individual's caste dharma. The activities of Christian missionaries were greatly restricted, and in some states legislation was enacted by the raja to make conversion almost impossible. The Surguja State Apostasy Act of 1945 sought to discourage conversion from "the Hindu religion" to "an alien faith." Under Hindu law as

[4] Vasishtha, quoted in J. H. Hutton, *Caste in India* (Bombay: Oxford University Press, 1963), p. 93.

applied in the princely states, a convert to another religion lost all of his civil rights including guardianship over his children and rights of inheritance. An 1894 judgment of the Chief Court of Mysore stated: "It does not seem necessary to quote from *Smritis* and Digests of Hindu law to prove that an apostate from Hindu religion who is expelled from caste loses his civil rights." [5]

Another threat to the integrity of the divinely ordained order was intercaste marriage, which if practiced extensively would soon lead to the breakdown of the entire social hierarchy. Hindu law positively prohibited inter-varna marriages, and in the princely states the law was enforced without exception. Even in British India this law was applied in the courts, and such marriages could be valid only if both parties formally renounced their religion and caste. Inter-varna marriages in general were not legalized in India until the enactment of the Hindu Marriages Validating Act of 1949.

The major components of the Hindu religiopolitical system continued to operate in the kingdom of Nepal until very recently. The king is worshiped as an incarnation of Vishnu, the god of preservation in Hindu mythology. Despite his divinity, at his coronation in 1956 King Mahendra, a *Kshatriya,* prostrated himself before the Brahman priests and symbolically guaranteed their ancient privileges: no Brahman may be executed, not even by the king. Before the promulgation of a new legal code in 1963 both criminal and civil law were based on the principle of caste inequality.

Neglect or violation of caste laws and customs entailed not only punishment by caste councils but legal prosecution in the courts. The highest religious functionary in Nepal was the *Rajguru,* a Brahman appointed by the government. He presided over an ecclesiastical court which dealt with caste matters and prescribed appropriate penance and purificatory rites for breaches of caste regulations. Under the Rajguru were assistant

[5] Cited in Donald E. Smith, *India as a Secular State* (Princeton, N.J.: Princeton University Press, 1963), p. 98. For other references to the traditional Hindu polity, see pp. 57–62, 94–98, 297–300.

ecclesiastical officers who exercised jurisdiction in caste matters over groups of villages.[6]

Even the constitution of Nepal (1959) emphasized the traditional concern of preserving the static sacral order. "Every citizen, subject to the current traditions, shall profess and practice his own religion as handed down from ancient times. Provided that no person shall be entitled to convert another person to his religion."[7] While pluralism is accepted (there are significant numbers of Buddhists and Muslims in Nepal), the emphasis is placed on the ancient traditions, and any serious disruption of society through religious change is forbidden.

This, then, is the Hindu version of the organic religiopolitical system: an ideology which represents the sacral society in terms of a caste hierarchy, mechanisms of socioreligious control which are largely internal, ultimately enforced by the sword of royal power. The divinity of the king embodies the cosmic totality which upholds the sacral order.

Ruler and Sacred Law: the Ottoman Islamic Polity. The egalitarianism of the early Islamic religiopolitical community had given way, before the beginning of the Ottoman Empire, to a quite different concept of society. "The medieval Muslim political view, like the Christian, was permeated by belief in a social structure based on distinct orders and estates. Unlike the *ummah* in which all Muslims were brothers and equals, a polity composed of these orders was seen as an organism pyramidally stratified and hierarchically arranged, fashioned and governed by the Creator."[8] In the eleventh century, Ibn Sina, influenced both by Platonic theories and Persian practices of class hierarchy, developed the idea of functionally differenti-

6 See B. L. Joshi and Leo E. Rose, *Democratic Innovation in Nepal* (Berkeley: University of California Press, 1966), pp. 51–52, 474, 486; Stanley Maron, Leo Rose, and Juliane Heyman, *A Survey of Nepal Society* (Berkeley: University of California, Berkeley, Human Relations Area File, 1956), pp. 112–114.

7 Nepal *Constitution* (1959), art. 5.

8 Niyazi Berkes, *The Development of Secularism in Turkey* (Montreal: McGill University Press, 1964), p. 10.

ated social orders in the context of the Islamic polity. His writings had a powerful impact on the political thought of the early Ottoman Empire. In the fifteenth century the jurist al-Dawwani held that the body politic was composed of four orders: men of knowledge (doctors of theology and law as well as secular intellectuals), warriors, businessmen (merchants and artisans), and farmers.[9] The parallel with the Hindu system of four original castes is striking, although al-Dawwani probably based his theory on Plato's three-class system.

According to the Ottoman-Turkish view, the function of the ruler, the Sultan, was to preserve this sacral order, to hold together the various estates of the society by giving to each no less and no more than it deserved. "Since God created every particle of the social universe for specific purposes and, thus, every individual should remain as God willed, the first principle was traditionalism." [10] Each group was segregated, assigned a separate status, and granted appropriate privileges by the ruler. This principle was extended even to the non-Muslim communities; under the *millet* system the Jewish, Greek Orthodox, Armenian Orthodox, and other religious communities were recognized as largely autonomous religiopolitical groups within the empire. The religious head of each community (for example, the Patriarch of the Greek Orthodox Church) administered the religious and civil law, schools, and other institutions of his millet. He had a respected place within the system so long as he maintained absolute loyalty to the sultan. All infidels, however, were second-class subjects.

The political authority of the Ottoman ruler rested on several religious considerations. First, he of course ranked highest in the divinely ordained social hierarchy described above. Second, from the Ottoman conquest of Egypt in 1517, the sultan acquired the title of Caliph, which related him to the whole tradition of Islamic political theory. Third, and most impor-

---

[9] See E. I. J. Rosenthal, *Political Thought in Medieval Islam* (Cambridge: Cambridge University Press, 1962); and Serif Mardin, *The Genesis of Young Ottoman Thought: A Study in the Modernization of Turkish Political Ideas* (Princeton, N.J.: Princeton University Press, 1962), pp. 96–99.

[10] Berkes, *op. cit.*, p. 11.

tant, the ruler enforced the shari'ah, the sacred law of Islam. The concept of the shari'ah is so central that government can only be understood as its corollary. As the point is stated by Mardin, "In Islam the law precedes the state and constitutes the principle guiding social cohesion." [11] In theory, the ruler had no legislative power and the shari'ah was regarded as a perfect and complete set of divine commands covering every aspect of man's life. In practice, however, based partly on pre-Islamic Turkish traditions, a considerable amount of secular legislation was produced by the Ottoman sultans and legitimized by various devices.

The ulama, those learned in Islamic law, constituted a separate estate and performed the judicial functions of the empire. The ulama were trained in law and theology in colleges founded and financed by the sultans. Upon graduation and appointment to a judicial post an *alim's* name was registered in an official ulama ledger. Most graduates became judges in the courts of justice, but some became "juristconsults" (*muftis*) whose function it was to interpret the shari'ah when new cases arose. These "written interpretations" (fatwa) acquired official authority in the Ottoman polity. The highest ranking mufti, the *shaykul-Islam,* was appointed by the sultan-caliph and exercised considerable authority over the affairs of the empire. Given the all-encompassing scope of the shari'ah, at least in theory and intent, the range of the shaykul-Islam's pronouncements was wide indeed. "His official statements related not only to matters of religious policy, but also such major concerns of the state as declarations of war, relations with non-Muslim states, taxation, and innovations such as the use of coffee or tobacco and the introduction of inventions such as the printing press." [12] While the ruler was clearly more powerful than the shaykul-Islam, he also depended on the latter to legitimize his decisions and hence found it desirable to avoid conflicts whenever possible.

Despite the existence of this ulama hierarchy, the Ottoman religiopolitical system was an *organic* one. There was no

11 Mardin, *op. cit.,* p. 83.
12 Berkes, *op. cit.,* p. 15.

autonomous ecclesiastical structure. Professor Berkes has made
the point most emphatically: "The *ulama* order differed from
the Christian clergy in its nature, function, and organization. The hierarchy which developed within that order bore
no resemblance to the Catholic or Orthodox clerical hierarchy.
They did not constitute a spiritual corps organized through a
church. Religious matters were organized not through an
autonomous church but by the state through the order of
ulama which constituted an official and temporal body." [13]
This quotation underlines the basic distinction made in this
analysis and also serves to introduce our discussion of *church*
religiopolitical systems, Buddhist and Catholic.

CHURCH RELIGIOPOLITICAL SYSTEMS

Church religiopolitical systems have three major components: an integralist religious ideology; a relatively developed
ecclesiastical structure which exercises extensive control over
society; and a political authority which may be superior to,
subordinate to, or in a relatively equal partnership with, the
ecclesiastical establishment (see Figure III.1). The first component, the ideology of a comprehensive religious ordering of
society, is the same as in organic systems. The existence of a
well-organized ecclesiastical structure with independent mechanisms of social control constitutes the major difference, with
the consequent three possible relationships to the political
authority.

An important distinction must be made at this point between churches which relied heavily on coercive mechanisms of
social control and those which integrated society chiefly by
fostering, through education and example, a common religious
culture. The religiopolitical system which developed in the
Buddhist kingdom of Burma, for example, was clearly an example of the latter. The Sangha transmitted no divine law for
the governance of society, propounded no theory of sacral social organization, maintained no system of monastic landlordism, exercised no coercive control over the behavior of the

13 *Ibid.,* p. 16.

laity. Nevertheless, it is quite clear that the Sangha was a powerful integrating factor in the society. In every village there were monks who transmitted the same sacred tradition, especially through the primary school which existed in every monastery, through the sermons delivered on every *poya* day, and the festivals organized by the monks. The Sangha's influence over society had a mild, nonauthoritarian, and noncoercive character, yet it was extremely effective.

The legitimacy of the near-absolute Burmese monarch was established by various religious ideas and practices — the Hindu doctrine of royal divinity, court rituals performed by Brahmans, the doctrine of karma, the belief that he was a future Buddha, his role as builder of pagodas and chief patron of the Sangha. The king appointed the *Sangharaja* ("primate of the Sangha"), supported the disciplinary authority of the entire ecclesiastical hierarchy by his temporal power, instituted reforms of the Sangha, and in general sought to promote the purity and prestige of the monastic order. In return, the Sangha supported the royal authority. In addition to their more general role as agents of social control, monks sometimes intervened on behalf of the government with admonitions to the people of a particular district to pay their taxes. Popular attitudes of veneration for the Sangha, rather than coercive ecclesiastical institutions, made the support and cooperation of the monks extremely useful to the king.[14]

There was never any doubt that government was dominant in the Burmese system and that the church was subservient to the ruler. As we shall see in the next section, however, the Buddhist church had the potentiality for a successful challenge to the temporal power and demonstrated this fact in Tibet. But the Buddhist church first developed important coercive institutions to regulate Tibetan society on its own, as the Catholic church had already done in early medieval Europe.

As stated above, there are three basic forms of church religiopolitical system: (1) church over government, (2) government

[14] See E. Sarkisyanz, *Buddhist Backgrounds of the Burmese Revolution* (The Hague: Martinus Nijhoff, 1965); Donald E. Smith, *Religion and Politics in Burma* (Princeton, N.J.: Princeton University Press, 1965).

over church, and (3) bipolar balance of power. The differences
among these three patterns are significant but should not be
exaggerated. Thus a government of laymen could be just as
zealous to promote the faith as a dominant church, and some
of the strongest arguments for royal absolutism did in fact
come from the clergy. In all three patterns there was an extensive fusion of religious and political structures and functions.
Common adherence to the integralist religious ideology was
the crucial factor, and the serious disruption of the traditional
order, the real conflict between church and state, could come
only when elites in either structure repudiated important aspects of the ideology. Figure III.1 presents the basic typology
of religiopolitical systems developed in this chapter.

Church over Government: the Lamaist Theocracy of Tibet.
The term "theocracy" has been applied to virtually every kind
of traditional religiopolitical system and in common usage has
no precise meaning. As used here, "theocracy" refers to a
church system in which the political structures are clearly subordinate to the ecclesiastical establishment.

Buddhism alone among the three major Asian religions
developed an impressive ecclesiastical institution, the Sangha
or monastic order. Buddhism was essentially a religion of per-

FIGURE III.1 *Typology of Tradition Religiopolitical Systems*

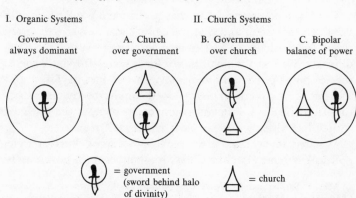

I. Organic Systems   II. Church Systems

Government   A. Church   B. Government   C. Bipolar
always dominant   over government   over church   balance of power

= government (sword behind halo of divinity)   = church

sonal salvation, however, and as such produced no integralist concept of society. In Burma the religion retained much of its original character despite the elaboration of a Buddhist civilization. In Tibet, on the other hand, we find a form of Mahayana Buddhism — strongly influenced by other religious elements — developing powerful coercive institutions of social control.

The Buddhism which was introduced into Tibet from India in the seventh century A.D. had already undergone major transformations in belief and ritual. In the influential school of *Vajrayana* ("Vehicle of the Thunderbolt"), it was associated with cults of feminine divinities (feminine counterparts or wives to the Buddhas or *bodhisattvas*) and the practice of magicoreligious rites. In Tibet it also assimilated indigenous Shamanist practices. Buddhism became established in the eighth century through the vigorous patronage of the king Thi-Sron Detsan, despite the opposition of the nobility who remained loyal to the native Bon religion.

The order of monks grew steadily as large monasteries were founded, endowed with state lands, and given the right to collect tithes and taxes by the Tibetan sovereigns. The fortunes of Buddhism later declined with the breakdown of centralized authority; the landed nobility and the large monasteries became largely independent centers of power. By the fourteenth century the monastic order was divided into numerous fiercely contending sects.

A major reformation led to the emergence of the *Gelugpa* ("Yellow Hat") sect in the fifteenth century. The head of the new sect later became known as the first Dalai Lama, and under the fifth Dalai Lama, the Yellow Church in 1642 achieved temporal power and proceeded to unify the country religiously and politically. At the invitation of this ambitious Buddhist hierarch, a Mongol prince, Gu-shri Khan, conquered Tibet and then handed it over to the Dalai Lama. The latter was confirmed in his title by the Chinese emperor a few year later. Some rival sects (especially the Red Church) were forcibly suppressed, and many of their monasteries were annexed by the

Yellow Church.[15] Thus was inaugurated the Tibetan theocracy which endured until its destruction by the Chinese Communists after the revolt of 1959.

The fifth Dalai Lama deliberately set about creating an ideology which would legitimize his consolidation of temporal and spiritual power and perpetuate the theocratic polity. This was achieved through a special reincarnation dogma, which states that forty-nine days after the death of each Dalai Lama the deceased is reincarnated in the body of a new-born baby, who must then be found through divination. But the spirit of the original Lama was an emanation of the special protective divinity of Tibet, *Avalokiteshvara,* the Bodhisattva who rules over terrestrial matters, and thus each succeeding Dalai Lama is a reincarnation of this divinity. The Mahayana texts describe the enormous powers of Avalokiteshvara: "Faced with any mortal danger — fire or water, monster or demon, fall from precipice or hit with thunderbolt, host of armed enemies or swords of executioners, witchcraft or fell disease — the afflicted on mere invocation will be rescued by Avalokiteshvara." [16] In the Mahayana tradition a Bodhisattva could take the form of a universal sovereign just as he could take the form of a monk. The Dalai Lama's attributes by virtue of this reincarnation were thus considerable.

The Dalai Lama's temporal power was reinforced by other spiritual considerations as well. The early Buddhist doctrine of the Three Jewels or Three Refuges was expressed in the formula: "I take refuge in the Buddha; I take refuge in the Dharma; I take refuge in the Sangha." In Tibetan Buddhism, however, the very ancient Indic notion of the Guru (teacher) also received great emphasis, and the Guru became identified with the Lama. The Lama was believed to control access to the Three Jewels, and one text even equated him with each of

[15] Tsung-lien Shen and Shen-Chi Liu, *Tibet and the Tibetans* (Stanford: Stanford University Press, 1953), pp. 42–44; Helmut Hoffman, *The Religions of Tibet* (New York: Macmillan Co., 1961), pp. 160–182.

[16] Nirmal C. Sinha, "The Skyabs-Mgon," *Bulletin of Tibetology,* vol. 5, July 1968, p. 36. Professor Sinha is Director of the Namgyal Institute of Tibetology in Gangtok, Sikkim. See also his book, *Prolegomena to Lamaist Polity* (Calcutta: Firma K. L. Mukhopadhyay, 1969).

them. However, the standard formula in Tibet and Mongolia became: "I take refuge in the Lama; I take refuge in the Buddha; I take refuge in the Dharma; I take refuge in the Sangha." The most important official title of the Dalai Lamas became Lord of Refuge. Sovereign Lord of Refuge is the title used in the 1963 constitution promulgated by Dalai Lama XIV from exile in India.

The doctrine of reincarnate lamas was later applied to the abbots of the major monasteries, the heads of other sects, and other high-ranking members of ecclesiastical hierarchies. Only the Dalai Lama, however, was recognized as the incarnation of Avalokiteshvara, and on this basis his power was held to be absolute. All the monasteries of Tibet, whatever the sectarian background of their hierarchies, recognize the divinity of the Dalai Lama. The second highest ecclesiastic is the Panchen Lama, head of the Tashilhunpo monastery, who is the reincarnation of Amitabha, the "Buddha of Infinite Light," but as such has no claim to temporal power. The dogma of reincarnate lamas solved the problem of succession for the headship of the numerous monasteries as well as for the Tibetan polity as a whole, since monastic celibacy precluded the principle of hereditary succession.

The Tibetan form of church polity has been described as "a system of very impressive solidarity: the great hierarchial power structure of Tibetan Buddhism, with all its drive toward assumption of monolithic control." [17] The integralist ideology was provided by the theory of the absolute rule of a god; the monasteries and governmental structures constituted the mechanisms by which he ruled. While theoretically absolute ruler of all the people and owner of all the land, in practice the Dalai Lama's power was limited by the thorough training he received from the senior lamas during his childhood and by the Tibetan ruling class consisting of landed noblemen and church hierarchs.[18]

[17] Robert B. Ekvall, *Religious Observances in Tibet: Patterns and Function* (Chicago: University of Chicago Press, 1964), p. 13.
[18] Pedro Carrasco, *Land and Polity in Tibet* (Seattle: University of Washington Press, 1959), pp. 217–218.

The Yellow Church hierarchy consists of four ranks of reincarnated lamas or Living Buddhas. Only the Dalai Lama and
the Panchen Lama are in the highest rank; the second consists of the abbots of the four great monasteries of Lhasa, who
are eligible for appointment as regent during the minority of
the Dalai Lama. Fifty or sixty abbots of large, landed monasteries constitute the third rank, and the fourth is made up of
lesser reincarnations. But the reincarnation lamas constitute
only 1 per cent of the monastic population; below them are
the rank and file monks and nuns. It is estimated that fully
one-sixth of the population of Tibet is found in the monasteries.[19]

The large monasteries are vast complexes, small cities in
themselves, with a high degree of self-sufficiency. The Dre-
Pung, the most powerful monastery of Lhasa, with a reported
population of 7,700 monks, is reputed to be the largest monastery in the world. Many of the monks are students, for the
monasteries operate a well-organized educational system with a
fixed curriculum emphasizing the study of Buddhist dialectics
and monastic discipline. The full course of study runs fifteen
or sixteen years, after which the student monk may apply for
an examination for one of four types of academic degrees. Examinations for the two higher degrees are conducted under
government supervision.[20] Whatever education the laity receive is given by the monks, and the primary aim of literacy is
to gain access to the sacred books, at least to the elaborate
rituals which have been committed to writing.

The economic dominance of the religious institution was
probably without parallel in history. "In 1917 the revenue of
the Tibetan government was estimated at £720,000, while the
church received from its estates an estimated £800,000. The
government spent out of its income the value of about £274,000
in grants for the support of monasteries and the performance
of ceremonies." [21] The peasant who worked on the landed
estate was bound in a relationship of serfdom to the abbot

19 *Ibid.*, p. 126; Ekvall, *op. cit.*, p. 86.
20 Shen and Liu, *op. cit.*, pp. 77–84.
21 Carrasco, *op. cit.*, p. 123.

exactly like the serf of a landed noble. The authority of the Dalai Lama over the head lama of the monastery was exercised directly through the Monastic Council of the ecclesiastical bureaucracy. No lay official of the government exercised any control over the church.

The Dalai Lama was of course also the head of the secular governmental hierarchy. A cabinet of four ministers — the leader of which was a lama while the other three were laymen — jointly headed the civil administration of the entire country. A special corps of 175 monk officials trained in secular administration occupied key posts in the bureaucracy. Their secular counterpart was a corps of 175 lay officials recruited from the nobility, and the usual pattern was for each important office to be headed by one monk and one lay official. This principle of parallel administrative control was applied throughout the government; even the war office was "under the joint charge of two commanders-in-chief, one clerical and one secular." [22] Tibet was divided into one hundred administrative districts which also had this dual control, reflecting the Dalai Lama's dual role as temporal and spiritual ruler.

The unique Tibetan system of church integralism, then, had three key components: an integralist ideology which posited the absolute temporal authority of the Dalai Lama as a god incarnate; a highly developed ecclesiastical structure which through monastic landlordism controlled extensive areas of social and economic life; and the complete dominance of the ecclesiastical establishment over the civil government.

Government over Church: the Spanish Catholic Empire in America. The integralist concept which exerted a powerful influence on the development of Spanish American civilization over the three centuries of colonial rule was that elaborated by Saint Thomas Aquinas. The social philosophy of Thomism was based on "the ecclesiastical unity of civilization." [23] Society is a hierarchical system; in this graded social order, each

[22] Shen and Liu, *op. cit.*, p. 115. See also H. E. Richardson, *Tibet and Its History* (London: Oxford University Press, 1962), pp. 18–22.

[23] Ernst Troeltsch, *The Social Teaching of the Christian Churches,* vol. 1 (New York: Harper and Brothers, 1960), p. 280.

class has distinct duties and prerogatives. The various classes, ranks, and orders are radically unequal, yet society is a unity because each group serves a higher end, is directed by a super- natural agency, and contributes to the realization of the divine design for the universe. In Troeltsch's words: "There is no uniform moral ideal, which would imply the same formal goal for the training of each individual. There is, rather, a distribu- tion of parts, classes, and services in an architectonic whole, which mutually complete and support each other, whose inner unity lies in the ecclesiastical authority, which relates the whole to the Divine Will, executes this Will, distributes the various parts, and assumes responsibility for the whole." [24] Closely related was the patriarchal principle, that the lower ranks give humble obedience and gratitude, the ruling classes command and exercise paternal care.

Thomist theory profoundly influenced intellectual life, and legitimized the sociopolitical realities of the Spanish empire.[25] But no particular capacity for theoretical abstraction was re- quired on the part of the masses; the text which was taught, preached, and believed was simply: "For there is no power but of God; the powers that be are ordained of God." [26] All insti- tutions which exercise power do so by divine right; the exer- cise of power is itself proof that God has given it. In the eigh- teenth century a Peruvian clergyman offered the following argument in defense of political absolutism: "Whether the prince uses his power well or badly, this power is always con- ferred by God. . . . Even if his government is so tyrannical that he ceases to be a prince and becomes a demon, even so . . . we must maintain fidelity, not allowing ourselves any other recourse than calling upon God, the King of Kings, that He may opportunely help us in our tribulations." [27] Submission to the

[24] *Ibid.,* p. 276.

[25] Richard M. Morse, "The Heritage of Latin America," in Louis Hartz, ed., *The Founding of New Societies* (New York: Harcourt, Brace and World, Inc., 1964), pp. 155–157.

[26] Romans 13:1.

[27] Quoted in Frederick B. Pike, "Catholicism in Latin America since 1848," in the forthcoming *The Christian Centuries,* vol. 5 (London: Darton, Longman & Todd Ltd.).

authority of the hacienda landlord, lay or clerical, was continu-
ally preached on the same principle, and it was still possible
for the archbishop of Guadalajara in the twentieth century to
write in a pastoral letter: "As all authority is derived from
God, the Christian workman should sanctify and make sublime
his obedience by serving God in the person of his bosses." [28]

In addition to this general legitimation of existing sociopolitical structures, the church had mechanisms of its own for the
regulation of society. It had a formidable arsenal of religious
instruments of coercion. In an age of unquestioning belief,
the clergy held the keys to the kingdom of heaven. In a day
when men feared eternal hell, the priest controlled the sacraments and hence the only means of salvation. Through the
confessional, he had access to the believer's innermost thoughts
and could control his actions by imposing penance, withhold-
ing absolution, or threatening excommunication. The Inquisi-
tion in the seventeenth and eighteenth centuries became a
powerful weapon in the hands of those intent on stifling all
freedom of intellectual inquiry and expression. Well-to-do individuals were also condemned during this period so that the
church could confiscate their wealth.

Education was a complete monopoly of the church. The first
school was founded by the Franciscan order in 1505, and the
religious orders played the major role in extending education
throughout the empire. The first universities were founded in
Mexico City and Lima in 1553; although the initiative came
from the Spanish crown, the institutions were administered by
priests.

The economic power of the church was immense. By the end
of the colonial period the church held one-half of all the productive land in Mexico. Many monasteries and individual prelates received large grants of land from the crown, and other
properties were willed to the clergy by devout laymen. Part of
the church land was in the form of *encomiendas,* large estates
which were worked by Indians in varying degrees of serfdom.

The Spanish crown was completely committed to the sacred

---

[28] Quoted in Clarence Senior, *Land Reform and Democracy* (Gaines-
ville: University of Florida Press, 1958), p. 19.

duty enjoined by Pope Alexander VI to propagate the Catholic faith in the New World. There was, in fact, the concept of what has been called a "church state," described as "a political organization which is invested with the transcendent purpose of the Church and which seeks to combine its secular functions with a religious mission." [29]

The relationship which developed between the Spanish crown and the Catholic church in America was one of intimacy based on clearly defined royal dominance. This relationship had its roots in the *real patronato* ("royal patronage"), by which the Spanish kings, as patrons and defenders of the church, had acquired the right to nominate suitable candidates for ecclesiastical office who were then installed by the Pope. The Pope in distant Rome could not supervise the establishment of the church in America, and thus it was not surprising that in crossing the Atlantic the rights of royal patronage expanded enormously. As Mecham noted: "The union of altar and throne was much more intimatè in America than in Spain. Indeed, it is difficult to conceive of a more absolute jurisdiction than that which the kings of Spain exercised over all the ecclesiastical affairs of the Indies." [30]

A papal bull in 1501 granted the Spanish crown the use of the tithes in America as partial compensation for the heavy expenses incurred in its Christianizing mission of conquest. Whereas in Spain the church was supported by tithes, in the new world these were paid to the royal treasury, and the crown was responsible for the maintenance of the ecclesiastical establishment. In many cases the tithes were insufficient to pay the clergy's salaries, and the additional funds were drawn from the general revenues.

The kings zealously defended their right to nominate the higher clergy — archbishops, bishops, and canons. This power was exercised on behalf of the crown by the viceroys, councils, and governors. In 1609 the right of royal patronage was ex-

[29] Silvio Zavala, *New Viewpoints on the Spanish Colonization of America* (Philadelphia: University of Pennsylvania Press, 1943), p. 25.

[30] J. Lloyd Mecham, *Church and State in Latin America* (Chapel Hill: University of North Carolina Press, 1966), p. 12.

tended to the appointment of lesser ecclesiastics. The power of appointment to parishes was exercised by the viceroy, although he was expected to choose between two candidates presented by the prelate. The laws commanded the viceroys to appoint always the best candidates: clerics of sound learning, piety, and purity of life.

Royal permission was required for the holding of church councils and synods, although the subjects most frequently considered were purely religious matters of doctrine, ritual, and discipline. The viceroy attended these meetings in person, and decisions of the councils had to receive the royal assent before being sent to the Pope for approval and publication.

Papal bulls, briefs, and rescripts could not be published in the New World before they had been examined and approved by the Council of the Indies and the viceroy. Civil and ecclesiastical authorities were commanded by law not to obey any papal bull which had not received such approval, and on numerous occasions viceroys stopped the circulation of unauthorized papal documents.

One of the important functions of the viceroy was to oversee and maintain the doctrinal purity and good discipline of the clergy. As vice-patron of the church, he was responsible for helping the bishops to effect reforms and used his temporal power to bring rebellious clerics into line. Those who refused to obey were expelled and sent back to Spain.

Royal dominance of the church was thus a prominent feature of the traditional religiopolitical system of Spanish America. "Never before or since did a sovereign with the consent of the pope so completely control the Catholic Church within his dominions. . . . The king was more than a patron in America; he exercised quasi-pontifical authority." [31] Indeed, it is likely that most of the clergy had a much stronger sense of loyalty to the king than to the Pope.

The Spanish crown benefitted greatly from its intimate association with the Catholic faith, for the church was frequently a more effective agency of extending and consolidating the

[31] *Ibid.*, p. 36.

royal dominions in the New World than the civil government. The close link with religion established and sustained the legitimacy of the temporal ruler. There were occasional conflicts between viceroy and archbishop, but the three centuries of colonial rule were characterized by a relatively harmonious relationship. And despite royal dominance, the church emerged from the colonial era with great prestige, power, and wealth.

Bipolar Balance of Power: Church and State in Colombia. The seamless fabric of Spanish Catholic tradition in America was rent by the revolt from the motherland which began in 1810. The rejection of monarchy and the emergence of almost a score of republics in the years which followed meant that, whatever survived of the old order, the traditional society of Spanish America would never again be completely intact. Indeed, the republics which emerged from the decapitated empire suffered from a lack of legitimacy for generations thereafter, and for some the question is still not settled and constitutes one of the factors in their continued political instability.

We are here primarily concerned with the Colombia of the years 1884 to 1930, a long period of conservative rule in which a particular kind of traditional religiopolitical system was built.[32] Not only was Colombia a republic, but it had just passed through thirty-one years of liberal anticlerical rule in which church and state were separated, church property nationalized, cemeteries secularized, and other radical measures adopted. It is therefore necessary to speak advisedly of a "traditional" system being "built." Colombia, 1884 to 1930, deserves attention because it well illustrates the third form of the church religiopolitical system, that in which church and state constitute a bipolar balance of power in society. Important aspects of this system survive to the present day.

In 1884, President Rafael Núñez inaugurated his conservative program designed to restore stability to Colombia. The problem, as he saw it, was as much moral and spiritual as po-

---

[32] For the general background of this period see Robert H. Dix, *Colombia: the Political Dimensions of Change* (New Haven: Yale University Press, 1967); and Benjamin E. Haddox, *Sociedad y Religión en Colombia* (Bogotá: Ediciones Tercer Mundo, 1965).

litical and economic, and he called his program "La Regeneración." He conceived of church and state as the two pillars of society, and the responsibility of social regulation as rightly shared by these coordinate powers. The constitution of 1886 declared that the Catholic religion was an essential element of the social order. The 1888 concordat with the papacy, which is still in force, made it clear that this concept was to be seriously implemented. A later liberal president commented that in fact, what was involved was "the surrender of the very attributes of civil power to the Church of Rome." [33]

The concordat assigned to the church sweeping powers in the field of education. According to article 12: "In the universities, colleges, schools, and other centers of learning, education and public instruction will be organized and directed in conformity with the dogmas and morals of the Catholic religion." [34] Catholic religious instruction was to be obligatory in these institutions, using textbooks selected by the hierarchy and taught by church-approved professors. But control of education was to extend far beyond religious instruction: "The government will prevent, in the conduct of literary and scientific courses, and in general, in all branches of instruction, the propagation of ideas contrary to Catholic dogma and to the respect and veneration due the Church." The Catholic educational system in Colombia developed rapidly with the aid and encouragement of the government and is today the largest in Latin America. Three-fourths of the nation's secondary schools are owned and administered by the church.

Article 3 of the concordat stated: "Canonical legislation is independent of the civil law, and forms no part of it, but it will be solemnly respected by the authorities of the Republic." [35] The coercive power of the state was thereby placed at the disposal of the church in the enforcement of canon law, and this relationship continues to exist. Thus the Ministry of National Education in 1959 issued a resolution which denied a

[33] Carlos Neissa, *Clero y Cultura* (Bogotá, 1966), p. 97.
[34] Mecham, *op. cit.,* p. 128. The entire text of the concordat is given on pp. 126–131.
[35] *Ibid.,* p. 127.

teacher's certificate to a Protestant woman on the ground that
under canon 2314 of the Code of Canon Law, her religious situation "deprives her of the moral authority necessary for the
educational mission." [36] She had been married by the civil ceremony, and under canon 1099 was guilty of concubinage.

The concordat itself was ratified by the Congress in 1888 but
included the following provision in Article 31: "Agreements
between the Holy See and the government of Colombia for
the encouragement of Catholic missions among the barbarian
tribes will require no additional approval on the part of Congress." [37] An Agreement on Missions between the Vatican and
the Colombian government was signed in 1928, but replaced
by a new Agreement in 1953. The latter treaty, signed during
the proclerical dictatorship of Laureano Gómez, and of course
with no congressional approval required anyway, essentially
placed three-fourths of Colombian territory and 10 per cent of
the country's population under the temporal control of the
church. The government agreed to make substantial annual
payments to support the civilizing work of the missions among
the Indians. Education was to be a complete monopoly of the
church. The chief prelates of the missions were to have control
over the assignment of government officials to the territories.
Article 12: "Civil functionaries for Mission territories will be
appointed from among those who can be recommended from
every point of view and who are known to be favorable to the
Missions and Missionary religious. . . . The complaint of the
Head of a Mission shall be sufficient cause for the dismissal of
employees of the Government, if the facts are proved." [38]

The following article of the Agreement explicitly defined
the secondary and auxiliary role of the government even in the
economic development of the mission territories. The head of
each mission "will combine with the primary purpose of his
charge, which is that of Christian civilization, that of promot-

[36] The resolution is quoted in its entirety in Gonzalo Castillo Cárdenas,
The Colombian Concordat (Cuernavaca, Mexico: Centro Intercultural
de Documentación, 1968), pp. 5/23–5/24.

[37] Mecham, *op. cit.,* p. 131.

[38] Cárdenas, *op. cit.,* pp. 5/19–5/20.

ing the material prosperity of the territory and of the Indians established in it." He will therefore seek to develop the most appropriate industries and will assume primary responsibility for the promotion of economic growth. "The Government of Colombia, for its part, pledges itself to help the Heads of the Missions in the development of agriculture and industry and effectively to support as much as possible the properties of the Indians." [39] The charge has been made that the economic institutions which have evolved under church control in fact bear a strong resemblance to the old hacienda system in which coercion was used to keep the Indian laborers on the estate. [40]

The political power of the Catholic hierarchy sometimes extended beyond the broad scope delineated in the concordat and other ecclesiastical treaties. The hierarchy's influence with the leadership of the Conservative Party was often decisive, and before 1920, it was commonly reported that the president of the republic was in fact chosen by the archbishop of Bogotá. [41] Theocratic tendencies were clearly in evidence. However, a formal theocratic structure did not develop as in Tibet, and the basic concept behind the concordat was that of a partnership between church and state. The theory, in fact, was explicitly stated just two years before the signing of the concordat by Leo XIII in his encyclical Immortale Dei. God has given charge of the human race to two powers, the ecclesiastical over divine things and the civil over human things. "Each in its kind is supreme, each has fixed limits within which it is contained. . . ." [42] While the Colombian church tended to dominate the state at certain times, the basic model was that of a bipolar balance of power.

As the concordat bound church and state together juridically, elaborate public ceremonies have sought to reinforce the tie in popular sentiment. In 1903, the Republic of Colombia

[39] *Ibid.*, p. 5/20.

[40] Neissa, *op. cit.*, pp. 92–94.

[41] John F. Bannon and Peter M. Dunne, *Latin America: An Historical Survey* (Milwaukee: Bruce Publishing Co., 1947), p. 659.

[42] Etienne Gilson, ed., *The Church Speaks to the Modern World: The Social Teachings of Leo XIII* (Garden City, N.Y.: Image Books, Doubleday and Co., 1954), p. 167.

was first consecrated to the Sacred Heart of Jesus, and since then the act of dedication has been renewed annually on June 21, the appropriate feast day. On this occasion a vast procession — led by an image of the Sacred Heart and including the president and his cabinet, the cardinal and hundreds of priests and nuns, a contingent of the armed forces and several military bands, and thousands of uniformed school children — marches from the national cathedral in Bogotá to the Basilica of the National Vow for the solemn ceremony. In 1968 the Colombian ambassador to the Vatican in an address on this occasion expressed thanks to God because the republic had been guided and elevated "from the very moment in which His Heart was incorporated into the existence and even essence of the nation. . . ." [43] The Apostolic Administrator pronounced the blessing on the sacred conclave, while in the background the military bands softly played the national anthem. The president in a fervent prayer then renewed the consecration of the republic to the Sacred Heart.

[43] *El Tiempo,* June 22, 1968.

CHAPTER IV

The Secularization of Polities

HAVING EXAMINED in some detail the two basic types of traditional religiopolitical systems, with their variations, we must now seek to analyze the processes of differentiation by which they are being transformed into modern secular polities.

AN OVERVIEW OF SECULARIZATION

In general, secularization is characterized by (1) the *separation* of the polity from religious ideologies and ecclesiastical structures, (2) the *expansion* of the polity to perform regulatory functions in the socioeconomic sphere which were formerly performed by religious structures, and (3) the *transvaluation* of the political culture to emphasize nontranscendent temporal goals and rational, pragmatic means, that is, secular political values.

These three aspects of secularization are universal in the development of modern polities over the past century and a half. They are universal at least in substance, although vestiges of the traditional system may remain. In the United Kingdom, for example, it is clear that the polity has vastly expanded its functions in the fields of law and education at the expense of traditional religion and that the political process is basically a very secular and pragmatic one. The continued constitutional link between church and state, which goes contrary to the separational aspect of secularization, has little significance other than as a symbol of continuity with the past. The state church shares this symbolic function with the monarchy itself.

In the contemporary third world, governments committed to secularization find that the separational and expansionist aspects can be achieved in many cases without encountering serious obstacles, since the process is largely one of legislation, and the changes are widely approved by members of the dominant elites. In the context of a participant and competitive political system, with universal suffrage and opposition political parties, however, the secularization of political culture becomes a much more problematical enterprise. Can secular mass politics develop in a profoundly religious society? [1]

Precisely because of the modernizers' awareness of this problem, a more radical form of secularization has been attempted in several cases. Thus we can add to the first three aspects: (4) the *dominance* of the polity over religious beliefs, practices, and ecclesiastical structures. This involves the expansion of the polity into what is recognized as the purely *religious* sphere in order to destroy or radically alter religion. This radical secularization, associated with revolutions in France, Mexico, Russia, and Turkey, sought both to destroy ecclesiastical temporal power, which constituted an actual or potential challenge to the state, and to change drastically the value system of the population to bring it into conformity with the revolutionary ideology.

These four aspects of secularization, which will be analyzed in detail later in the chapter, are represented graphically in Figure IV.1.

In general, the saliency of the first two aspects of secularization is related to the type of traditional system undergoing secularization. Thus, polity separation has great significance in the secularization of church religiopolitical systems, relatively little in organic systems (see Figure IV.2). For example, the decision to separate church and state in Chile in 1925 was re-

---

[1] For detailed examinations of two major experiments in secularization see Niyazi Berkes, *The Development of Secularism in Turkey* (Montreal: McGill University Press, 1964); and Donald E. Smith, *India as a Secular State* (Princeton, N.J.: Princeton University Press, 1963).

FIGURE IV.1   *The Secularization of Polities*

   Traditional Religiopolitical system

   1. Polity-Separation Secularization

   2. Polity-Expansion Secularization (After 1)

   3. Polity-Transvaluation Secularization (After 1 and 2)

   4. Polity-Dominance Secularization (Combined with 2)

 = Society   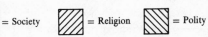 = Religion   = Polity

garded as momentous and provoked sharp debate on the theological, ideological, political, constitutional, and legal implications of the move. By contrast, the deletion from the Turkish constitution in 1928 of the clause recognizing Islam as the state religion caused hardly a stir; the center of the Islamic concept of polity was elsewhere.

Polity expansion is important in both types of traditional

FIGURE IV.2   *Salience of Aspects of Secularization for Different Systems*

	Polity Separation Secularization	Polity Expansion Secularization
Church Religiopolitical Systems	X	X
Organic Religiopolitical Systems		XX

systems, but is at the very heart of secularization in organic systems. Thus, in Turkey it was Kemal's complete abolition of the shari'ah (Islamic law) and its replacement with secular legal codes based on European models which dealt the death-blow to the Islamic state.

SECULARIZING REGIMES

We must now examine the basic types of secularizing regimes in the third world. Secularization is proceeding in large part without conscious direction throughout the entire area, as the secular values associated with modern education, science, technology, and economic development, disseminated with increasing effectiveness by the media of mass communications, make their impact on the political culture. However, in addition there are regimes which, for various reasons, are consciously committed to the secularization of the polity, and these require special attention here.

Western imperialist regimes in Asia and Africa have been powerful secularizers. Western powers deposed sacred kings (as in Burma), replaced Islamic criminal law with secular penal codes (as in northern Nigeria), refused to deal with their subjects on the basis of a sacral social hierarchy and actually legislated against it (as in India), undermined sacral economic institutions of monastic landlordism (as in Ceylon), sidetracked sacral educational systems by introducing secular government schools and Christian missionary schools (as in Egypt), and in general drastically reduced the prestige and influence of the indigenous religions in social and political life.

The impact of the Western secularizers was so keenly felt and so deeply resented precisely because they were of a different religion. Whereas in some cases the colonial rulers actively sought to encourage the propagation of Christianity, in others they were sincerely motivated to promote what we would today call "modernization," however disastrous their policies may have appeared to the defenders of Hinduism, Buddhism, or Islam.

Nationalist revolutionary regimes, such as those in Mexico and Turkey, sought to effect the radical form of polity-dominance secularization. In both cases there was an ideological conflict between a political movement of intense nationalism and a religious structure of universalist orientation. In both cases there was a compelling desire to establish the true sovereignty of the modern state over jurisdictional areas "usurped" by ecclesiastical authority. In both cases drastic measures were taken by the regimes to break the hold which traditional religion had on the people, an influence which was held largely responsible for their poverty, ignorance, superstition, and general backwardness. Even today the Nasser regime in Egypt, while much less aggressive in its policies toward Islam, operates from similar ideological assumptions.

The Communist revolutionary regime in Cuba has pursued the secularization of the polity with clearer ideological guidelines than those provided by nationalism. However, Fidel Castro has not proceeded against the Catholic church with the same ruthlessness which was manifested in the Mexican Revolution. It is important that major aspects of secularization had been effected within a few years of Cuba's independence from Spain in 1898, partly under the aegis of a North American military governor. In 1958, on the eve of Castro's take-over, the legal status of the church in Cuba was very similar to that in the United States. But the great majority of the clergy were Spaniards, and the hierarchy was ultraconservative and allied to the ruling elite. After the revolution, Castro expelled all foreign priests, nationalized without compensation all educational institutions under religious management (including the Catholic University), and instituted the teaching of Marxism-Leninism in public schools. The social and political influence of the church was broken, but it had never been nearly as great in Cuba as in other Latin American countries.[2]

Liberal regimes, with varying degrees of democratic political participation, have accounted for a great deal of the secularization which has taken place throughout the third world. In nineteenth-century Latin America, the Liberals fought many fierce battles in the cause of secularization against Conservative Parties closely allied with church hierarchies. While Western imperialist regimes in Asia and Africa were carrying out their drastic programs of secularization, native elites of strong ideological conviction in Latin America were pursuing similar objectives. With widely varying success the Latin American Liberals struggled for the separation of church and state, religious liberty, the establishment of civil marriage, the secularization of cemeteries, the abolition of special legal rights of the clergy (*fueros eclesiásticos*), the termination of church control over education, and in some cases the nationalization of church-owned land.[3]

Both Liberals and Conservatives in nineteenth-century Latin America were, for the most part, members of a small elite which was socially, economically, and politically dominant. The Liberals, although espousing an ideology associated with democratic ideals, had no thought of permitting the participation of the masses in politics. In Latin America as in Asia and Africa, mass participation did not become a basic premise of politics until after World War II (although it is still often denied in practice). Overt governmental policies of secularization have become more difficult, given the traditional religious value systems of such a large part of the electorate. Prominent among the secularizing regimes of liberal *democratic* orientation have been India, Tunisia, and Indonesia during part of its postwar history.

[2] See Leslie Dewart, *Christianity and Revolution: The Lesson of Cuba* (New York: Herder and Herder, 1963).

[3] For a useful study of the ideological and political conflict in Argentina during the 1880's, see Nestor Tomás Auza, *Católicos y Liberales en la Generación del Ochenta* (Cuernavaca, Mexico: Centro Intercultural de Documentación, 1966).

This brief survey indicates the wide range of ideological positions from which secularizing regimes have proceeded. Western imperialist, nationalist revolutionary, Communist, and liberal democratic regimes have all perceived some aspects of secularization as basic to their political programs.

POLITY-SEPARATION SECULARIZATION

We now come to a detailed analysis of the four aspects of secularization outlined earlier. Polity-separation secularization involves the severance of connections, or the decision not to create the connections in the first place, between religion and the polity. Polity separation may be accompanied by polity-expansion secularization, but the two are fundamentally different. Polity separation frequently results in the *contraction* of the polity, as the government ceases to perform traditional religious functions — the appointment, payment, and supervision of the clergy, the building and maintenance of places of worship, royal participation in rituals and festivals, and so on.

As shown in Figure IV.2, polity-separation secularization in general has great significance in the modernization of church religiopolitical systems, and much less in organic systems. There is, however, another variable which cuts across this typology of traditional systems: the extent of religious pluralism. To put it simply, separation of church and state may have little meaning in a society which has no church and in which 97 per cent of the population professes the same religion. Whatever significance polity separation has in these circumstances is clearly symbolic and usually means that the ruling elite associates the idea of a secular state with its image of modernity.

However, into this same picture introduce a religious minority of 25 per cent, and the proposition of a secular state assumes the dimensions of a question of some gravity. While the significance may still be mostly symbolic, the minority will feel threatened by any constitutional arrangement between religion and polity which might tend to relegate it to second-class citizenship or to limit its freedom of religion. Even if these apprehensions should be unfounded, their very existence in the minds of members of the minority community has already exacerbated the problem for a government presumably committed to national integration.

The strenuous efforts of Jawaharlal Nehru to create the structure of a secular state in India must be interpreted largely in terms of the two decades of Hindu-Muslim conflict which preceded independence and which led to the partition of the subcontinent. Various other elements in Nehru's thought strongly confirmed the commitment to secularism, but it was above all the fundamental sociological fact of religious pluralism which dictated the policy.

We shall now examine three patterns of polity-separation secularization found in various parts of the third world: revolutionary disestablishment, constitutional disestablishment, and nonestablishment.[4]

Revolutionary Disestablishment. In this type of separation the whole apparatus of a relatively modern and secular government is substituted wholesale for that of a traditional religiopolitical regime. This completely revolutionary change was wrought by various Western imperialist powers in Asia and Africa. In such cases the new government simply started to function along its own lines without attempting to assume the religious role of the old regime. As the colonial administrators saw it, representatives of a European Christian government were in any case disqualified from interference in the religious affairs of their Hindu, Buddhist, or Muslim subjects.

In the preceding chapter we discussed the religiopolitical system of the Buddhist kingdom of Burma. The Buddhist monarch was regarded as divine and also as a future Buddha. He built and adorned pagodas, sent monks as missionaries to the animists, regulated the dates for the observance of the Buddhist Lent, and held annual examinations to promote learning in the sacred texts. The king appointed the primate of the Sangha (monastic order) and supported the entire hierarchy,

---

[4] See J. Milton Singer, *The Scientific Study of Religion* (New York: Macmillan Co., 1970), especially Chapter 19, "Church and State in Complex Societies." This study examines religion in relation to a wide range of social, psychological, cultural, economic, and political questions.

enforced the punishment of heretical or schismatic monks, settled disputes within the order, and initiated extensive ecclesiastical reforms. Clearly, the prosperity of Buddhism and the
purity of the monastic order were major concerns of the ruler.

The demise of sacred kingship came with the British abolition of the monarchy following their annexation of Upper
Burma in 1886. Most of the traditional religious functions of
the king were dropped entirely, and the internal discipline of
the monastic order deteriorated seriously under a British government committed to a policy of religious neutrality.[5] In this
very radical case of polity-separation secularization, the substitution of secular for traditional regime was virtually complete.

The substitution has been just as complete in successful internal revolutions, whether nationalist (Mexico, Turkey, Egypt)
or Communist (Cuba). While the new government is composed
of members of a native elite, its political and ideological orientation is just as foreign to the traditional culture as is that of
the Western imperialists. The revolutionary ideology, in fact,
is generally not only foreign but definitely hostile to existing
religious structures. Unlike the nineteenth-century imperialists,
the twentieth-century revolutionaries affirm the urgent necessity
of radical social change. For this reason, polity separation is
seen as. but the first step, and the revolutionary ideology demands virtually totalitarian control by the state in order to
eradicate traditional elements held to be inimical to radical
social change. This leads to polity-dominance secularization, in
which the government reaches far into the sphere of even private religious practices in order to restructure society.

Constitutional Disestablishment. Contrasted with the wholesale substitution of a basically secular regime for a traditional
one is the constitutional process by which religion and state
are separated, both remaining intact after the connections between them are severed. There is continuity in both ecclesiastical and political institutions before and after polity separation
takes place. This process is associated with the modernization
of church religiopolitical systems, particularly with the West-

5 Donald E. Smith, *Religion and Politics in Burma* (Princeton, N.J.:
Princeton University Press, 1965), pp. 38–80.

ern Christian phenomenon of separation of church and state.

The pattern of secularization in Chile has been one of gradual change, with periodic adjustments in church-state relations
culminating in a peaceful and mutually satisfactory separation
in 1925. The early constitutions of Chile all accorded Catholicism a special status as the exclusive religion of the state. The
Constitution of 1823 explicitly prohibited the public and private exercise of other religions and even excluded non-Catholics
from citizenship. Religious toleration developed, however, as
restrictive constitutional provisions went largely unenforced.

By the middle of the nineteenth century, secular attitudes
were in the ascendant at various levels of society. Two prominent Chilean intellectuals, Lastarria and Bilbao, popularized
the ideas of Comte, Rousseau, Montesquieu, and Bentham,
and their anticlerical writings squarely placed the blame for
Chile's backwardness at the door of the Catholic church.[6] During the 1870's and 1880's, governments controlled by Liberals
and Radicals abolished the special clerical privilege of trial by
ecclesiastical tribunal, and by secularizing the cemeteries they
deprived the church of a powerful weapon of social control —
the threat of excluding a person from burial on consecrated
ground.

By the end of World War I, there was widespread indifference, especially on the part of men, to Catholic religious observances. President Arturo Alessandri argued that the privileged position of a particular church inevitably compromised
the principle of equal citizenship in a modern state and also
restricted the freedom of the church. After initial opposition
the Catholic hierarchy came to accept the proposition that
separation would benefit the church as well as the state. In
Mecham's words: "The ecclesiastical and governmental officials
therefore entered into a friendly, businesslike agreement, the
former promising no resistance to separation, the latter guar-
anteeing to the church title to its vast properties, the right to

6 William Rex Crawford, *A Century of Latin American Thought* (Cambridge: At the University Press, 1945), pp. 69–74.

conduct its own schools, and financial aid over a brief transitional period." [7] The disestablishment was embodied in the constitution of 1925, which is still in force.

Nonestablishment. In the two preceding forms of polity-separation secularization, the traditional connections between religion and polity are severed; here we examine the situation in which, as a matter of conscious choice, no religion is officially connected to the polity. This of course was the experience of the United States in 1789, confirmed by the no-establishment clause of the First Amendment to the Constitution. Various states of the Union, on the other hand, had official churches which were later *disestablished,* the last (Massachusetts), not until 1833.

The achievement of political independence by Asian and African states in the two decades which followed World War II permitted them a similar option with respect to the constitutional status of religion. In a number of cases the independent states proceeded to ratify the polity-separation secularization which had been forcibly imposed by their former colonial rulers. The constitutions of India and Ceylon, for example, made no mention of special status for any religion and clearly outlined the structure of a secular state.

In a number of Asian and North African countries the option for nonestablishment upon achievement of independence was clearly related to the ideological evolution of nationalist movements. In the struggle against European imperialism in the first three decades of this century, religious symbols and clerical groups frequently played a major rule.[8] By the end of the 1930's, however, many of the nationalist movements were strongly influenced by secularist and socialist ideologies, and these were dominant by the time political freedom was won.

In Indonesia, the first major nationalist organization was the religiously based Sarekat Islam (founded in 1912). Inde-

---

[7] J. Lloyd Mecham, *Church and State in Latin America* (Chapel Hill: University of North Carolina Press, 1966), p. 219.

[8] This subject is treated in some detail in the following chapter.

pendence, however, was won under the leadership of secularists such as Sukarno and Sjahrir.[9] The Provisional Constitution drafted by these leaders simply stated in article 29: "The State shall be based upon belief in the God of all Mankind." [10] But faith in God, it was clear from Sukarno's speeches, had nothing of specifically Islamic content and, as a concept, had been deconfessionalized.[11]

In the third world a unique constitutional arrangement based on religious pluralism is that found in Lebanon. The population of the country is almost evenly divided between the two major groups, Christians (Maronite, Greek Orthodox, Greek Catholic, Armenian) and Muslims (Sunni, Shi'a, Druze). Under the unwritten National Pact proclaimed in 1943, the president of the republic must be a Maronite Christian and the prime minister a Sunni Muslim. Each of the religious communities is represented in Parliament in proportion to its numerical strength, and the same principle is applied in filling cabinet posts and even administrative positions. This uniquely Lebanese political system, frequently referred to as a "confessional democracy," poses very serious problems for future political development.[12] Probably nowhere in the world is it more axiomatic that the state cannot be identified with one particular religion. However, the Lebanese system is one in which the process of polity-separation secularization has a long way to go. In a sense the system is one not of nonestablishment but of the establishment of all religions, or at least of all religious communities.

POLITY-EXPANSION SECULARIZATION

We come now to the second major aspect of the secularization of polities. Here the polity extends its jurisdiction into

[9] See Fred R. von der Mehden, *Religion and Nationalism in Southeast Asia* (Madison: University of Wisconsin Press, 1963), p. 94.

[10] Quoted *ibid.*, p. 95.

[11] See C. A. O. Van Nieuwenhuijze's chapter on deconfessionalized Muslim concepts, *Aspects of Islam in Post-Colonial Indonesia* (The Hague: W. van Hoeve Ltd., 1958), pp. 180–243.

[12] See Leonard Binder, ed., *Politics in Lebanon* (New York: John Wiley & Sons, Inc., 1966), pp. 25–29, 127–129.

areas of social and economic life formerly regulated by religious structures. The polity expands its functions at the expense of religion.

Most of the measures of polity-expansion secularization have been motivated by two principal concerns: to establish the full internal sovereignty of the state and to effect major social reforms. Many of the modernizers are scandalized by a situation in which so many important aspects of law or education, for example, are controlled by traditional religious structures. To them, the concept of a modern polity demands that these vital areas be brought directly under state control. Even if all the religiously based laws or educational institutions were admirably adapted to the needs of present-day society, their secularization would still be demanded in the name of a modern polity.

In most cases, however, the first motive is reinforced by a second: namely, the conviction that at present, traditional laws or educational institutions are perpetuating a static, backward, and unjust social system and that meaningful social reform can only be brought about by a legislating state which brings these problems fully within its jurisdiction. To cite just one example: throughout the Muslim world the modernizers have been profoundly disturbed by the existence of the institution of polygamy, which is unquestionably sanctioned by Islamic law. Eliminating polygamy by state legislation therefore necessarily entails the secularization of law, at least in part.

We shall now examine four major areas into which the polity is expanding in the process of secularization: law, education, social structure, and economy.

Secularization of Law. Striking parallels emerge from the comparative study of the secularization of law in the Hindu, Muslim, and Catholic countries of the third world. During the medieval period, all three of these religious systems included impressive systems of law. The process of secularization has been long and uneven, starting in the fifteenth century in Catholic Europe but not until the eighteenth and nineteenth centuries in Hindu and Muslim countries. In all three cases, family law (marriage, divorce, adoption, and so on) has been the last area to undergo secularization, and the process in some countries is still far from complete.

Saint Thomas Aquinas devoted an important section of the *Summa Theologica* to his treatise on law. Church canon law was drawn from a variety of sources, secular as well as religious, and by the thirteenth century was of impressive scope. The ecclesiastical courts (bishops' courts and papal courts), which enforced the canon law, gradually expanded their jurisdiction. "In course of time . . . the church went beyond the purely ecclesiastical sphere and entered the domain of lay jurisdiction in criminal cases; and as an important aspect of its rise to a position of dominance in the medieval world it ultimately acquired a jurisdiction which was truly criminal in character and so extensive in scope that it materially curtailed the criminal jurisdiction of medieval territorial states." [13] By the end of the fifteenth century, however, the civil courts of the temporal powers were rapidly expanding their jurisdiction at the expense of the ecclesiastical courts. Roman law, an essentially secular law of pre-Christian origins devised by men to regulate society, became the dominant legal system of continental Europe.

In colonial Spanish America, therefore, the most fundamental secularization of law was an inheritance from Europe and did not have to be fought over. Furthermore, the state's dominance over the church was virtually complete. There were, nevertheless, two important issues which occupied the attention of secular, modernizing elites from the early decades of the nineteenth century — the clergy's privilege of trial by ecclesiastical tribunals and the question of civil marriage and divorce.

The fuero eclesiástico exempted the clergy from the control of the ordinary tribunals and permitted them trial by ecclesiastical courts. In 1795 a royal decree reduced the criminal jurisdiction of the latter, and thereafter clerics accused of serious

[13] H. D. Hazeltine, "Canon Law," *Encyclopedia of the Social Sciences* (New York: Macmillan Co., 1937), vol. 2, p. 182.

offenses were tried by the common courts. After independence the Liberals in many countries attacked the fueros on the ground that they made the clergy a separate and privileged class and violated the basic principle of equality before the law. This clerical privilege was abolished in Argentina as early as 1819, in Mexico and Peru in 1856. In Colombia a fuero is still in force, although the jurisdiction of the ecclesiastical tribunals has been narrowed considerably.[14]

The nineteenth-century Liberals also attacked the church's exclusive control over family law. In Peru and other countries the civil code prescribed that "marriages in the republic shall be celebrated with the formalities established by the Church in the Council of Trent." [15] The religious ceremony was sufficient and had full legal effect once the marriage was registered in the civil register. Non-Catholics were placed under a severe hardship, since the code recognized no valid marriages outside of the Catholic church.

The Liberals won their fight in Uruguay in 1885, when civil marriage was made compulsory and the only legal form of matrimony. In the following two decades civil marriage was established in a number of other countries, including Argentina, Brazil, and Ecuador. In Peru the civil marriage of non-Catholics was legalized in 1897, but it was not until 1934 that legislation prescribed civil marriage for Catholics as well.

The conflict between church and state on the issue of civil marriage was a real one, involving a serious clash of jurisdictions. Canon law states explicitly that "between baptized persons there can be no valid contract of marriage without there being a sacrament." [16] State legislation created a legally valid contract of marriage without the sacramental aspect and in effect made the latter an optional matter for the individual Catholic.

The conflict was even sharper on the issue of divorce, since

[14] Antonio Copello, *El Fuero de los Eclesiásticos: Su Regulación en el Derecho Concordatario Colombiano* (Barcelona: Herder, 1967). On the general problem see Mecham, *op. cit.*, pp. 29–30, 132, 165, 225.

[15] Quoted in Mecham, *op. cit.*, p. 173.

[16] Code of Canon Law of 1917, Canon 1012 (2).

canon law states flatly: "Valid marriage ratified and consummated can be dissolved by no human power and by no other cause than death." [17] Nevertheless, one by one, fifteen of the Latin American republics have established absolute divorce (that is, divorce which allows remarriage), several of them in the 1930's. The five countries which still do not permit divorce are Argentina, Brazil, Colombia, Chile, and Paraguay.[18]

Hindu criminal law had already been displaced by Islamic law throughout the Mughal Empire long before the British became concerned with judicial administration in India at the end of the eighteenth century. Muslim criminal law (with substantial modifications) continued as a system of general law applicable to all persons until 1832. The plan adopted by Warren Hastings in 1772, however, provided that marriage, inheritance, and related matters would continue to be decided on the basis of the law of each religious community. While the British enacted a secular penal code and codes of civil and criminal procedure in the 1860's, they did not dare to extend this principle to the area of family law, which they rightly regarded as intimately connected to their subjects' religious beliefs and practices. With relatively few changes, this is the system which continues to function in present-day India; Hindu law and Muslim law are applied in the ordinary civil courts on matters of marriage, divorce, adoption, inheritance, and succession.

The Republic of India is constitutionally committed to the principle of a common secular law for the entire population. Thus, article 44 directs: "The State shall endeavor to secure for the citizens a uniform civil code throughout the territory of India." Thus far, however, the most significant step has been the enactment of a series of measures which have unified and reformed the Hindu law of marriage, divorce, succession, guardianship, adoptions, and maintenance. While the aim of the original Hindu Code Bill was chiefly codification, over a period of years the emphasis gradually shifted to social reform.

The Hindu Marriage Act of 1955 confirmed the validity of

17 Code of Canon Law of 1917, Canon 1118.
18 Mecham, *op. cit.*, p. 173.

all forms of intercaste marriage.[19] Polygamy was made illegal, despite the traditional religious sanctions which supported it. The most radical innovation was the provision for divorce, which was completely foreign to Hindu law. As the conservatives pointed out in the parliamentary debate, in Hinduism (as in Catholicism) marriage is a "sacrament" (*sanskara*); it is one of the ten sacraments necessary for the regeneration of men of the three highest castes, and the only sacrament for women and Shudras. Despite the protests of the Hindu Mahasabha leaders that according to Manu, marriage is a sacrament and hence an inviolable and indissoluble union, the provision for divorce was approved. Equally revolutionary provisions were contained in the other pieces of legislation: the Hindu Succession Act recognizes the rights of a daughter as a simultaneous heir along with a son, widow, and others, and the Hindu Adoptions and Maintenance Act permits the adoption of daughters as well as sons. In these cases also, the traditional Hindu law was defended on the basis of the spiritual concepts underlying it, but to no avail.[20]

These far-reaching changes in the Hindu law in India have firmly established the legislating state as the central authority in the regulation of society. Religious legal texts, no matter how ancient and sacred, have no inherent authority in the present setup. However, the fulfillment of the constitutional directive to establish a uniform civil code for all citizens still appears to be far in the future, primarily because the Muslim minority is not at all prepared to give up its distinctive law, the shari'ah.

For two centuries, a code of Hindu law called the *Muluki Ain,* based on the ancient texts, was applied in the courts of Nepal. During this period of rule by a native oligarchy, the Ranas, there were none of the secularizing influences such as those with which the British confronted India. Under the Muluki Ain, no Brahman could be executed and different pen-

19 Before the special legislation of 1949, marriage between persons of different varnas (the four original castes) was strictly forbidden by Hindu law.

20 Donald E. Smith, *India as a Secular State*, pp. 265–291.

alties were prescribed for the same offense according to the castes of the individuals involved. After the palace revolt of 1950 which overthrew the Ranas and restored the king to power, the stage was set for reform under the aegis of an enlightened monarch determined to promote a cautious program of modernization. In 1963 a new legal code was promulgated which established equality before the law, forbade certain forms of caste discrimination, legalized intercaste marriages, prohibited polygamy, and guaranteed to women new rights relating to divorce and inheritance.[21]

The pattern of the secularization of law in the Muslim world is somewhat more complex, given the vast geographic region and large number of countries involved. The shari'ah remained basically unchallenged at the middle of the nineteenth century in those areas still under Muslim rule. In the Ottoman Empire the authorities promulgated various codes based on European models (the Commercial Code of 1850, the Penal Code of 1858, and so on), but these were understood as supplementing rather than displacing Islamic law. Indeed, the new law coexisted with such shari'ah rules in force as the death penalty for apostasy. Nevertheless, the dichotomy in the law, Western and Islamic, became progressively clearer, and "the criminal and commercial law became almost wholly secularized, while the family law remained rigidly Islamic." [22] Furthermore, the two systems of law were applied in separate tribunals. The shari'ah courts which dealt with family law were staffed by ulama trained in the traditional Islamic sciences, while the secular courts were presided over by Western-educated judges.

From 1915 onward there were cautious reforms even of the family law, not through overt secularization (as had happened in the case of criminal and commercial law), but by the use of

[21] Bhawan Lal Joshi and Leo E. Rose, *Democratic Innovation in Nepal* (Berkeley: University of California Press, 1966), pp. 474–475.

[22] J. N. D. Anderson, *Islamic Law in the Modern World* (New York: New York University Press, 1959), p. 90. The process was of course not uniform throughout the Muslim world, and it was not until 1959 that the government of Northern Nigeria replaced the Islamic criminal law with a secular, Western-based penal code.

variant legal interpretations other than those of the dominant Hanafi school. The next major landmark, however, came with the Turkish Revolution and the decision in 1926, after two years of intensive debate, to reject the shari'ah entirely in favor of a new civil code based on the Swiss model. Marriage was made an entirely secular matter, and the new code was applied to Muslim and non-Muslim alike. Polygamy was prohibited, and women were accorded the same rights as men with respect to divorce, inheritance, and succession.[23]

As Anderson has emphasized, "it is the family law that has always represented the very heart of the shari'ah, for it is this part of the law that is regarded by Muslims as entering into the very warp and woof of their religion." [24] While significant changes in family law have been brought about by legislation in a number of countries, only in Tunisia has the problem been dealt with as decisively as in Turkey. In the rest of the Muslim world serious questions remain.

In Tunisia, the Personal Status Code of 1956 created a unified legal system in which all Tunisians — Muslims and Jews — were brought under the jurisdiction of the secular civil courts. As in Turkey, the shari'ah courts were abolished. The new code prohibited polygamy, established the equality of the sexes with respect to marriage and divorce, and introduced legal adoption, an institution which did not exist in the shari'ah.[25]

In Pakistan the question of family law has produced serious controversy which is by no means settled even now. An official seven-member commission appointed in 1955 was dominated by modernists, including three women and only one member of the ulama. In its report the commission in fact repudiated

23 Berkes, *op. cit.*, pp. 465–473. Both Roman Catholic canon law and Hindu law regard marriage as a sacrament, and the problem of the modernizers in these settings was to *introduce* provisions for divorce. In traditional Islamic law, marriage was a contract, and the right of divorce was exercised unilaterally by the man simply repeating "I divorce thee" three times. The Muslim modernizers, therefore, sought to restrict divorce by repudiation and to equalize the rights of men and women.

24 Anderson, *op. cit.*, p. 39.

25 Charles A. Micaud, *Tunisia: The Politics of Modernization* (New York: Frederick A. Praeger, 1964), pp. 145–149.

the traditional role of the ulama in the interpretation of law, declared that Islam is a progressive religion, and recommended a number of provisions corresponding to the modernists' vision of what a contemporary Muslim society should be. In a bitter note of dissent the Maulana condemned the efforts of his colleagues to propose Western legal innovations in the name of Islam. "In Islam the provisions of the Holy Qur'an and the Sunnah, be they in the form of basic principles or individual laws, are authoritative and final for all occasions and for all epochs between the time of revelation and doomsday." [26]

No action could be taken on the report until after the military coup of 1958. In 1961, General Ayub Khan promulgated the Muslim Family Laws Ordinance, which restricts (but does not prohibit) polygamy and limits divorce by unilateral repudiation through various procedures intended to safeguard the rights of women. The changes are not nearly as radical as those in Turkey or Tunisia, but the opposition of the ulama has been intense, and it is doubtful that even these reforms could have been implemented by any other than a military government.

The secularization of law has proceeded at different paces in various parts of the third world. In the Theravada Buddhist countries the problem is nonexistent, since Buddhism never developed a corpus of civil or criminal law. In Catholic Latin America relatively few problems remain, solely in the field of family law. In Hindu and Muslim countries the displacement of traditional criminal law came much later but is now virtually complete. On the other hand, the reform and secularization of family law does remain a problem and a serious one in many parts of the Muslim world.

Secularization of Education. By the end of the eighteenth century the British government in India had accepted the traditional duty of an Indian ruler to patronize the classical religious learning of the country. In 1781, the government founded the Calcutta Madrasa to promote Islamic studies, and eleven years later the Banaras Sanskrit College as its Hindu counterpart. However, in 1823 when the Committe of Public

[26] Cited in Donald E. Smith, ed., *South Asian Politics and Religion* (Princeton, N.J.: Princeton University Press, 1958), pp. 42–43.

Instruction voted to establish a Sanskrit College in Calcutta, this entire policy came under vehement attack from the Hindu reformer, Raja Rammohan Roy. The proposed Sanskrit College, he wrote, could only impart "what was known two thousand years ago with the addition of vain and empty subtleties since then produced." [27] He wanted the money to be used to employ European gentlemen to teach the Indians mathematics, chemistry, and other useful sciences.

The British themselves were divided on this question, the "Orientalists" favoring the prevailing policy and the "Anglicists" urging the adoption of western liberal education through the medium of English. In 1835 the committee made the historic decision in favor of the latter. Oriental learning, with its strongly religious orientation and content, was rejected in favor of a secular Western curriculum. Teachers in government schools were strictly forbidden to engage in any discussion of religious beliefs with their students. Having rejected Hindu and Islamic learning, the government made every effort to avoid the least suspicion that its schools were serving the interests of Christianity. India thus became one of the first countries in the world to have a thoroughly secular system of public schools. Under the grants-in-aid system instituted in 1854, Christian missionary and other religious schools received substantial aid for the teaching of the standard secular curriculum and could impart their own religious instruction. However, the government schools remained uncompromisingly secular.

In traditional Hinduism there was no well-established general system of education. Elementary education was imparted in Hindu *pathsalas,* but this was largely a monopoly of the upper castes and especially of the Brahmans, and higher education was decidedly so. Furthermore, the traditional schools were heavily dependent on the patronage of the ruler. By the early nineteenth century the pathsalas had declined seriously and provided no framework within which educational modernization could have taken place.

27 William Theodore de Bary, ed., *Sources of Indian Tradition* (New York: Columbia University Press, 1958), p. 593.

The situation was very different in Burma and Ceylon, the Buddhist countries which came under British rule. The monastic order, the Sangha, was represented in virtually every village, and each monastery was also a school (the Burmese word *kyaung* means both "monastery" and "school"). Almost every boy attended the monastery school for a time, and in the nineteenth century the Buddhist countries had the highest literacy rates throughout what is now called the third world.

The British extended their system of government schools from India to Burma but, in 1866, also attempted a daring experiment, namely, to integrate the monastic schools into their educational program. The proposal was that if the monks would modify their curriculum by introducing secular subjects such as arithmetic and geography, to be taught by qualified laymen, the government would provide books, equipment, and money for buildings. The primate of the Sangha opposed the plan, and the majority of the monks remained aloof and distrustful.

Nevertheless, the government pursued this basic policy for over fifty years. The lieutenant governor of Burma stated in a 1912 resolution that the vital problem was to improve the monastic schools. "The alternative course — to abandon this system, which is closely bound up with the national life and religion of the people, to deprive the vast army of *pongyis* [monks] of what is perhaps their greatest sphere of usefulness to the community, to remove from them the opportunity of inculcating in the rising generation the tenets of Buddhism, with its admirable moral precepts and discipline, and to substitute instead a vast and costly network of lay schools . . . appears to the lieutenant governor to be opposed to the best interests of the country, and to every principle of good government." [28] The number of government-registered monastic schools rose to 3,418 in 1916, but the number of unregistered kyaungs was over 16,000.

By 1920 it was clear that the experiment had failed. The prestige of the monastic schools rapidly declined in the follow-

[28] Cited in Donald E. Smith, *Religion and Politics in Burma,* p. 62.

ing two decades, as it became clear to the more progressive Burmese that these institutions were irrelevant to the new social and economic order and that the subjects taught in government and mission schools opened the door to better jobs. Essentially, it was the monks' unwillingness to accept a limited amount of educational secularization which finally led to the virtual demise of the traditional system.

Islamic educational institutions have fared better in some situations. In Tunisia, the traditional Islamic school, the *kuttab,* was found in virtually every town and village. Near the end of the nineteenth century there were about 1,100 of these schools in which a single teacher drilled his students in the memorization of the Qur'an. Promising students went on to studies at the Zitouna, the mosque-university comparable to al-Azhar in Cairo, which produced a class of men learned in Islamic law and theology, the ulama. The policy of the French Protectorate, which began in 1881, was to scrupulously avoid any governmental interference in this traditional system. However, among the general effects produced by the Protectorate were "the slow development of the idea of a modern state, of public education as a state responsibility, and of mass education as an ideal" and "the steady move away from a theocentric, static, and self-sufficient culture." [29] The Protectorate government created a Western secular system of education with two-thirds of the instruction in French and one-third in Arabic.

Without governmental pressure, a significant movement developed in the first decade of this century to modernize the kuttab by integrating modern subjects and methods with the traditional emphasis on Islam and the Arabic language. By the end of the Protectorate period (1954) the modern Qur'anic schools had virtually replaced the traditional kuttab. After independence Bourguiba moved quickly to create a unified national system of education, building chiefly on the public Franco-Arab schools but also integrating the modern Qur'anic

---

[29] Leon Carl Brown, "Tunisia," in James S. Coleman, ed., *Education and Political Development* (Princeton, N.J.: Princeton University Press, 1965), p. 146.

schools. The religious schools had managed to modernize themselves sufficiently to remain relevant but by the same token had invited assimilation by the state in this process of polity-expansion secularization.

At the other end of the Islamic world, in Indonesia, a movement for the reform of the religious schools also began in the early twentieth century. The modernized schools taught secular subjects (arithmetic, history, literature, geography), utilized a modern organizational pattern (regular class hours, examinations, marks, diplomas), employed chiefly lay (non-ulama) teachers, and even educated girls. By 1954 there were about twelve thousand of these *madrasas* with a million and a half pupils, while two million still studied in the more traditional Islamic schools. After describing this educational reform movement, Clifford Geertz concluded that "a strong and active parochial school system (if I may adapt this Catholic Christian term to Muslim uses) is not, in an Islamic country and certainly not in Indonesia, an enemy but an ally of the secularist modernizing elite. It is an ally not because it promotes the ideals of a militant and totalistic secularism (ideals that only a small minority of these elites themselves hold) but because it allows, and in fact encourages, an established religious tradition with a powerful hold on the minds of the population to come to terms with the modern world, neither simply rejecting nor simply capitulating to it but becoming part of it." [30]

Roman Catholic education has demonstrated greater flexibility than any other traditional system of the third world in responding to the challenges posed by modernization. In the nineteenth century, church domination of education was one of the prime targets of the Liberals in all the Latin American countries.[31] Today the church remains an important educational agency, despite the powerful attacks carried out by the

[30] Clifford Geertz, "Modernization in a Muslim Society: The Indonesian Case," in Robert N. Bellah, ed., *Religion and Progress in Modern Asia,* (New York: Free Press, 1965), pp. 106–107.

[31] For a detailed discussion of the role of anticlerical positivism in the thinking of many Latin American educators and other intellectuals, see Leopoldo Zea, *The Latin-American Mind* (Norman, Okla.: University of Oklahoma Press, 1963).

secularists. Nevertheless, the balance has shifted decisively to the modern state as final authority in the field of education.

In Argentina, for example, a statute enacted in 1884 made public education completely secular; religious instruction during school hours was forbidden. With the exception of the twelve years of the Perón era, this secular policy has been adhered to faithfully. At the present time the Catholic schools of Argentina account for only 5 per cent of the total school enrollment. At the other extreme, of course, is the case of the still highly traditional Catholic society of Colombia, where 75 per cent of the secondary schools are controlled by the church. In Colombia as elsewhere in Latin America, the Catholic secondary schools serve only the middle- and upper-class families which can afford to pay the high fees.

The content of Catholic education in the early nineteenth century obviously had much more in common with a modernizing West than the traditional Hindu, Buddhist, and Muslim educational systems. Although dominated by concepts of a theocentric universe and sacral social order and hostile to scientific inquiry, Catholic education nevertheless could and did absorb much that came from Europe without creating severe dislocations. There has been a long evolution which has enabled Catholic schools and universities to adjust gradually to the demands of modernization. The subjects taught in these institutions today hardly differ at all from those taught in state institutions, with the exception of the departments of theology in the Catholic universities or the religious instruction in secondary schools.[32] The content of Catholic education itself has thus undergone a process of gradual secularization. Among the thirty Catholic universities found today throughout Latin America are a number of institutions of impressive academic standards.

Secularization of Social Structure. As we have mentioned, in Catholic, Muslim, and especially Hindu societies, highly elaborated doctrinal legitimations of social inequality were devel-

---

[32] This fact underlies the continuing discussion over the raison d'être of the Catholic university in modern society. See *Universidad Católica Hoy* (Bogotá: Departamento de Educación, Consejo Episcopal Latinoamericano, 1967).

oped.[33] Traditional governments accepted and supported these sacral orders with their systems of rigid social hierarchy. There was no conflict so long as government and society were integrated by the same religious ideology. Polity-expansion secularization began when sections of the indigenous ruling elite, or a totally foreign ruling elite, rejected the religious basis of inequality and sought to bring about social change in the direction of equality through state intervention.

By positing the radical idea of a legislating state, the British in nineteenth-century India prepared the way for the modern concept of government as the regulator of society. The principle of equality before the law, which the British regarded as an elementary notion, was in fact revolutionary in the context of Indian history, and the 1860 Indian Penal Code which embodied this principle was in effect an attack on traditional Hindu caste society. Comparable changes in the Hindu kingdom of Nepal did not come until 1963. The British adoption of universalistic criteria in recruitment to the civil service (education and the passing of competitive examinations) represented another blow to the traditional caste hierarchy.

The British government in India was limited, however, in its role as the new regulator of society. As an imperialist regime it was not primarily concerned with the modernization of the country, and as a foreign Christian government it could not promote social reform without exposing itself to the charge that it was interfering with Hindu religious matters.[34] It was, therefore, only after independence that governmental intervention to promote social equality became prominent — legislation forbidding various acts of caste discrimination, government departments administering special aid to the ex-untouchables and other backward classes.

In Latin America, the concept of a hierarchical society, which was rooted in medieval theology, was restated and reinforced doctrinally by various writers at the beginning of the

[33] See Chap. II.

[34] For an excellent discussion of the relationship between nationalism and reform see Charles H. Heimsath, *Indian Nationalism and Hindu Social Reform* (Princeton, N.J.: Princeton University Press, 1964).

sixteenth century. "A person convinced of these arguments could not help but acquire attitudes of acceptance of the differences between groups (especially economic and racial differences) and rationalize them as facts within the divine order of the universe." [35] The first major ideological challenge to these arguments came with the impulses generated by the French Revolution. The Declaration of the Rights of Man and Citizen was translated into Spanish and published in America in 1794. However, the first use to which the revolutionary ideology was put was to assert the equality of the native-born Creole elite with the Spanish ruling elite. And once independence was achieved, the Liberals who intellectually continued to profess the ideals of the French Revolution had no desire to destroy the basis of their own status as members of a ruling elite.

Throughout the nineteenth century, liberalism, with its profound distrust of governmental regulation, failed to accept the state as the regulator and reformer of an increasingly desacralized society. As Frederick B. Pike has pointed out: "Although events in the nineteenth and twentieth centuries altered the traditional pattern of relations between church and state in most Latin American countries, traditionalism remained largely unchallenged in regard to one important aspect of the social structure. While new middle groups were achieving positions of social, economic, and political importance, almost nothing was accomplished toward incorporating the vast lower mass into society." [36] Governments now recognize that the equalization of educational opportunities is a key step in approaching this major problem. Many ideological tendencies (socialist, populist, nationalist, Christian Democratic) now converge on the basic view that a major restructuring of society is the primary responsibility of the state.

Secularization of Economy. In all the traditional societies considered here, religioeconomic institutions were important. Systems of Islamic and Hindu religious endowments resulted,

---

[35] Orlando Fals Borda, *La Subversión en Colombia: El Cambio Social en la Historia* (Bogotá: Ediciones Tercer Mundo, 1967), p. 71.

[36] Frederick B. Pike, *The Conflict Between Church and State in Latin America* (New York: Alfred A. Knopf, 1964), pp. 20–21.

in some cases, in the accumulation of vast wealth in the form of landed property attached to mosques and temples. According to one theory of Hindu law, the god of the temple is a juridical person who owns the land which has been dedicated to him by a worshiper. Buddhist monastic landlordism continues to be a prominent economic institution in central Ceylon, despite the unfriendly policies of the government during the British period and the efforts of lay Buddhist reformers since independence. The Catholic church continues to be counted among the largest landlords in a number of Latin American countries.

Nevertheless, virtually everywhere in the third world, governmental programs of land reform are now expanding the regulatory jurisdiction of the polity to include economic relationships which were formerly considered sacred and inviolable. In the eyes of the modernizers, if there is any sacred relationship it is between the peasant and the land he tills, not between the land and the divinity or clergy to whom it was once offered.

This radical secularization of the economy has of course been most marked in countries which have experienced revolutions. When Mexico achieved its independence in 1821, one-half of all the productive real estate in the country was in the hands of the church. Each diocese had a highly organized fiscal institution called the *Juzgado* which functioned as a bank, receiving clerical revenues and making loans at interest.[37]

The Liberals sought to crush the church's economically based political power and enviously contrasted the empty state treasury with the ample financial resources of the clergy. In 1856, Liberal legislation prohibited ecclesiastical corporations from administering real estate other than that directly used for purposes of worship. Following a three-year civil war, Juárez issued an executive decree providing for the actual confiscation of ecclesiastical holdings. The church recouped much of its economic losses, however, during the long and conservative

[37] See Michael P. Costeloe, *Church Wealth in Mexico* (Cambridge: Cambridge University Press, 1967).

Díaz regime. The Mexican Revolution not only stripped the church of all agricultural lands but decreed that ownership of church buildings used solely for worship was vested in the state. In the revolutionary ideology, argrarian reform for its own sake became a much more important motive than in the anticlerical legislation enacted by the nineteenth-century Liberals.

POLITY-TRANSVALUATION SECULARIZATION

The first two major aspects of secularization, polity separation and polity expansion, involve profound *relational changes* among the three spheres of religion, polity, and society. The differentiation which occurs results in (1) the separation of polity and religion and (2) the expansion of the polity at the expense of religion in the regulation of society. Polity-transvaluation secularization, which we shall now attempt to analyze, involves *internal qualitative changes* within the polity: the secularization of political culture.[38]

Secularization of Political Culture. Sidney Verba has defined the concept "political culture" as follows: "The political culture of a society consists of the system of empirical beliefs, expressive symbols, and values which defines the situation in which political action takes place. It provides the subjective orientation to politics." [39] It is clear that the secularization of political culture is a far more complex matter than either polity-separation or polity-expansion secularization. To begin with, both of these aspects of secularization can be and are largely imposed by modernizing elites; decisions made in these processes are not referred to the masses for approval. The

---

[38] For a stimulating discussion of this subject see Gabriel A. Almond and G. Bingham Powell, Jr., *Comparative Politics: A Developmental Approach* (Boston: Little, Brown and Co., 1966), pp. 57–63. See also the excellent chapter on "The Formation of Political Values" in David E. Apter, *The Politics of Modernization* (Chicago: University of Chicago Press, 1965), pp. 266–312.

[39] Sidney Verba, "Comparative Political Culture," in Lucian W. Pye and Sidney Verba eds., *Political Culture and Political Development* (Princeton, N.J.: Princeton University Press, 1966), p. 513.

secularization of political culture, because it involves broadly
based changes in values, cannot be effectively directed by the
ruling elite within a short span of time. It is a long process in
which value changes are effected, gradually, by the formal educational system and by other means at the disposal of governments, but perhaps more importantly by a number of related
processes (technological changes, industrialization, urbaniza-
tion, economic growth, and so on) over which governments in
fact have very limited control. The few cases in which governments have attempted to secularize general culture and hence
political culture rapidly and coercively constitute a special
category, polity-dominance secularization, which is considered
in the next section.

Underlying the secularization of political culture is the decline of explicitly religious values, generally throughout the
society. Religiosity and piety are no longer highly valued socially. Material values rank higher than otherworldly values,
and concern with ethical social relationships based on universalistic norms takes the place of beliefs and rituals rooted in
specific religious traditions. There is growing scepticism concerning the truth or validity of traditional religious doctrine,
and less concern with transmitting religious ideas in the socialization process. Religious values no longer motivate importantly; the Indonesian Muslim is no longer prepared to
sacrifice and save for thirty years in order to make the journey
to Mecca. People do not think about religion much; it occupies
a diminishing part of their consciousness. There is growing
tolerance of religious values foreign to one's own culture and
a growing relativism based on scepticism of all religious truth
claims.

This secularization of values has been evident in the history
of the West since the seventeenth century and is now broadly
based in Western society. The same process began with the
elites of the third world in the nineteenth century and is now
slowly spreading to the masses. Is this thoroughgoing secularization of the general culture really necessary in order to produce a secular *political* culture? It is certainly possible for
individuals to perceive religion as a purely private matter of

faith and to be intensely devout personally while functioning
politically in a completely secular manner. Clearly there are
many such individuals in contemporary Western society.
However, for an adherent of one of the major religions of the
third world (with the possible exception of Theravada Buddhism) to regard religion as a private matter means that he has
already abandoned large segments of the traditional religious
system, that his world view has already undergone radical secularization. In the West, general cultural secularization has in
fact accompanied and facilitated the secularization of political
culture and it seems likely that the process will be similar in
the third world.[40] We must now consider the secularization of
two major facets of political culture, namely, attitudes and
values relating to legitimacy and group identity.

Secularization of the Basis of Legitimacy. In all traditional
religiopolitical systems, government was in some sense divine.
The king was himself a god or at the very least an agent of a
god. His function was the maintenance of a sacral sociopolitical order. The legitimacy of governments was based primarily
on their divine nature and function. No single fact more
clearly marks the end of the traditional age than governments
no longer claiming legitimacy on grounds of divinity. Vestiges
of the old theory still remain, but their weakness is evidenced
by the disinclination of regimes to put all of their eggs in the
basket of divinity. Thus, spokesmen for an allegedly divine
government will insist that it is also the people's government
and, furthermore, an effective government.

Three major secular legitimations of rule are commonly
offered. First, this is an *ideologically true* government. That is,
the regime is fully committed to the principles and blueprint
provided by the ideology and hence is related to some ultimate
truth. This approach, expressed by Communist and other ideological regimes, has obvious affinities with traditional notions
of divine government. Second, this is *the people's government*.
This approach may reflect several backgrounds: nationalism
(for example, a post-independence government in contrast with

[40] See Bernard Eugene Meland, *The Secularization of Modern Cultures*
(New York: Oxford University Press, 1966).

former foreign imperialist rule), democracy (a government elected by universal suffrage), or socialism (a government representing workers and peasants). Third, this is an *effective government.* That is, it is legitimate because it gets things done. This highly pragmatic approach to the question of legitimacy is increasingly influential in the industrially more developed societies, capitalist and Communist alike.

Religion thus ceases to be a potent source of legitimacy for governments, politicians, or political movements. A prime minister's ostentatious religiosity is no longer sufficient to establish him as a good prime minister; he is judged on his performance in the realm of the temporal. The goals of government are no longer determined by religious ideas; governments are expected to promote the physical health, social welfare, and economic prosperity of the people as well as to advance national power and prestige. Where religious dogma conflicts with programs of social welfare (such as birth control), the dogma is ignored or even repudiated. Both nature and society are desacralized, and government understands its function to be their rational manipulation in such a way as to maximize human welfare. As the ends of government are increasingly secular, so also the means. Religion becomes largely irrelevant to decision making, and astrology, divination, supernatural signs, prayers, and directives of religious authorities no longer guide the activities of governments.

When speaking of the secularization of political culture, not only do we refer to the decline of religious values in the understanding and motivations of political life but also to the development of positive secular values — egalitarianism, humanism, materialism (in the sense of predominantly this-worldly concerns), rationality, and a pragmatic problem-solving orientation. Both the ends and means of politics are increasingly informed by these values in a secular political culture.

Secularization of Group Identity. As Verba points out, "The first and most crucial problem that must be solved in the formation of a political culture, if it is to be capable of supporting a stable yet adaptable political system, is that of national identity." [41] It is necessary that individuals who are by legal definition citizens and hence part of the nation-state come to *feel* that they are part of it. The question of a sense of identity with the nation and loyalty to the nation-state is for the individual a serious problem "in many ways similar to that of religious identification." [42] Verba does not develop this point further, but the rise of nationalism in the West involved precisely the *displacement* of religious values and loyalties by those associated with the nation as the prime orientation to social and political life. "Modern nationalism has displaced religion as the chief factor in human group relationships." [43] A fundamental aspect of the secularization of political culture is therefore the development of a secular national identity.

In the Hindu, Buddhist, and Muslim countries the basic conflict between religion and nation as the prime political value was partly obscured by anti-imperialist nationalist movements in which religious forces participated as an important ally, especially in the early decades of this century.[44] As the European rulers were Christians engaged in the Westernization of their colonies, opposition could as logically be led by Burmese monks as by Burmese nationalists, by Algerian ulama as by Algerian nationalists. With the achievement of independence, however, the underlying conflict between religion and nation became more evident.

There were of course many efforts to manipulate religion in order to strengthen the commitment to nation. Thus, M. A. Jinnah produced the totally un-Islamic notion of a Muslim *nation* within British India, and after the creation of Pakistan, secularized politicians (civilian and military) continued to associate Islam with the nation with the object of creating ultimately a strong sense of Pakistani national identity. In other Muslim countries, however, the tension between religion and

[41] Verba, *op. cit.*, p. 529.

[42] Verba, *loc. cit.*

[43] Salo Witmayer Baron, *Modern Nationalism and Religion* (New York: Meridian Books, Inc., 1960), p. 7.

[44] This alliance between religion and nationalism is analyzed in some detail in Chap. V.

nation has been recognized more openly, and governments have seen the necessity of secularizing political culture in order to establish the nation. Mustafa Kemal declared in 1925: "The Turkish Revolution signifies a transformation far broader than the word revolution suggests. . . . It means replacing an age-old political unity based on religion with one based on another tie, that of nationality." [45]

While religion was relegated to a subordinate place under nation in countries where one faith was overwhelmingly dominant, in other countries religious pluralism resulted in efforts to exclude religion entirely from the definition of nation. Secular nationalists in Syria sought a territorial definition of nation which included both Muslims and Christians, while their counterparts in India spoke of an Indian nation composed of Hindus and Muslims. Religious pluralism posed the problem in its most acute form — a true sense of national identity could develop only on a secular basis, for any religious definition of nation would exclude an important segment of the population.

The secularization of political culture thus involves the secularization of beliefs and sentiments about nationality. In this sense the secularization of American political culture, while its legal basis was formed at the end of the eighteenth century, has been a continuing process which is not yet complete. The normative assertion that Americans are a "Protestant nation" was a powerful one in our political culture until recent decades; this idea was not finally laid to rest until the election of John F. Kennedy in 1960. And overtones of the idea of "Christian nation" still linger.

POLITY-DOMINANCE SECULARIZATION

The first three processes of secularization (polity separation, expansion, and transvaluation) can be observed very widely throughout the world. The phenomenon of polity-dominance secularization has occurred in a few countries, chiefly France, Mexico, Russia, Turkey, and China during periods of revolu-

[45] Quoted in Berkes, *op. cit.*, p. 470.

tionary upheaval. Despite its limited distribution, the phenomenon is of great significance and because of its peculiar
features must be distinguished analytically from the other
three forms of secularization.

Polity-separation secularization severs the ties between religion and polity; polity dominance creates new institutional ties
in order to bring religion under control. Polity-expansion secularization involves the growth of the polity at the expense of
religion in the regulation of society; polity dominance goes beyond this to deny to religion any area of autonomy whatsoever.
Polity transvaluation involves the secularization of political
culture in a gradual process in which nongovernmental and
noncoercive factors are important and possibly crucial; polity-
dominance secularization involves an open governmental attack on the religious basis of the general culture and the
forcible imposition of a secular ideology on the political culture. The polity takes over religion, in order to drastically re-
duce its influence (or even eradicate it) or to restructure and
reform it, thus bringing it into line with the modernizing program of the regime. In denying any autonomy to the religious
sphere, the state operates on totalitarian premises, although
its overall philosophy need not be explicitly totalitarian.

The Mexican Revolution which erupted in 1910 was bitterly
opposed by the Catholic clergy, who feared the educational
and agrarian reforms which were soon incorporated into the
revolutionary program. The revolutionaries stood in the tradition of the anticlerical liberalism of the nineteenth century,
and some of them were atheists. They claimed that their reforms were "not aimed at the Church in its spiritual sphere,
but at the clergy in their temporal activities." [46] Over a period
of thirty years, however, it became clear that the matter was
not so simple. The goal of the Revolution came to be defined
as a major restructuring of society, and it was not enough to
put an end to the political activities of the clergy. The political culture of the country had to be secularized, and this involved radical changes in both education and religion under a

[46] Mecham, *op. cit.,* p. 381.

dominant polity. Apart from more or less rational considerations, during several periods fanaticism was evident on both sides, and state attacks on the church clearly constituted persecution of Catholicism.

The constitution of 1917 declared that church buildings were the property of the nation, forbade religious corporations or personnel from administering schools, prohibited the establishment of monastic orders, recognized no juridic personality in religious institutions, gave to the state legislatures the exclusive power to regulate the number of priests to be permitted within their respective states, prohibited foreigners from functioning as ministers of religion, and deprived the clergy of the right to vote. The constitutional provisions were not enforced, however, until President Calles issued a series of drastic laws implementing them early in 1926. State governments exercised their constitutional prerogative; the state of Tabasco authorized six priests for the entire territory, and other states were equally severe in their restrictions. In the bitter conflict which developed, the Catholic hierarchy suspended religious services, and for three years (1926 to 1929) no masses were celebrated in Mexico.

After a short period of church-state conciliation, a new educational plan was introduced. General Plutarco Calles, one of its originators, declared in 1934: "It is necessary that we enter into a new phase of the Revolution which I shall call the psychological revolutionary period; we must enter into and take possession of the minds of children, the consciences of the young, because they do belong and should belong to the Revolution. . . . It is absolutely necessary to drive the enemy out of that entrenchment where the clergy has been, where the Conservatives have been — I refer to Education." [47] The Constitution was amended to provide for "socialistic" education, and in a number of states teachers were required to make an ideological declaration which stated in part: "I declare that I am an atheist, an irreconcilable enemy of the Catholic, Apostolic, Roman religion, that I will endeavor to destroy it, detaching con-

[47] Quoted *ibid.,* p. 406.

sciences from the bonds of any religious worship, and that I am ready to fight against the clergy anywhere and wherever it may be necessary." [48]

In 1936 a new administration suspended the antireligious campaign, but despite the general easing of tensions, serious disputes over education have continued to arise from time to time. The anticlerical laws have not been repealed but have remained unenforced as a tacit understanding between church and state has developed. Since 1940, even presidents of the republic have been able to declare publicly their Catholic faith.

We have already touched on various aspects of the secularization which was a vital part of the Turkish Revolution. However, the abolition of the caliphate and the shari'ah (polity separation and polity expansion, respectively) were accompanied by legislation suggestive of polity dominance, such as the law abolishing religious orders and their cloisters. In fact, from 1923 until 1928, Kemal engaged in various experiments of religious reform, convinced that Islam was essentially a natural and rational religion which had to be rescued from the obscurantism of the ulama who posed as its sole authentic interpreters. Radical religious reforms were also the only way the state could safeguard individual freedom. As Berkes stated the Kemalist position: "Freeing the conscience could be effected only when and insofar as the theocratic concept was eliminated from the body of the religious outlook." [49] The modernization of religion had to accompany the modernization of the state.

In 1924, a Department of the Affairs of Piety was established by the government to manage the administrative affairs of religion and promote the governmental reforms of Islam. One of its activities was the preparation of textbooks on religion for children. Under Kemal's leadership, Turkish took the place of Arabic in the sermons and call to prayer, and after a long struggle, he initiated the recital of the Qur'an in Turkish in 1931. He was determined to make the sources of Islam accessible to the people, thereby undermining the reli-

[48] Quoted *ibid.*, p. 407.
[49] Berkes, *op. cit.*, p. 482.

gious monopoly of the ulama. Kemal also established a Faculty of Divinity which devised a modern curriculum within which Islam could be studied. In 1928, the Constitution was amended to delete the provision that Islam was the state religion. According to Berkes, Mustafa Kemal "ceased to evince interest in reforming religion after 1928 and came to the conclusion that the course of development of the religious consciousness of the people could not and should not be led by the state or by secular personalities." [50] This, in fact, has been the conclusion reached by most of the revolutionary secularizing regimes after a decade or two in power.

The Lamaist theocracy of Tibet, previously described, has been obliterated by Chinese Communist rule in one of the harshest manifestations of polity-dominance secularization. Following the invasion of 1950, Dalai Lama XIV sought to appease the Chinese in an effort to moderate their policies. The new rulers, on the other hand, recognized the tremendous hold which the Dalai Lama had on the minds and hearts of the Tibetan people and made no effort to remove him directly. By 1957, however, it was clear that intensive Chinese propaganda had not succeeded in weakening traditional Tibetan values, and land reform and other revolutionary measures were postponed. A press campaign in 1958 roundly denounced religion and declared that the Lord Buddha was a reactionary.[51] Revolts in the eastern part of the country spread, and in 1959 Chinese repression of an uprising in Lhasa itself led to the flight of the Dalai Lama to India.

According to Professors Snellgrove and Richardson: "Since 1959 the Chinese rulers have completely destroyed the mainsprings of Tibetan civilization." [52] Many monasteries have been leveled to the ground, many monks have been killed, imprisoned, or forced to become laborers. The traditional economic system, dominated by lay and monastic landlordism,

[50] *Ibid.,* pp. 495–496.

[51] Tsepon W. D. Shakabpa, *Tibet: A Political History* (New Haven: Yale University Press, 1967), p. 316.

[52] David Snellgrove and Hugh Richardson, *A Cultural History of Tibet* (New York: Frederick A. Praeger, 1968), p. 268.

has been totally demolished. "A new generation of young
Tibetans, taken early from their parents, has been systematically trained to despise all traditional social and religious
values, and to work with the new rulers toward the development of an entirely different material order. Every village has
been visited and purged by teams of ideological workers; the
village temple has ceased to exist . . . the landlord and the
religious state have been replaced by 'The People' and 'The
Party.' " [53]

[53] *Ibid.*

CHAPTER V

Religion and Politicization

THE MOVEMENT from traditional elite politics to mass participation politics is one of the fundamental characteristics of the
process of political development. Since the turn of the century,
religious symbols, issues, organizations, and leaders have played
an important role in the induction of the masses into the
political process. Stated in its simplest terms: in traditional
societies, religion is a mass phenomenon, politics is not; in
transitional societies, religion can serve as the means by which
the masses become politicized.

The role of religion in politicization in some ways runs
counter to the processes of secularization discussed in the preceding chapter. The secularization of law in the Muslim world,
for example, is a clear case of polity-expansion secularization.
However, the formation of mass political parties with an
Islamic ideology is also a fact. Does this mean that the processes
of secularization are superficial, and that religious values and
consciousness simply assume different institutional forms? My
answer is in the negative. Both processes, the secularization of
polities and the involvement of religion in politicization, are
taking place simultaneously. However, secularization is by far
the more fundamental process, and it will in time devour the
phenomena of religious political parties and ideologies. The
political sphere has its own raison d'être, and participation in

politics offers its own gratifications and generates its own motivation.

The involvement of religion in the politicization of the masses, then, is an important but short-lived process characteristic of the politics of transitional societies. It is important to note the *nature* of the two Muslim institutions mentioned above. The *shari'ah,* which developed over a period of many centuries, stood at the center of the traditional Islamic polity but is now being rapidly replaced by secular law. That which represents the survival of Islamic ideas and values is a political party, and all political parties live an uncertain and precarious existence. In short, crucial and stable traditional forms are dead or dying; neo-traditional elements are encased in highly fragile forms.

Fundamental changes are taking place in the relationship between elites and masses in the third world. Within the political system the center of gravity moves gradually from the elite to the masses. Partly as a consequence of the political phenomenon, within the religious system a parallel development takes place — the gradual shift of religious authority from the clerical elite to the laity. Laicization is a major fact in all four religious systems; the laity are assuming an increasingly important role as religious leaders and doctrinal interpreters. Within Hinduism, Buddhism, and Islam this development is related to the emergence of new Western-educated intellectual elites who regard the traditional religious elites as incapable of making the necessary adjustments to the modern world. But this must be understood not simply as the challenge of an old elite by a new one; laicization takes place in the context of democratic assumptions which deny the right of any elite to speak authoritatively for the whole society. Within Catholicism, in Latin America and throughout the world, the new emphasis on the laity (theological motivations and rationalizations aside) reflects the basic fact that influence in modern society is increasingly correlated with influence among the masses.

One of the themes of this chapter is the transformation of

traditional religious elites into modern clerical interest groups. In traditional religiopolitical systems, ecclesiastical hierarchies occupied a vital position. As sacred elites whose legitimizing powers were necessary to the established authority of kings, they could maneuver near the center of power to augment their prerogatives and influence. Part of their importance at royal courts was based on their influence with the masses, but this was secondary to their inherent sacral character and the necessity of their being intimately associated with the exercise of royal power. The modernization of clerical groups not only involves organizational changes to improve internal coordination but, more importantly, the greatly increased emphasis on their capacity to influence large numbers of people. In a modernizing society, inherent sanctity alone may mean irrelevance, but demonstrated capacity to mobilize the masses, especially in the political sphere, guarantees recognition. Not only clerical interest groups but lay religious groups in the modern mold emerge to join the struggle for influence. In some cases lay associations are the creations and instruments of ecclesiastical hierarchies; in others they are completely autonomous.

The second theme concerns the lay politician as manipulator of sacred symbols and organizer of movements and groups which bear these symbols. We have already noted the process of laicization within the religious system itself, and we must now see its relevance to politicization. As mentioned, interest groups of laymen may be created by clerical hierarchies. However, where ecclesiastical organization is weak (especially in the cases of Hinduism and Islam), lay interest groups easily emerge as the leading spokesmen for the religious interests in society. Whereas religious interest groups may be either clerical or lay, within the political party of religious orientation we find an organization which is overwhelmingly associated with laymen. Even those political parties which are founded with overt or covert ecclesiastical support soon function quite independently of the clerical hierarchy.

This chapter is divided into two major sections: an analysis of the political actors related to religion and an analysis of patterns of politicization. The first will seek to identify the major kinds of actors (individuals and groups) involved in the interaction of religion and politics; the second will discuss the principal kinds of situations in which various combinations of political actors interact in ways which promote the politicization of the masses. Each point can only be illustrated with a few examples drawn from various parts of the third world. In many cases the structures and phenomena observed bear an important systemic relationship to the religion involved, and these relationships will be made clear.

POLITICAL ACTORS RELATED TO RELIGION

Individual Political Leaders. Individual clerics or religious functionaries have made a great impact on the political scene in a number of countries. Perhaps the most impressive political leadership has been provided by a few outstanding Buddhist monks. U Ottama, the first major nationalist leader to emerge in Burma, began his struggle against the British in 1920. Buddharakkhita organized the powerful United Monks Front which helped to bring S. W. R. D. Bandaranaike to power in Ceylon in the 1956 elections; three years later he organized the conspiracy which carried out the assassination of the prime minister. Tri Quang is the militant monk who led the movement to overthrow the Diem government in South Vietnam in 1963, and other governments thereafter.[1]

In all three of these cases the monks were prominent and skillful politicians in their own right. Buddharakkhita, for example, was vice-president of a political party (the SLFP) and had numerous other political connections. Nevertheless, all three of them had their political base in Sangha organizations.

1 On U Ottama, see John F. Cady, *A History of Modern Burma* (Ithaca, N.Y.: Cornell University Press, 1958), pp. 231–232, 250–253. On Buddharakkhita, see Donald E. Smith, "The Political Monks and Monastic Reform," in D. E. Smith, ed., *South Asian Politics and Religion* (Princeton, N.J.: Princeton University Press, 1966), pp. 489–499. On Tri Quang, see Jerrold Schecter, *The New Face of Buddha: Buddhism and Political Power in Southeast Asia* (New York: Coward-McCann, Inc., 1967), pp. 145–165.

Father Camilo Torres of Colombia, on the other hand, in his short-lived career as revolutionary and guerrilla fighter (he was killed by government troops in 1966), was condemned by the Catholic hierarchy and received very little support from his fellow clerics. He joined hands with Marxist revolutionaries, impelled by what he regarded as his Christian duty in the face of the massive social injustice of Colombian society.[2]

Prominent lay politicians who have effectively utilized religious symbols have been found in all four religious traditions. Among the important Hindu nationalists were: Tilak, who used religious festivals for anti-British propaganda; the Bengal terrorists, who identified Mother India with the goddess Kali whose worship required bloody sacrifices (political assassinations); and Gandhi, whose elaborate theory of nonviolent resistance, rooted in Hindu concepts, also spurred the Indian nationalist movement.[3] U Nu was the Buddhist lay politician par excellence, appealing to the masses by his piety, his retreats to the monastery, his pagoda building, and other meritorious acts. Jinnah used Islamic symbols to intensify the Indian Muslims' sense of separate national identity and, on this basis, demanded a separate state, Pakistan. Eduardo Frei, Jacques Chonchol, and other leaders of Chile's Christian Democratic Party — inspired originally by the writings of another Catholic layman, Maritain — have attempted to map a route of democratic modernization in keeping with their society's religious heritage. President Frei's public use of explicitly Catholic symbols is much less than, say, U Nu's use of Buddhist symbols; this factor could be expected to vary with the degree of political sophistication of the population.

Religious Interest Groups. Clerical interest groups are of two main types: those which constitute official ecclesiastical hierarchies and those which are composed of a segment of the

[2] See German Guzman, *Camilo Torres* (New York: Sheed and Ward, Inc., 1969).

[3] On the Extremists, see Maganlal A. Buch, *Rise and Growth of Indian Militant Nationalism* (Baroda, India: Atmaram Press, 1940). On Gandhi, see Joan V. Bondurant, *Conquest of Violence: The Gandhian Philosophy of Conflict* (Princeton, N.J.: Princeton University Press, 1958).

nonofficial clergy. Politically the most important clerical hierarchies are the Catholic bishops of each Latin American country, organized through periodic national episcopal conferences and a permanent secretariat located in the national capital. The bishops issue pastoral letters on a wide range of subjects, many of them with significant political implications. The Chilean hierarchy's 1962 pronouncement, "On Social and Political Responsibility in the Present Hour," for example, is widely credited with having been a significant factor in events leading to the electoral victory of the Christian Democrats in 1964. Through their ecclesiastical bureaucracy, the bishops can marshall considerable resources to exert political pressure on governments.[4]

The Buddhist ecclesiastical hierarchy in Burma disintegrated through lack of government support after the British conquest, but in central Ceylon a part of it has survived to this day. The *Mahanayakes* ("archbishops") of the two major chapters of the Siam sect, together with the monks under their jurisdictions, have been very effective in fending off all state-sponsored reforms which would jeopardize the traditional monastic landlordism of the area. The Mahanayakes convene their councils, issue their pronouncements, command substantial financial resources, and enjoy high social prestige. However, the values, interests, and demands of this group are highly traditional, as are its basic methods of exerting political influence — individual contacts with high officials rather than mobilization of the masses.

The ulama of al-Azhar, the thousand-year-old mosque-university in Cairo, have long enjoyed the status of an official ecclesiastical hierarchy and, in the early nineteenth century, constituted a major center of political power. Their autonomy, and their political influence, has declined drastically in the twentieth century, however, and the institution is now completely dominated by the government. By the legislation of 1961, the rector of al-Azhar is recognized as "the Grand Imam

[4] See Thomas G. Sanders, "The Chilean Episcopate," Institute of Current World Affairs, newsletter no. 13, 1968.

with the final say in all matters related to religious affairs.
. . ."[5] The shadow of an official Islamic hierarchy thus exists
in the United Arab Republic, but it is in fact a docile instrument of the government and incapable of independent action
as an interest group.[6]

Clerical associations are far more important as interest groups
than clerical hierarchies throughout the Hindu, Buddhist, and
Muslim areas, and in some of the Latin American countries
the extent of their influence comes close to that of the Catholic
hierarchy. In India an association of Hindu holy men, the
Bharat Sadhu Samaj, has agitated for national legislation banning cow slaughter. In Ceylon, the United Monks Front, organized in 1956, had its greatest strength in Colombo and the
coastal areas, as contrasted with the Buddhist hierarchy's
stronghold in the central Kandyan area. The Front's well-organized activities in the elections of that year included house-to-
house campaigning, the sponsoring of public meetings, and
the publication of campaign literature. After the victory of
their candidate, the Front continued to function as an aggressive and powerful interest group, issuing press releases and
pressuring the government to implement its program quickly.[7]
In Burma there have been a large number of such Sangha associations, the oldest and best known being the Young Monks
Association with headquarters in Mandalay.

In most of the Muslim countries there are one or more
ulama associations. In various countries — Algeria and Indonesia
to select just two examples — these groups provided much of
the early leadership in the struggle against Western imperialism. Ulama associations have been most active since independence on such issues as the defense of traditional Islamic law,

[5] Law 103 of 1961, art. 9, quoted in Daniel Crecelius, "Al-Azhar in
the Revolution," *Middle East Journal,* vol. 20 (Winter 1966), p. 45.

[6] See *ibid.,* pp. 31–46.

[7] On the origins of the Bharat Sadhu Samaj, see Donald E. Smith, *India
as a Secular State* (Princeton, N.J.: Princeton University Press, 1963), pp.
260–261. On the United Monks Front in the 1956 elections in Ceylon, see
W. Howard Wriggins, *Ceylon: Dilemmas of a New Nation* (Princeton,
N.J.: Princeton University Press, 1960), pp. 193–207, 342–348, 355–358.

agitation for the creation of Islamic states, and opposition to secularizing trends in state educational policy.

Like the Sangha groups, the ulama associations are essentially voluntary organizations which a qualified individual cleric joins. It is not uncommon to find several such organizations in a country, based on different regions, theological persuasions (usually reflecting study at different traditional colleges of Islamic learning), ideological inclinations, or simply loyalty to different prominent leaders among the ulama. The proliferation of such voluntary clerical interest groups is solely a phenomenon of the twentieth century and is itself a significant index of politicization, quite apart from the important role which these groups have played in the politicization of the masses.[8]

In Latin America various religious orders have long played a major role in educational, economic, and political affairs. Unlike the Hindu, Buddhist, and Muslim clerical associations mentioned earlier, the Franciscans, Dominicans, Jesuits, and other orders have long traditions rooted in distinctive spiritual emphases within a church framework. They are subject to the authority of the bishops in whose dioceses they function but have frequently operated with considerable independence. One of the most effective of these groups is the Centro Bellarmino of the Jesuits, located in Santiago, Chile. The center is a complex of interrelated organizations, some oriented toward research, others toward the training of laity, and still others toward action programs in such areas as labor union organization and low-cost housing. A number of the Jesuit priests of the center have Ph.D.'s in the social sciences, and the major theme of their work is the relationship of the church and the individual Catholic to social change. The center has been an important source of ideas for the Christian Democratic Party now in power, and the Jesuits have many close friends among cabinet ministers and other high-ranking officials.[9]

8 For a discussion of ulama organizations in Pakistan see Leonard Binder, *Religion and Politics in Pakistan* (Berkeley, Calif.: University of California Press, 1961), pp. 28–33.

9 The center is discussed in some detail in Chap. VII.

Also of concern are the religion-oriented interest groups of a predominantly lay character. A most aggressive spokesman for Hindu interests has been the Rashtriya Swayamsevak Sangh (RSS), founded in 1925 during a time of violent Hindu-Muslim conflict in India. The RSS ideology holds to the concept of a Hindu Nation and urges the creation of a Hindu State in which the religious minorities would be relegated to the status of foreigners. The RSS has concentrated on the indoctrination and paramilitary training of youth and has never entered politics directly.[10] However, it has provided much of the leadership and organizational strength of the Jana Sangh, a political party.

Buddhist lay groups have included the Young Men's Buddhist Association — a group, patterned after the YMCA, that was active in the early years of the Burmese independence movement. The All-Ceylon Buddhist Congress has been a vigorous pressure group on behalf of the interests of Buddhism and the Buddhist community. This organization produced a major document on Buddhist grievances which had a significant effect on the 1956 elections, and during the period of the two Bandaranaike administrations (1956 to 1965) it saw most of its demands carried out.

The most important Muslim lay group has been the Muslim Brotherhood which has substantial strength in Egypt, Syria, and elsewhere in the Middle East. The Brotherhood was founded as a nonpolitical organization in 1928 by an Egyptian schoolteacher, Hasan al-Banna. The Brotherhood has frequently been critical of the ulama for their docile acquiescence in the un-Islamic setup of the society around them. Issuing a militant call for a return to the fundamentals of the Islamic polity and society, the Brotherhood has used modern organizational means to pursue its ends.[11] Toward the end of World

---

[10] See J. A. Curran, Jr., *Militant Hinduism in Indian Politics: A Study of the RSS* (New York: Institute of Pacific Relations, 1951).

[11] See Ishaq Musa al-Husayni, *The Moslem Brethren: The Greatest of Modern Islamic Movements* (Beirut: Kayat's, 1956). See also Manfred Halpern, *The Politics of Social Change in the Middle East and North Africa* (Princeton, N.J.: Princeton University Press, 1963). Halpern devotes a

War II, the organization shifted its emphasis to direct political action. The Jama'at-i-Islami (Islamic Association), a very important group in Pakistan, was founded by Mawlana Mawdudi in 1941, and has drawn much of its ideological inspiration from the Muslim Brotherhood. While devoting its major efforts to propaganda and especially the indoctrination of Pakistani youth, the Jama'at has also functioned as a political party in parliamentary and presidential elections.[12]

Catholic lay interest groups in Latin America are also a product of the twentieth century, although there were important European antecedents at the end of the nineteenth century. A worldwide program of the "lay apostolate" called "Catholic Action" was set forth by Pope Pius XI in 1930. Laymen were called to be active collaborators with the hierarchy in the task of Christianizing the largely secular society in which the church now found itself. The laity were instructed in the church's social encyclicals and organized in functional groups (workers, university students, professional men, and so on) to seek practical ways of influencing society. Clerical supervision was prominent, for the Catholic Action units were organized at the diocesan level and under the direct control of the bishop. Political action as a group was forbidden; the training in Catholic Action programs would attempt to prepare laymen as individuals for a responsible political role. However, much of the leadership of present-day Christian Democratic parties received its initial inspiration and training in the Catholic Action movement in the 1930's.[13]

Today Catholic trade unions and youth organizations are found in all the urban centers of Latin America and constitute a significant political force.[14] Behind the Catholic hierarchy's

---

chapter to this movement which he describes as "neo-Islamic totalitarianism," pp. 134–155.

12 See Charles J. Adams, "The Ideology of Mawlana Mawdudi," in Donald E. Smith, *South Asian Politics and Religion*, pp. 371–397.

13 Much useful information on the general background of Catholic Action is contained in Gianfranco Poggi, *Catholic Action in Italy* (Stanford, Calif.: Stanford University Press, 1967).

14 For an excellent detailed study of the Latin American Catholic trade union movement see Efrén Cordova, "El neosindicalismo cristiano en

final conflict with Perón in 1955 was the fact that both church and regime aspired to control the most important functional sectors of society. More recently the church has been active in the creation of peasant organizations. In 1961, for example, the archbishop of one state in the northeast of Brazil assigned four priests to organize peasant unions, and a few years later these claimed a membership of two hundred thousand.

Even though hierarchical control of lay groups has frequently been reaffirmed (Pius XII in 1951 spoke of Catholic Action as "an instrument in the hands of the Hierarchy" [15]), these groups have been exercising much more independence, especially since Vatican Council II. The most startling developments have occurred in Brazil, where radicals of the *Juventude Universitaria Católica* ("Catholic University Youth"), despite the open hostility of the hierarchy, in 1960 formed what amounted to a "united front" with Communist groups in the National Student Union.[16]

On another continent has developed a uniquely Hindu interest group, the caste associations which have become active in Indian politics since independence. Although the institution of caste is supported by strong religious authority, scriptural and philosophical, the caste associations are mostly concerned with totally secular issues involving the educational, economic, and political interests of their respective castes. They are chiefly concerned not with questions of ritual purity, religious prerogatives, or status in the caste hierarchy (although the last mentioned was an issue thirty years ago) but with concessions on school fees, representation in state cabinet ministries, ap-

---

América Latina: CLASC," *Revista de Ciencias Sociales,* vol. 12 (Rio Piedras, P.R., 1968), pp. 255–295. CLASC refers to Confederación Latinoamericana Sindical Cristiana. The author emphasizes the recent radicalization and secularization of the movement.

[15] Poggi, *op. cit.,* p. 65.

[16] See Thomas G. Sanders, "Catholicism and Development: The Catholic Left in Brazil," in Kalman H. Silvert, ed., *Churches and States: The Religious Institution and Modernization* (New York: American Universities Field Staff, 1967), pp. 81–99, and the same author's "Catholics and the UNE" (New York: Institute of Current World Affairs, 1967), newsletter no. 4.

pointments, and patronage. Involvement in politics is thus secularizing the basic significance of the caste group. The caste associations are another form of bridge between tradition and modernity; one is born into a caste but must join the association in order to become a member. It thus involves a transition from the purely ascriptive group to the voluntary association characteristic of modern societies.[17]

The religious sect is another political actor of some consequence. The term "sect" is used here to refer to a subdivision of one of the four major religions; the sect has distinctive doctrines, practices, and ecclesiastical organization which differentiate it from the main body and/or other sects. There are numerous Hindu sects, some of them well-organized ecclesiastically. The most significant politically has been the Arya Samaj, a reform sect founded in 1875 which developed an aggressive anti-imperialist, anti-Western and anti-Christian stance.[18] Since independence it has continued to function as a vigorous spokesman for Hindu interests, sometimes with a decided anti-Muslim emphasis.

In Islam there are numerous Sufi orders which are active politically. In North Africa, the *marabouts,* leaders of Sufi brotherhoods, played a major political role in the preindependence period during which they were sometimes allied with the imperialist powers. There is a long history of rivalry and conflict between the marabouts and the ulama.[19] In the Sudan, as we shall see, Muslim sects have provided the bases of opposing political parties. Also there are the syncretist sects of South Vietnam. The Hoa Hao sect, concentrated in the southwest, claims 90 per cent of the non-Khmer population of one province. The Cao Dai sect is a blend of Mahayana Buddhism,

[17] See Lloyd I. Rudolph and Susanne Hoeber Rudolph, *The Modernity of Tradition: Political Development in India* (Chicago: University of Chicago Press, 1967). The first half of this book is devoted to a careful analysis of caste in modern Indian politics.

[18] See Norman G. Barrier, "The Arya Samaj and Congress Politics in the Punjab, 1894–1908," *The Journal of Asian Studies,* vol. 26 (May 1967), pp. 363–379.

[19] See F. S. Vidal, "Religious Brotherhoods in Moroccan Politics," *Middle East Journal,* vol. 4 (1950), pp. 427–460.

Confucianism, Taoism, and Catholicism. Both exercised political functions in areas of their strength, maintained private armies, and strongly opposed the efforts of the Diem government in 1955 to 1956 to consolidate the country politically and militarily.[20]

The last religious interest group to be discussed is a nonassociational one: the religious community (Asian terminology), or confessional group (European equivalent). In societies characterized by religious pluralism, each community may become in some sense a political actor. Religious communities become politicized in conflict situations where the real issues are frequently social, political, and economic. Religion derives its chief importance from its function as a symbol of group identity and self-esteem. The phenomenon of religious communities as political actors has a long history in Catholic-Protestant conflict in the West and is still very much a factor in the politics of Northern Ireland. In the contemporary third world this phenomenon is largely limited to South and Southeast Asia. In the Middle East, if we leave aside the Arab-Israeli conflict, which is international, and only partly based on differences in religious community, the communal issue is significant only in Lebanon. In Latin America the Protestant minority has sometimes been placed under extreme pressures, as in Colombia in recent decades. The two sides have been so unequally matched, however, that the Protestant community has never been able to assume a positive political role in the same way that minorities in South and Southeast Asia have done.

In India, Pakistan, Ceylon, Malaysia, and Lebanon, the religious communities have been exceedingly important. Interest groups and political parties have been formed to further communal interests; constitutional provisions have recognized the communities as political units; political and administrative posts have been filled on the basis of communal quotas established by law; and in the case of Pakistan a new state was created for a minority religious community.

---

[20] See Bernard B. Fall, "The Political-Religious Sects of Vietnam," *Pacific Affairs,* vol. 28 (September 1955), pp. 235–253.

Religious Political Parties. Political parties of religious orientation can be classified under four categories: communal, sect-based, traditionalist, and modernizing parties. The first two function in societies marked by communal or sectarian competition, and it is this rivalry which provides the basic orientation of the parties. An ideological distinction is used to classify the religious parties which function in societies without significant communal or sectarian conflict, and these are labeled either "traditionalist" or "modernizing" parties.

The communal party arises in response to the actual or latent conflict of a religiously pluralist society. In British India the Muslim League, founded in 1906, and the Hindu Mahasabha, founded in 1923, sought to articulate and champion the interests of their respective communities which, both were convinced, were being ignored, harmed, or betrayed by the leadership of the Indian National Congress which professed secular nationalism. The major Hindu party since independence has been the Jana Sangha, which maintains a definite anti-Muslim bias despite the existence of liberal elements within the party.[21]

The essential raison d'être of a communal party is of course the protection of communal interests; it may range from highly traditionalist to moderately progressive on issues relating to the interpretation of its own religion. Thus the Westernized leadership of the Muslim League, which fought tenaciously for the creation of a *Muslim* state (a state run by Muslims), fought equally tenaciously against the effort to make Pakistan an *Islamic* state (a state ruled by traditional Islamic law as interpreted by the ulama). Of course, with the creation of Pakistan, the Muslim League ceased to be a communal party and had to address itself to a totally different set of problems related to nation building. After 1947, it became essentially a modernizing party, although little modernization was accomplished.

Sect-based political parties are found in the Sudan. The first political party, Ashiqqa, was founded in 1943. A second, more moderate party called Umma ("Islamic Community") was then

---

21 See Craig Baxter, "The Jana Sangha: A Brief History," in Donald E. Smith, ed., *South Asian Politics and Religion,* pp. 74–101.

formed, based on the support of the 1.5-million-member Ansar sect. This is the sect that had been founded by the Mahdi, the messianic figure who created an Islamic polity which governed the Sudan from 1881 to 1898. The Mahdi's grandson, head of the sect, also became president of the Umma party. The Ashiqqa then aligned itself with the 1.5-million-member Khatmiya sect, the rival religious group which had been dominant before the Mahdist revolt. Since independence in 1955, the sectarian base of the Ashiqqa (renamed the "National Union Party") has weakened, but the Umma-Ansar tie remains strong. One writer suggested: "The great weakness of the parties lies in their attempt to reach the population through the intermediary of the religious leaders — al-Mahdi and al-Mirghani — thus putting modern instruments of political participation in the hands of traditional groups and leaders." [22]

Traditionalist parties are committed to the preservation or restoration of religious values and institutions in society. Their quest for political power is legitimized by a vision of the ideal religiopolitical system of the remote or recent past. Some traditionalist parties are organized and directed by religious functionaries but draw their official memberships from the ranks of both clergy and laity. Such clerical parties have evolved out of ulama associations. In Indonesia, the Nahdatul Ulama was formed in 1926 to provide orthodox leadership to the Muslim masses on questions of Islamic law, relations with the government, and education. By 1935, it had developed a strong base in East Java and claimed 67,000 members. In 1952, the Nahdatul Ulama started to function as a political party, and in the 1955 parliamentary elections emerged as the third-largest party.[23]

The most important religious party in the Middle East is the Muslim Brotherhood which has been characterized by a fundamentalist Islamic ideology, a tight hierarchical organization, and an emphasis on conspiracy and violence as a mode of political action. A doctrinal emphasis on Islamic socialism makes it difficult to classify this party simply as traditionalist.

[22] I. William Zartman, *Government and Politics in Northern Africa* (New York: Praeger, 1963), p. 135.

[23] Fred R. von der Mehden, *Religion and Nationalism in Southeast Asia* (Madison, Wis.: University of Wisconsin Press, 1963), p. 138.

Some writers have used the term "neo-traditionalist," others see it as socialist. As noted (footnote 11), it has also been described as "neo-Islamic totalitarianism." It is included here because the radically Islamic orientation is closer to the traditionalist than the modernizing end of the continuum.[24] In 1948, the efforts of the Egyptian government to dissolve the organization were countered by the assassination of the premier, Nuqrashi Pasha. For some time after the military coup of 1952, the Brotherhood had good relations with the regime but was suppressed following an attempt on Nasser's life by a Muslim Brother in 1954. Other unsuccessful assassination attempts have been made by the Brotherhood since then.

Traditionalist Catholic parties of a strongly elitist character have existed in a number of the Latin American countries since the early years of independence. These have usually been designated by the official name of "Conservative Party," and their political ideology has contained a strong theological element. The Conservative Party of Ecuador, for example, stated its *political* program in the following terms: "The end of man is God, whom he should serve and adore in order to enjoy after death the beatified possession of divinity. . . . The purpose of the state is to facilitate religious action so that its subjects will not lack the necessities of the spirit and will be able to obtain in the next life the happiness which can never be achieved in this." [25] Conservative parties in general have reaffirmed the Thomist notions of a static hierarchical society — each individual in his proper rank as divinely ordained — and have frequently constituted the political arm of the three traditional elites: the landlords, the military, and the church hierarchy. Conservative parties in some cases have made the necessary adjustment in order to function within a democratic setup, but the adjustment has been a reluctant one, for the

---

[24] For statements of the Brotherhood's ideological position, see Kemal H. Karpat, ed., *Political and Social Thought in the Contemporary Middle East* (New York: Frederick A. Praeger, 1968), pp. 115–126.

[25] Quoted in George I. Blanksten, "The Politics of Latin America," in Gabriel A. Almond and James S. Coleman, eds., *The Politics of the Developing Areas* (Princeton, N.J.: Princeton University Press, 1960), p. 502.

essential ideological orientation has been authoritarian and antagonistic to mass political participation.

Modernizing political parties of religious orientation are also found in both Muslim and Catholic countries. The Masjumi of Indonesia played a major political role in the decade after independence, leading the first two cabinets and sharing power in various coalition governments thereafter. By the end of 1958, however, the process of parliamentary democracy had deteriorated seriously, and Sukarno's "guided democracy" replaced party government. In contrast to the orthodox Nahdatul Ulama, the Masjumi's ideological roots were found in the modernist Islam of Muhammad Abduh in the early twentieth century. Egyptian modernism and reformism directly inspired the founding, in 1912, of the Indonesian Muhammadiyah, a nonpolitical Islamic movement, and Muhammadiyah has provided a large part of the Masjumi party's leadership and ideological support. The emphases have been: a rational approach to Islam, the emancipation of the individual Muslim, and the synthesis of what has proved to be sound in Western thought with the Islamic tradition.[26]

The Christian Democratic parties of Latin America represent a modernizing Catholic political force. They have become politically significant only since the end of World War II, but today exist in every Latin American country except Honduras and Haiti. The Christian Democrats form the government of Chile and are of major significance in Venezuela, Peru, and El Salvador. Ideologically they are poles apart from the traditionalist Catholic parties; they ally with the democratic Left, and in fact are sometimes referred to as "Christian Socialists." Their political philosophy draws on the social encyclicals of the church, but more fundamentally on the concept of Christian humanism expounded by Maritain and others. While rejecting Marxist prescriptions, the Christian Democrats concur

[26] The cultural and ideological background of both Nahdatul Ulama and Masjumi are explored in Robert R. Jay, *Religion and Politics in Rural Central Java* (New Haven: Yale University Southeast Asia Studies, 1963), and Clifford Geertz, *The Religion of Java* (Glencoe, Ill.: Free Press, 1960).

with many aspects of the Marxist critique of capitalist society.[27]

Table V.1 represents a summary of the major points of the analysis thus far and includes some of the salient points regarding the political actors in relation to religion. A small number of actors not discussed in the text are included.

The political expression of Hinduism, it is clear, is dominated by two basic orientations: the *laity* and *communalism*. Religious functionaries, individually or collectively, have played no significant political role; on the other hand, there have been very prominent lay spokesmen for Hinduism in the political sphere. Hindu interest groups and political parties have not concerned themselves with developing a Hindu ideology for modern society but have been strongly oriented toward defending the interests of their community in communal conflict. The caste associations fit into this same pattern of group competition. The political expression of Buddhism is chiefly characterized by the *political monkhood:* outstanding individual monks and powerful monks' associations rather than clerical hierarchies. Buddhist laymen have also been important, but the absence of any kind of Buddhist political theory is reflected in the fact that there have been no explicitly Buddhist political parties.

Islamic religiopolitical actors have extended over the whole range of possibilities, reflecting the diversity of the geographically vast Muslim world. The ulama have played a very important role in the past, but their influence has been declining rapidly over the past few decades, especially in the absence of an effective ecclesiastical organization. Western-educated lay spokesmen for Islam are clearly in the ascendant. Muslim communal organizations have been strong in pluralist societies, but in overwhelmingly Muslim societies the conflict has been no less intense over the ideological and practical issues of Islamic state versus secularism. The strong ideological concern is reflected in the number of Islamic political parties, traditionalist and modernizing.

---

[27] See Edward J. Williams, *Latin American Christian Democratic Parties* (Knoxville: University of Tennessee Press, 1967).

TABLE V.1 *Political Actors Related to Religious Systems*

	Hinduism	Buddhism	Islam	Catholicism
I. Individual leaders				
A. Religious functionaries		Political monks: U Ottama (Burma); Buddharakkhita (Ceylon); Tri Quang (So. Vietnam).	Political ulama: Jamal ad-Din Afghani (throughout Middle East); Abul Kalam Azad (India); Shabbir Ahmad Usmani (Pakistan); Ben Badis (Algeria).	Political priests: Manuel Hidalgo (Mexico); Camilo Torres (Colombia); Dom Helder Câmara (Brazil).
B. Laymen	B. G. Tilak, Aurobindo Ghose, V. D. Savakar, M. K. Gandhi, M. R. Golwalkar (India).	U Nu (Burma); S. W. R. D. Bandaranaike (Ceylon).	Sayyid Ahmad Khan, Muhammed Iqbal (India); M. A. Jinnah (Pakistan); Mohammed Natsir (Indonesia).	Gabriel García Moreno (Ecuador); Eduardo Frei (Chile).
II. Interest groups				
A. Clerical hierarchies		Sangharaja and ecclesiastical hierarchy (Thailand); Burma until end of 19th century. Hierarchies of Siam sect in Ceylon.	Ulama of al-Azhar in Cairo, now dominated by the government.	National episcopate (bishops and archbishops) of each Latin American country.
B. Clerical associations	Bharat Sadhu Samaj – association of holy men (India); weak organizationally and politically.	Young Monks Association, Presiding Monks Association, and many others in Burma. United Monks Front in Ceylon.	Nahdatul Ulama (pre-1952 Indonesia); Jamiat Ulama-i-Hind (India); Society of Reformist Ulama (Algeria).	Religious orders: Franciscans, Dominicans, Jesuits.
C. Lay interest groups	Rashtriya Swayamsevak Sangh (RSS) of India; strongly communal (anti-Muslim) orientation.	Young Men's Buddhist Association (Burma and Ceylon); All-Ceylon Buddhist Congress.	Jama'at-i-Islami (pre-1947 India); Muslim Brotherhood (pre-1945 Egypt); Muhammadiya (Indonesia).	Branches of Catholic Action (university student, professional, and labor groups).

D. Caste associations	Gujarat Kshatriya Sabha; Vanniya Kula Kshatriya Sangham (Madras state).
E. Religious sects	Arya Samaj	Ansar and Khatmiya (Sudan); Ahmadiya (Pakistan); Qadiriyya (throughout Muslim world); Tijaniyya (North and West Africa).
F. Religious communities	Hindus in India and Pakistan (conflicts with Muslims).	Muslims in India and Pakistan (conflicts with Hindus); Muslims in Malaysia (conflicts with Chinese); Muslims in Lebanon (conflicts with Christians). Buddhists in Ceylon (conflicts with Hindus, Christians); Buddhists in Burma (conflicts with Muslims); Buddhists in So. Vietnam (conflicts with Catholics). Syncretist sects: Hoa Hao and Cao Dai (So. Vietnam).
III. Political parties		
A. Communal parties	Hindu Mahasabha, Jana Sangh (India).	Muslim League, Majlis Ittihad-ul-Muslimin (India).
B. Sect-based parties		Umma and National Union Party (Sudan).
C. Traditionalist parties		Nahdatul Ulama (Indonesia); Jama'at-i-Islami (Pakistan); Muslim Brotherhood (Egypt and Syria); Nation Party (Turkey); Fidaiyan-i-Islam (Iran). Conservative Party (Argentina, Colombia, Ecuador, Chile, etc.); Partido de Acción Nacional (Mexico); Unión Cívica (Uruguay).
D. Modernizing parties		Muslim League (Pakistan); Masjumi and Partai Muslimin Indonesia (Indonesia). Christian Democratic Party (Chile, Venezuela, Peru, El Salvador).

The political expression of Catholicism in contemporary Latin America varies greatly throughout the area. However, it is clear that while the hierarchy alone spoke for the Catholic religion in the nineteenth century, this is no longer the case. Catholic Action, and certainly the Christian Democratic parties, are not the docile instruments of the bishops. As in Islam, ideological conflicts between exponents of the traditional religious society and a modern, open, and valuationally pluralist society continue to divide the religious leadership, both clerical and lay.

PATTERNS OF POLITICIZATION

The word "religion" has been used several hundred times without a definition. Without attempting a definition now, it may be suggested that four basic elements would have to be taken into account in any attempted definition. A religion may be analyzed according to: group identity, societal regulation, ecclesiastical organization, and belief system. Religion as group identity refers to the existence of *religious communities,* groups composed of individuals who are bound together by the same or similar religious symbols. Religion as societal regulation refers to the existence of *socioreligious structures* which regulate the internal social life of a religious community. Religion as ecclesiastical organization refers to the existence of *clerical institutions,* groups of specialists who are professionally concerned with religious teaching and ritual. Religion as belief system refers to the existence of *religious ideologies,* more or less coherent bodies of doctrine.

Using these categories, we shall attempt to analyze the kinds of situations in which religion is related to politicization. By identifying various kinds of phenomena prominently associated with the four elements, we can analyze the basic interactions of religion and politics.

The notion of *conflict* is central to our understanding of the nature of politics. Politicization — the drawing of people into active participation in the political process — takes place as people become conscious of conflicts which are perceived as relevant to their lives. We would suggest here that politicization has been taking place in the third world partly as the result of conflicts involving religious communities, socioreligious structures, clerical institutions, and religious ideologies. These four categories are obviously not completely separate, watertight compartments. For example, what are classified as conflicts of religious communities may also involve socioreligious structures, clerical institutions, and religious ideologies; however, it is the religious community (or religion as group identity) which provides the essential key to understanding the conflict.

We have assumed thus far that these conflicts relating to religion are real. The assumption is valid in that for many millions of people throughout the third world, religious values are deeply cherished, and issues relating to religious communities, socioreligious structures, clerical institutions, and religious ideologies are real and, indeed, fundamental issues. At the same time we have no desire to minimize the equally significant fact that behind many religious conflicts there are essentially secular political interests. Politicians, clerical and lay, are engaged in manipulating religious symbols as one technique in the struggle for power, sometimes cynically but more often through the same process of rationalization by which interests become disguised as principles in politics everywhere. From this point of view, we must recognize still another kind of conflict — the conflict of political interests which cuts across, and in some cases clearly dominates, the conflicts over ostensibly religious issues.

Conflicts of Religious Communities. Our first point is that politicization takes place as large numbers of individuals come to think of themselves as members of political collectivities determined by religious identity. Individuals perceive their personal interests as significantly related to the welfare of their religious community presently in conflict with its opponents.

Conflicts of religious communities have taken two forms: (1) a religious community attempting to overthrow a foreign imperialist power of a different religion, and (2) the conflict between two or more indigenous religious communities. In both cases religious symbols are used to mobilize the masses, producing attitudes and actions of opposition to the rivals or enemies

of the community. Both of these kinds of communal conflict
have been found in Asia-Africa but not in Latin America. In
Latin America there were no religious differences between ruler
and ruled in the colonial period, nor have there been large politically articulate minorities since independence. Protestant
groups have often struggled over issues of religious liberty but
have never constituted a cohesive political force with a wide
range of demands like minority religious communities, say, in
South Asia.

The role of religion as group identity in anti-imperialist nationalism could be documented at great length, drawing upon
many examples from Hindu, Buddhist, and Muslim countries.
Most of the examples of religious nationalism come from the
first three decades of the twentieth century. By World War II
the leadership of most nationalist movements was held by relatively secular politicians, many of them strongly influenced by
Marxism. Independence was won with the secularists in control, but the religious forces in many of these societies experienced a revival of influence shortly thereafter.

The basic affirmation of religious nationalism was simply
that differences in religious group identity constituted an unbridgeable chasm between rulers and ruled, that European
Christian governments had no moral right to govern Hindus,
Buddhists, or Muslims, and that these illegitimate foreign
rulers had to be overthrown by whatever means were available.
For the Indonesian, the *kafir* ("infidel") government of the
Dutch stood as an intolerable affront to the subject Islamic
community. The leader of Sarekat Islam, H. O. S. Tjokroami-
noto, proclaimed Islam as a "binding social factor and national
symbol." [28] In Indonesia, religion was the only major traditional factor unifying a people sharply divided by geography,
language, culture, and precolonial history. As Islam constituted
the nationality of the Indonesian, at least in early nationalist
thought and in popular sentiment, apostasy (especially in the
form of conversion to Christianity) represented an act of dis-
loyalty to the Muslim's nationality as well.

[28] Cited in von der Mehden, *op. cit.,* p. 12.

Conflicts of two or more indigenous religious communities have had many of the same characteristics as anti-imperialist conflicts. The Hindu-Muslim conflict leading to the partition of India in 1947 is the classic example, but there are various other important cases. After independence and partition, Hindu-Sikh tensions became a prominent feature of politics in the Punjab. A militant Sikh political party, the Akali Dal, sought to mobilize the entire community behind the demand for a separate Sikh state within the Union of India. After the movement for the creation of linguistic states developed, the Sikh demand assumed the form of an agitation for a Punjabi-language state, which involved the partition of the then bilingual (Punjabi and Hindi) state of Punjab. While language constituted the official basis and justification for the demand, which was conceded in 1966, the motivating force behind it was clearly religious and communal. While most Punjabi Hindus claimed Hindi as their mother tongue, all Sikhs claimed (and with considerably greater accuracy) that their language was Punjabi. In any event, the creation of a Punjabi-language state also meant the creation of a Sikh-majority state, which was the real point of the agitation.[29]

In the history of Algeria, from 1920 to independence, one can see elements of both these types of communal conflict, anti-imperialist and anti-*colon*. While not an indigenous community, many generations of French colons (colonization began in 1830) had grown up in Algeria and considered it their home. The nationalist struggle of Arabic-speaking Muslim Algerians was directed against both a foreign power and a dominant minority community. In this struggle, Islam (along with the Arabic language) became a powerful sustaining symbol of group identity. The Society of Reformist Ulama, founded in 1931, was led by the dynamic nationalist Shaykh Ben Badis. His strongest attacks were launched against the French and Algerian protagonists of cultural assimilation, who envisaged

[29] See Baldev Raj Nayar, *Minority Politics in the Punjab* (Princeton, N.J.: Princeton University Press, 1966); and the same author's essay, "Sikh Separatism in the Punjab," in Donald E. Smith, ed., *South Asian Politics and Religion*, pp. 150–175.

equality and prosperity for the Algerian Muslim through French naturalization. In 1938 he declared: "Naturalization — that is, the option of a Muslim for a people which is not Muslim — includes the rejection of the divine laws which regulate him and the adoption of human and profane laws." [30] Rejecting the political leadership of the Westernized Algerian elite, which was hardly distinguishable culturally from the French rulers, Ben Badis and his followers established a network of primary Qur'anic schools. In these schools conducted by the ulama, the children began each day by chanting in unison: "Islam is my religion, Arabic is my language, Algeria is my country."

Significant politicization has taken place, then, as clear-cut religious group identities have drawn the battle lines of political conflict. This is not to suggest, however, that the causal relationship is unidirectional. In all of the cases cited above, political conflict greatly strengthened and reinforced the sense of religious group identity. Furthermore, in other cases one could go so far as to state that political conflict virtually *created* a religious identity. We shall illustrate this point by reference to two examples: the Hindu "community" in the early twentieth century and the Mahayana Buddhist "community" in South Vietnam in the 1960's.

While Theravada Buddhists in Ceylon, Burma, and Thailand had long traditions as national entities, and Muslims everywhere had a strong attachment to the ummah (Islamic Community), the Hindus had no comparable unifying self-concept. Caste and, to a lesser extent, sectarian loyalites constituted the basis of all social and political organization. Caste constituted a formidable obstacle to the growth of any sense of nationalism, and for this reason the relationship between Indian nationalism and Hindu social reform was extremely important.[31] From the middle of the nineteenth century down to Gandhi, social reform was a predominant nationalist motif. The liberal Moderates thought in terms of an Indian nation

[30] Quoted in Joan Gillespie, *Algeria: Rebellion and Revolution* (New York: Frederick A. Praeger, 1960), p. 45.

[31] See Charles H. Heimsath, *Indian Nationalism and Hindu Social Reform* (Princeton, N.J.: Princeton University Press, 1964).

("the Indian National Congress"). In the 1920's, however, il-
liberal communalists such as V. D. Savakar began to speak of a
"Hindu nation." What was often forgotten in the heat of controversy between secular and Hindu nationalists was that the
latter's ideology was almost as antitraditional and contrary
to the reality of Indian society as the former's. Despite the
profound divisions which were the essence of the Hindu caste
order, under the pressure of conflict with both the British and
the Muslims, some sense of a Hindu community emerged.

The Buddhist crisis in South Vietnam began on May 8,
1963, when government troops in Hue fired on a large crowd
of demonstrators protesting a government order which forbade
the display of the Buddhist flag. The firing produced eight
Buddhist martyrs. The Diem regime, with extraordinary obdu-
racy, failed to discern the explosive potential inherent in the
situation: a government dominated by Catholics, 10 per cent
of the population, stood pitted against the Buddhists who represented 70 per cent.

For most Vietnamese Buddhists, the sense of religious communal identity had been weak and politically unimportant. In
marked contrast to Burma and Ceylon, Buddhism in Vietnam
played no part in the nationalist struggle against Western imperialism. The Mahayana Buddhism of the country (like that
of China and Japan) embraced a number of sects with significantly different tenets and practices, and sectarian loyalties
were more important than Buddhist self-consciousness. Con-
fucian values were also a prominent element in Vietnamese
culture and tended to blur the sense of Buddhist identity.

Confident that it could easily control this vaguely defined,
disunited Buddhist majority, the Catholic Diem regime pursued a course of action which in fact helped to produce a militant organized Buddhist opposition. The Buddhist identity
was forged by a combination of government repression and the
monks' leadership in creating an organized resistance. Both
factors were important: the vivid perception of an external
threat and the internal organization necessary to confront it.
With these developments, the monks were in a position to
mobilize the Buddhist masses for political action. After six

months of mass demonstrations and dramatic acts of self-im-
molation by monks, the government was overthrown by a military coup.[32]

Conflicts of Socioreligious Structures. Polity-expansion secularization (see Chapter IV) involves the expansion of state functions at the expense of traditional religion in the regulation of
society. This expansion has been most prominent in the areas
of law, education, social structure, and economy. The process
of polity expansion has naturally produced many sharp conflicts. In most cases secularization conflicts over these issues
have taken the form of clerical groups pitted against governments, and the clergy have on occasion mobilized mass support
for their position. Such cases of politicization are based on
both conflicts of socioreligious structures and of clerical institutions.

Not all secularization conflicts have taken the form of cleri-
calism-anticlericalism, especially in the context of Hinduism
which has very little organized ecclesiastical structure. Thus
the debate over the secularization of Hindu law (it was of
course described in other terms at the time) was an important
political controversy in India from 1947 to 1955. The controversy was waged by laymen on both sides, in Parliament, in the
press, and from public platform. It was an important issue in
the 1950–1951 general elections, and in that campaign
Nehru declared that he would stake his prime-ministership on
the Hindu Code Bill. The Hindu political parties (Hindu
Mahasabha, Jana Sangh, and Ram Rajya Parishad) led the
opposition to the bill. Even the overwhelming Congress electoral victory did not settle the issue, however, and the controversy continued until final passage of the legislation several
years later.[33]

Other secularization conflicts in India have been generated
by the breakdown of the sacral social hierarchy under the im-

---

[32] See Charles A. Joiner, "South Vietnam's Buddhist Crisis: Organization
for Charity, Dissidence and Unity," *Asian Survey*, vol. 4 (July 1964), pp.
915–928; Robert Scigliano, "Vietnam: Politics and Religion," *ibid.*, vol. 4
(January 1964), pp. 666–673.

[33] See Donald E. Smith, *India as a Secular State*, pp. 277–291.

pact of modern egalitarian norms actively promoted by government. In some cases the political manifestations of this conflict have been extremely important. The Justice Party, founded in 1917 in Madras, attacked the religious, social, economic, and political dominance of the small Brahman community. The leaders of this movement emphasized their Dravidian racial identity and Tamil cultural heritage. They condemned caste as a tool of Brahman oppression. "It is the Aryans who have introduced this birth distinction, which they have elaborated into the system of Varnashrama Dharma with its concomitant evils. It was that civilization which brought about illiteracy in the country, the pedestal on which is erected the exclusive oligarchy of Brahmans." [34] The Justice Party allied itself with the British government, since Brahman leadership was prominent in the Congress, and only slowly responded to the growing sentiment of Indian nationalism.

Under the dynamic leadership of E. V. Ramaswamy Naicker, the Justice Party was reorganized in 1944 as the *Dravida Kazagham* ("Dravidian Federation") and rapidly became a mass movement. It became atheistic and anti-Hindu as well as anti-Brahman, for Naicker insisted that the whole elaborate structure of Hindu religion was an opiate designed to perpetuate priestly power. The glorification of Tamil language and culture led to the development of a Tamil nationalism which demanded the creation of a sovereign Dravidian state. The splinter party which seized the leadership of the movement, the DMK (Dravidian Progressive Federation), was victorious in the 1967 elections and formed the Madras state government. In the political maneuvering and compromise, however, both its separatism and its anti-Brahmanism had been greatly toned down.[35] But the entire Dravidian movement was a remarkable example of politicization generated by conflict over the socioreligious caste structure.

Conflicts of Clerical Institutions. Conflicts involving cleri-

[34] Quoted in Robert L. Hardgrave, Jr., "Religion, Politics, and the DMK," in Smith, ed., *South Asian Politics and Religion*, p. 214.
[35] See Robert L. Hardgrave, Jr., *The Dravidian Movement* (Bombay: Popular Prakashan, 1965).

cal institutions have no necessary relationship to the phenomenon of politicization. The conflict here is the struggle for corporate clerical influence in society, with clashes over the boundaries of spheres of influence. Such conflicts occupy a considerable part of the history of the West in the premodern period.

Although far more prominent in church systems, such conflicts were found within all traditional polities in which the political process was essentially one of adjusting and accommodating the interests of different individuals and elites close to the center of power. Appeals for the support of the peasantry in any conflict were rare and usually regarded as illegitimate, as the masses were understood to be outside the system. The higher-ranking members of the clerical institution operated politically within this basic framework, reinforcing and enlarging their power whenever possible. Vallier has thus characterized the traditional politics in which the Latin American Catholic hierarchy was involved: "The clergy's energies were largely consumed by short-run maneuverings, by building up viable coalitions with other power groups, and in bargaining." [36] Strong personalities in church and state sometimes clashed and entered into protracted conflict with each other. [37]

In nineteenth-century Latin America the conflicts between church and state sometimes touched fundamental issues, for the Liberal leaders repudiated the integralist Catholic ideology which had legitimized the traditional system. However, the secularization conflicts which erupted over such questions as clerical control of education, marriage law, cemeteries, and so on were fought out by representatives of the same privileged classes. Only in the twentieth century have such conflicts become a significant factor in the politicization of the masses.

A clerical institution's potentiality for significant influence

[36] Ivan Vallier, "Religious Elites: Differentiations and Developments in Roman Catholicism," in S. M. Lipset and Aldo Solari, eds., *Elites in Latin America* (New York: Oxford University Press, 1967), pp. 192–193.

[37] See Hubert H. Bancroft, "The Struggle between an Archbishop and a Viceroy in Seventeenth-Century New Spain," in Frederick B. Pike, ed., *The Conflict between Church and State in Latin America* (New York: Alfred A. Knopf, 1964), pp. 78–88.

in contemporary society is highly correlated with organizational coherence and effectiveness (see Chapter I). The failure to organize and mobilize lay followers has frequently meant defeat at the hands of secularizing forces, especially antitraditionalist governments. The ulama of Egypt in the early nineteenth century held "a rich, independent, and powerful stronghold in the mosque-university of al-Azhar." [38] Whereas most traditional Muslim systems approximated the organic model, in Egypt during this period the religiopolitical reality was closer to the church model. Al-Azhar enjoyed a high degree of autonomy, elected its own head, controlled a network of religious schools, and dominated the judicial system. Its influence over the urban masses was a major political factor.[39] By the early twentieth century the ulama were on the defensive, however, as Western-educated laymen usurped their traditional functions and prerogatives. After World War I, al-Azhar became a political ally of the king, and it was the secular nationalists who sought mass support in the struggles against both the monarchy and the British. The ulama gradually withdrew from political life, and when religion again became an important ideological issue, it was the Muslim Brotherhood, not the men of al-Azhar, who championed Islam. After the 1952 coup, the abolition of the shari'ah courts and the virtual secularization of al-Azhar itself constituted massive blows against Islamic tradition, but the ulama had no organizational resources, no mechanism for the mobilization of lay supporters to defend Islam against an aggressive modernizing regime.[40]

Conflicts of clerical institutions have been associated with politicization when the ecclesiastics have perceived the fundamental importance of mass support and have effectively organized it. The Burmese order of Buddhist monks, although

[38] Nadav Safran, *Egypt in Search of Political Community* (Cambridge, Mass.: Harvard University Press, 1961), p. 28.

[39] See Afaf Loutfi El Sayed, "The Role of the Ulama in Egypt during the Early Nineteenth Century," in P. M. Holt, ed., *Political and Social Change in Modern Egypt* (London: Oxford University Press, 1968), pp. 264–280.

[40] Crecelius, *op. cit.*, pp. 36–37.

not well organized above the level of the monastery, has struggled continuously since independence to maximize its influence in society. At times this fundamental drive of the Sangha was overshadowed by the dramatic and ostentatious religiosity of Premier U Nu, who had his own reasons for promoting a revival of Buddhism in Burma. What in fact developed was a basic alliance between the leading Sangha associations and U Nu's political party (the AFPFL, and after the split, the "Clean" AFPFL later renamed the "Union Party"). Essentially, the Sangha leadership yearned for a return to the traditional setup in which their institution would occupy a central place.

The whole movement for a constitutional amendment to make Buddhism the state religion originated not with U Nu, but with several powerful Sangha associations in 1956.[41] U Nu and the cabinet yielded to the importunities of leading senior monks. After the AFPFL split and a period of military rule, the 1960 election campaign was waged largely on U Nu's pledge to make Buddhism the state religion. Although some monks supported his opponents, the vast majority rallied to U Nu's side and became his most effective propagandists in the towns and villages. After his overwhelming victory, U Nu appointed a State Religion Advisory Commission composed of eighteen leading monks and seventeen Buddhist laymen. The state religion amendment, adopted in 1961, committed the government to the general promotion of Buddhism; it was to honor and protect the Three Jewels (Buddha, Dharma, and Sangha) and consult the leading monks formally and on a regular basis regarding its religious policy. Accompanying legislation provided for instruction in the Buddhist scriptures in all state schools, the establishment of new schools in monasteries, the observance of Buddhist sabbath days as official holidays, and the installation of Buddha images in courts, schools, and other public buildings. While many of these provisions seemingly only had symbolic significance, the net effect was to reestablish the Buddhist ecclesiastical institution near the center of power and in a place of prominence in national life.

[41] See Donald E. Smith, *Religion and Politics in Burma* (Princeton, N.J.: Princeton University Press, 1965), pp. 230–280.

The state-religion conflict was unquestionably one of the few political issues since independence which had some real meaning for the Burmese peasant who still lived in an essentially traditional village society. Among other things, it meant the reaffirmation of the values embodied by the Sangha, which was represented in virtually every village. The politicization of the masses through religion was thus very significant. However, this victory for the Sangha did not come about because the monks succeeded in organizing and mobilizing their lay followers. It was rather the case of an alliance between the clerical institution and a mass-based political party led by a charismatic figure.

The organizational weaknesses of the Sangha were exposed a few weeks later when U Nu decided to push through an innocuous constitutional amendment designed to reassure the now-troubled religious minorities. The prime minister promptly found himself under severe attack from his former clerical allies, militant monks who now declared that the safeguards extended to the minorities effectively nullified the adoption of Buddhism as the state religion. The Union Sangha League, close ally of U Nu's Union Party, led the attack. On the day of the final vote, two thousand monks threw up a picket line around the building in which the parliamentary session took place in a futile attempt to stop a measure which they interpreted as a blow to their recently enhanced status as custodians of a state religion. The mobilization of two thousand monks was itself evidence that the Sangha could not be discounted as a political force of some significance. But it also revealed the Sangha's political limitations; it had failed (indeed, had never attempted) to organize the laity into a coherent interest group so that it could function effectively in a sustained conflict with the government or other political opponents. This failure was unquestionably related to the Sangha's raison d'être as a monastic body; the fact is that the Buddhist laity has no clear-cut role within the religious system which can be easily related to contemporary political problems.[42]

[42] See Samuel P. Huntington, *Political Order in Changing Societies* (New Haven: Yale University Press, 1968), pp. 194–196. Huntington argues

We must turn again to Latin America to examine political conflicts in which clerical institutions have demonstrated their ability to mobilize the laity independently, even in opposition to dictatorial regimes. In Argentina under Perón, as in Burma under U Nu, the church was the beneficiary of friendly government policies until the final conflict took shape. Perón came to power in 1943 with considerable support from the Catholic hierarchy, and one of his first acts was to issue a decree which stated: "In all the public schools of primary, post-primary, secondary and special instruction, the teaching of the Catholic religion will be imparted as ordinary material in the respective plans of study." [43] The military regime thus reversed a secular educational policy which had been in effect since 1884. The Catholic hierarchy, in turn, publicly urged the faithful not to support a party which advocated separation of church and state, the legalization of divorce, and the secularization of education — all positions espoused by Perón's opposition, the Democratic Union. With this support from the church, Perón was victorious in the elections of 1945–46 and 1947–48.[44]

Clerical cooperation was disrupted precisely because the regime's totalitarian aspirations were incompatible with the continued existence of another major structure of social control. In Mecham's words: "Since the church was the only major organization, group, or institution in Argentina not fully subjected to Peronista control, its influence and power had to be destroyed." [45] In November of 1954, Perón issued a strong denunciation of priests who were allegedly meddling in poli-

---

that interventions of the clergy in politics reflect "the general politicization of social forces and institutions" in transitional societies, rather than the social and organizational characteristics of particular clerical groups. But this simple generalization ignores the significantly different *degrees* and *kinds* of clerical involvements in politics: social, organizational, and doctrinal factors clearly explain many of the differences.

[43] Quoted in John J. Kennedy, *Catholicism, Nationalism, and Democracy in Argentina* (Notre Dame: University of Notre Dame Press, 1958), p. 196.

[44] J. Lloyd Mecham, *Church and State in Latin America* (Chapel Hill, N.C.: University of North Carolina Press, 1966), p. 247.

[45] *Ibid.,* p. 248.

tics, and a number of clergy were imprisoned. Catholic news-papers were closed, divorce was legalized, the teaching of religion in public schools was stopped, state aid to Catholic schools was cut off, and in May, 1955, a constitutional conven-tion was called to separate church and state. The Perón regime was overthrown, however, before this last step could be taken.

The church had formidable weapons of its own in the strug-gle with the state. The hierarchy's pastoral letters condemned the anti-Catholic attack, and Perón and his officials were ex-communicated by Pope Pius XII. But it was militant laymen in numerous Catholic Action groups who organized the anti-Peronista demonstrations. Catholic labor unions, Catholic student groups, Catholic medical associations, and others rep-resented precisely the kind of phenomenon a totalitarian re-gime could not tolerate, and the church's most effective weapon once the struggle was joined.[46] In the competition for influence in Argentine society, the effort was indeed being made to bring labor, business, professional life, and the uni-versities under clerical influence if not control, and since the regime also sought to dominate these areas of public life, the conflict was inevitable. The church's opposition to Perón was a major factor in the situation which prepared the way for his overthrow by the military in 1955.

Conflicts of Religious Ideologies. We come now to our fourth major area, one in which religion is examined in terms of belief system. Politicization in the third world has been signif-icantly furthered by various ideological conflicts involving religious and political belief systems. These are conflicts not only of general world views but of blueprints for society.

Ideological conflicts are in some cases closely related to conflicts of clerical institutions, but in other cases largely un-related. Two points must be made to substantiate this state-ment. First, a clerical institution may have no formulated ideo-logical blueprint for society but may nevertheless be intensely involved in the struggle for power. The Buddhist monks, for example, have scant ideational resources for the development

---

[46] For Peronista statements on Catholic Action, see Pike, *op. cit.*, pp. 183–196.

of a Buddhist political philosophy and have in fact made little effort to articulate one. Their *ideas* for the structuring of society are limited to a nostalgic yearning for the traditional past in which the Sangha occupied a place of prominence. Their ideological poverty, however, has not decreased one iota their eager participation in the power struggle. After the Mahayana Buddhist monks of South Vietnam had toppled their third government, American correspondents interviewing Thich Tri Quang were puzzled by his extremely vague replies to their questions concerning the Buddhist program for the country. The fact was that Buddhism provided no ideological guidelines.

Secondly, the ideological struggle may be waged more importantly by laymen than by clergy. This is clearly the case today and has been for several decades, in the case of Islamic ideological formulations. Throughout the Muslim world the ulama have been in continuous decline as the intellectual leaders of the community since early in this century. During this period, the ideological debate has raged with great intensity but the spokesmen for Islam have increasingly come from the ranks of the Western-educated professional classes. To a lesser extent the same can also be said of Latin American Catholicism. While important theological and ideological leads have come from the papal social encyclicals and the documents of Vatican II, the major part of Christian Democracy's ideological formulation and propagation is being performed by Catholic laymen.

The ideological conflict, then, must be analyzed in its own terms, and not simply as a function of the conflicts of clerical institutions. Serious conflicts of religious ideologies have occurred only in the Muslim and Catholic countries. This is an empirical fact which is largely explained by the concern with human history which is deeply imbedded in the Judeo-Christian-Islamic tradition. The theological assumptions of this tradition have given rise to ideological political parties, Islamic and Roman Catholic. The religions of Indic origin, Hinduism and Buddhism, promote a world view which is at best indifferent to history. There has developed no Buddhist ideology, and there have been no Buddhist political parties. The so-called Hindu political parties have no Hindu ideology and in fact are communal parties whose raison d'être is dependent on the existence of religious pluralism and the conflicts of religious communities.

Ideological conflicts involving religious belief systems have been both internal and external. The past half century has witnessed major ideological conflicts *within* these religious systems, conflicts which were in some cases fought out in the political arena. Both in Islam and in Catholicism the internal conflict might be described as that of traditionalism versus modernism. Modernism was primarily the result of the impact of ideas associated with the terms "liberalism" and "democracy." Seen from this perspective, the ideological conflict during certain periods might be described as a triangular struggle: traditional Islam versus modernist Islam versus secularism; or traditional Catholicism versus modernist Catholicism versus Marxism. The internal and external conflicts were interlocked.

In the case of Islam, the political manifestation of the traditionalist-modernist cleavage is well illustrated by the al-Azhar mosque-university. On the eve of the 1952 coup, "al-Azhar was suffering from the consequence of more than half a century of spasmodic reform and severe political crises arising from the general conflict between Egyptian modernists and traditionalists, a conflict which naturally revolved around al-Azhar and its system of education. For both groups this ideological confrontation had been crystallized in specific issues concerning the control of al-Azhar. . . . This struggle, then, between the two competing ideological orientations, influenced the issues and described the lines of battle for the more intense political struggle between parliament and king for control of al-Azhar and its system of religious education." [47] In far away Indonesia, the traditionalist-modernist cleavage took concrete institutional form in two political parties, Nahdatul Ulama and Masjumi respectively. Yet Masjumi had its ideological roots in the modernist Islamic movement led by Muhammad Abduh

[47] Crecelius, *op. cit.,* p. 31.

at al-Azhar, and an influential modernist organization, the Muhammadiyah, was founded in Indonesia in 1912. As noted earlier, Muhammadiyah continued to provide ideological and organizational support for Masjumi in the post-independence period.

Within Catholicism, the internal ideological conflict was reflected in splits within the old Conservative parties in several Latin American countries. In Chile, a group of young Catholic intellectuals, who had studied the social encyclicals at the Catholic University of Santiago, formed the National Young Conservative Movement and, in 1935, entered the Conservative Party. This party, the natural home of Catholics, was also dominated by a laissez-faire economic outlook which the young intellectuals found completely incompatible with the social encyclicals. Three years later they revolted to form their own party, the *Falange Nacional,* which in 1957 changed its name to Christian Democratic Party. Drawing deeply on the writings of Jacques Maritain, especially his emphases on pluralism, democracy, and "integral humanism," Eduardo Frei and his colleagues moved steadily away from the oligarchy-dominated Conservative Party and, in their increasing commitment to radical social change, found their natural ally in the Left.[48]

Both in Islam and in Catholicism, therefore, internal ideological cleavages of a fundamental nature produced important political consequences and conditioned the ideological encounters which took place later. We shall now turn to the external ideological conflicts, which involved religious responses to secularism and Marxism.

The conflict between Catholicism and secularism in the realm of ideas was largely fought out in the nineteenth century by a small elite divided into Conservatives and Liberals. The struggle generated no large-scale politicization, and ideological anticlericalism versus Catholicism did not come to approximate an issue of mass politics until the Mexican Rev-

[48] Williams, *op. cit.,* pp. 17–19; Ernst Halperin, *The Christian Democratic Alternative in Chile* (Cambridge, Mass.: MIT Center for International Studies, 1964); Paul E. Sigmund, "Christian Democracy in Chile," *Journal of International Affairs,* vol. 20 (1966), pp. 332–342.

olution. Even here, however, the struggle was far more over the church's power in society than over ideology per se. That is, it was basically a conflict of a clerical institution, although the revolutionaries also found it necessary during certain periods to mount powerful ideological attacks against the Catholic belief system itself.

The ideological conflict between Islam and secularism in the polity, however, has been a significant and continuing problem for a number of Muslim states from the Turkish Revolution to the present.[49] Perhaps most interesting has been the case of Pakistan which, in a sense, started in 1947 with a clean slate — a totally new political entity inheriting a secular parliamentary system but owing its birth to an overwhelming sense of Islamic group identity. In the ideological debate which ensued, and which continues, Islam as group identity has become complicated by Islam as belief system, particularly as political theory.

Jama'at-i-Islami, which is now (1969) one of the two political parties with significant strength in both West and East Pakistan, represents an ideological Islam which sees the traditionalist ulama as largely irrelevant to the contemporary scene (although it cooperates with them on occasion), the modernists as spineless imitators of the West, and the secularists as the archenemy of Islam. According to Mawlana Mawdudi, the Islamic state is ideological and all-embracing. "Its sphere of activity is coextensive with the whole of human life." [50] This totalitarian nature of the Islamic state simply reflects the awesome sovereignty of God, embodied in the sacred law, in its total application to human society. Islam, Mawdudi declares, is "the very antithesis of secular western democracy," since the latter is based on the sovereignty of the people, not God. No legislative enactment can be permitted which would contradict the sacred shari'ah, and no non-Muslim could have any significant part in governing a true Islamic state.

[49] See E. I. J. Rosenthal, *Islam in the Modern National State* (Cambridge, Eng.: Cambridge University Press, 1965).

[50] Sayyid Abul A'la Maududi, *The Islamic Law and Constitution* (Lahore: Islamic Publications, Ltd., 1960), p. 154.

Throughout the long and tortuous process of framing the 1956 Constitution of the Islamic Republic of Pakistan, the debate on the nature of a modern Islamic polity continued. The final product, predictably, was still essentially a Western parliamentary system, although it was specified that no legislation could be enacted which was "repugnant to the injunctions of Islam as laid down in the Holy Qur'an and Sunnah." [51] After the military coup of 1958, many of the same questions were debated in the drafting of the 1962 Constitution. And at the present time, under a new military government, the fundamental question of the relationship of Islam to the political order remains manifestly unsettled. Whatever the eventual outcome, it is clear that the ideological conflict over the Islamic state has been a factor in the politicization of Pakistanis. The debate has filtered down far below the level of the politicians and intellectuals, for the ulama in the most remote villages have some opinions on this subject.

The ideological conflict between religion and Marxism has been important in both Catholic and Muslim countries. Throughout Latin America, Conservative parties have regarded the relatively small Communist parties as the most serious threat to the established order and, along with the church hierarchy, have attacked them ideologically and politically at every opportunity. The most serious Catholic-Marxist confrontation, however, in which all political forces were largely polarized and seemingly balanced, took place in the Chilean elections of 1964 and 1965. Significantly, Catholicism was represented in this struggle not by a Conservative oligarchy, but by a progressive, left-of-center Christian Democratic Party which emerged victorious over a Socialist-Communist coalition (FRAP).

The Christian Democratic leadership has devoted vast amounts of time and energy to the exposition of what it regards as its distinctive ideological position. It seems acutely embarrassed by the fact that its concrete program seems to differ little from that of European Social Democrats with their Marx-

[51] Article 198(I).

ist background. Yet apart from the emphasis on Christian humanism, which clearly is different philosophically from the Marxist view, the Christian Democrats have been able to offer only a "communitarian" economic theory which is held to be an alternative to both capitalism and socialism.[52]

In the 1964 presidential election it was not ideology so much as Frei's general image as a devout Catholic which gave him an overwhelming majority of the women's vote. The fear of communism (although FRAP was led by a Socialist, Salvador Allende) drove many segments of the middle class to support Frei. For the common man, his promise of a "Revolución en Libertad" contained the most important elements of the Marxist program of socioeconomic change, plus the commitment to carry it out within the democratic framework.

The Marxist-Islamic ideological confrontation has an especially interesting history in Indonesia. *Sarekat Islam,* despite its name, was from its inception in 1912 an ideologically heterogeneous nationalist organization, accommodating devout Muslims and committed Marxists, middle-class merchants and the protagonists of class warfare. "Left-wingers came to see in the Sarekat Islam their weapon in a class struggle with non-Islamic colonial capitalist groups, and Marxism and nationalism rather than Islam became for them the chief motive forces. But the Muslim bourgeoisie regarded the Islamic movement primarily as the expression of group solidarity, integrated along the religious-cultural lines of modern Islam." [53] Serious efforts were made to synthesize Marxism and Islam, and some SI leaders pointed to the Qur'anic prohibition of usury, the Prophet's strong emphasis on equality, and other similarities. Nevertheless, the ideological tension between the two was fundamental, and successive congresses of the organization shifted the emphasis from one side to the other, resulting finally, in 1921, in the ousting of the Communist group and the clear-cut adop-

---

[52] This question is considered in Chap. VII.

[53] J. M. van der Kroef, *Indonesia in the Modern World* (Bandung: Masa Baru, 1954), pt. I, pp. 74–75, quoted in von der Mehden, *op. cit.,* p. 63.

tion of Islam as the basis of the movement's ideology and action.[54]

After independence the ideological struggle continued in the confused period of parliamentary politics. In 1954, a Western scholar observed: "The most significant political development in Indonesia in the past two years is the growing polarization of ideological extremes, represented on the one hand by the resurgence of the Indonesian Communist Party (PKI) and on the other by the growing cohesion of Islam as a political force." [55] During the subsequent period of "guided democracy," Sukarno proclaimed the national ideology of NASAKOM, an acronym for the three forces of Indonesian society, nationalism, religion, and communism, which he felt could and should coexist. In 1960, however, President Sukarno banned the Islamic party Masjumi for its alleged complicity in revolts in Sumatra and Sulawesi, and in the years following moved toward close ties with the PKI. Following the Communist coup attempt of September 30, 1967, however, the army, with the enthusiastic cooperation of Islamic organizations, launched a bloody campaign to wipe out the PKI. The ulama proclaimed a *jihad* ("holy war") against the atheist Communists, and in the massacres which ensued over 300,000 people were killed. With the political demise of Sukarno, a new major Islamic party, the *Partai Muslimin Indonesia,* was formed in 1968 to fill the ideological gap left by the disbanded Masjumi.[56]

We have attempted to examine the relationship between politicization in the third world and the four major aspects of religion: group identity (religious communities), societal regulation (socioreligious structures), ecclesiastical organization (clerical institutions), and belief system (religious ideologies). The

[54] This whole period is treated extensively in von der Mehden, *op. cit.,* pp. 54–71.

[55] Justus M. van der Kroef, "Communism and Islam in Indonesia: A Western View," *India Quarterly,* vol. 10 (October 1954), p. 314.

[56] See Allan A. Samson, "Islam in Indonesian Politics," *Asian Survey,* vol. 8 (December 1968), pp. 1001–1017.

word "politicization" has been used to refer to the process by which large numbers of people have been drawn into the political process. The major argument has simply been that religion in its four aspects has provided important points of relatedness, linkages of meaning, between the masses and the political process.

From another point of view, however, the process could be described as the politicization of religion. The four religions have interacted with the political process in very different ways over the past half century. In some cases the differences are accounted for by accidents of history — for example, the absence of politically significant religious pluralism in Latin America. In other cases, however, the differences reflect important systemic characteristics of the religions themselves — for example, the nature of their ecclesiastical organization or their ideational impulses (or lack of them) toward the formulation of ideologies. These findings are summarized in Table V.2.

TABLE V.2   *The Politicization of Religion*

Aspects of Religion	Hindu-ism	Bud-dhism	Islam	Catholicism
Group identity (religious communities)	X	X	X	
Societal regulation (socioreligious structures)	X		X	X
Ecclesiastical organization (clerical institutions)		X	X	X
Belief system (religious ideologies)			X	X

Religious Promotion of Secular Politicization. Thus far we have considered the politicization of the masses as a largely incidental by-product of religious conflicts. We must also take note, however, of a small segment of a religious institution within which theories and programs of politicization have been

evolving which have little to do with institutional self-preserva-
tion. This "disinterested" politicization effort indeed springs
from religiously rooted concepts of man and society, but essentially regards development (cultural, social, economic, and
political) as an end in itself. A number of the clerical intellectuals who espouse the "ideology of development" are in fact
convinced that the changes they seek will likely undermine the
institutional church within which they now operate. In particular, the kind of politicization they seek to promote, once
achieved, cannot really be directed by a church, political party,
government, or any other institution.

These remarkable developments have taken place within a
small segment of the Catholic church in Latin America, primarily in Brazil, but to some extent in Chile and other countries as well. The effort in Brazil led to the coining of the word
conscientização ("making people aware politically and socially") which in its Spanish form, *conscientización,* has now
gained currency throughout the remainder of Latin America.
Conscientización is precisely the psychological prerequisite, for
individuals and groups, of politicization at the deepest level
— that is, politicization which goes beyond the manipulative
mobilization of people by interested parties.

The concept of conscientización was developed by a Brazilian Catholic intellectual, Paulo Freire, in connection with a
program of adult literacy training. As Freire analyzed the
problem, the illiterate had an undifferentiated, magical perspective on reality. He saw his environment, both nature and
society, as the immutable given of life, to which attitudes of
pessimism, resignation, and fatalism were wholly appropriate.
His place at the bottom of the socioeconomic structure was
accepted. Existing methods of literacy training, Freire argued,
were paternalistic operations in which middle-class instructors
from another world attempted to hand down smatterings of
their culture to the masses, with the object of making them fit
into the existing structures of society better.

Freire's approach was to use the vocabulary of the illiterates
themselves and by dialogue to encourage the development of a
critical view of their environment, a consciousness of what
things could in fact be changed. In short, Paulo Freire re-

garded the skills of literacy as but a part of a general process of conscientización.[57] "Within the framework of a Christian humanist philosophy, he is concerned with the question of how the depressed masses can move toward full human existence as persons. This, he believes, can happen only as they are enabled to cut the umbilical cord with nature and with a sacralized social order and thus discover themselves as participants in a concrete historical process open to the future."[58] The politicization analyzed earlier was largely dependent on the continued vitality of traditional religious attitudes; the politicization envisioned here, however, although demanded in the name of Christian humanism, required a significantly secularized view of the world.

At the same time Freire was developing his method of literacy training (roughly, between 1960 and 1963), the Brazilian Bishops Conference, in cooperation with the government, started a nationwide campaign called the "Basic Education Movement" (MEB). MEB was run on behalf of the hierarchy by a group of remarkably independent laymen who came increasingly to define their educational task in terms of conscientización. Using the radio as their basic medium, the MEB leaders also distributed primers which reinforced the message of social change. The leadership itself was divided between the reformists who sought the integration of the depressed groups in society so that a major upheaval could be averted and the militants whose object was nothing less than a revolutionary transformation of society.

The revolutionary view was expressed in the following typical page from the MEB primer *Viver E Lutar* ("To Live Is to Struggle"):

> Peter came home much informed by his lesson.
> He came home informed that:
> Government is for everybody.

[57] See Thomas G. Sanders, "The Paulo Freire Method: Literacy Training and Conscientización" (New York: Institute of Current World Affairs, 1968) newsletter no. 12.

[58] Richard Shaull, *National Development and Social Revolution,* mimeographed (New York: Overseas Ministries, National Council of Churches, 1967), reprinted as CIDOC document 68/81, Cuernavaca, Mexico.

All should participate in government.
Some have more than they need; some have nothing.
Some earn an awful lot.
Many work and their work is exploited by others.
Lots of things are wrong in Brazil.
We need a complete change in Brazil.
WE NEED A COMPLETE CHANGE IN BRAZIL.[59]

By late 1963 and early 1964 MEB was embroiled in an ideological crisis in which the majority of the militants were ranged against the hierarchy. Meanwhile, in 1963 the Brazilian ministry of education launched a massive literacy campaign based on the Paulo Freire method. Both of these programs were brought to an abrupt halt by the military coup of April, 1964. Without any doubt, some of the upper- and middle-class support for the coup was based on the fear that conscientización, sponsored in part by radical Catholic elements, would soon give the masses "a voice commensurate with their numbers." [60]

[59] Henrique C. de Lima Vaz, "The Church and Conscientização," *America*, vol. 118 (April 27, 1968), p. 581.

[60] Sanders, "The Paulo Freire Method," *op cit.*, p. 11.

CHAPTER VI

Religious Values
and Political Culture

In Chapter V we analyzed the overt and relatively clear manifestations of the interaction of religion and the process of politicization. The intervention of clerical groups in politics, the functioning of religious political parties, and political conflicts over religious ideologies are all phenomena which can be observed and described with some measure of confidence. Some of the most vital questions concerning religion and politicization, however, are far more subtle, and the answers are far more elusive. These questions concern evaluative and attitudinal transfers from traditional religious orientations to new political experiences as politicization occurs. Do authoritarian religious values predispose individuals and societies to accept authoritarian political systems and do they impede the development of open, competitive, and participant systems? And do religious systems which view truth as proximate and even pluralist contribute to a political culture more favorable to democratic institutions? The great significance of such questions need hardly be argued.

In a transitional society today, religion is still the most important expression of the basic ideas, values, attitudes, and assumptions found in its culture. An anthropologist who had conducted field research in Burma for ten months reported:

"As in all field work, my guiding concerns and major interests were tempered by the actuality of the society under study and the historical flow of events while the field work was being done. The concentration on Buddhism [in this book] is a reflection of the simple fact that Buddhism is pervasive in the life of the people studied, for I had no explicit, before-hand commitment to go deeply into that subject as I did have in regard to economics and local social organization." [1] The anthropological literature dealing with Hindu, Muslim, and Latin American Catholic societies contains similar statements regarding the pervasiveness of religion in village cultures.

Politics in the third world, however, is not controlled by villagers, but by educated elites who have undergone considerable secularization. But even here the religious influence remains important, and the extent of secularization has frequently been exaggerated. A 1963 sample survey of Brazilian secondary schoolteachers, most of whom held university degrees, revealed a continued strong commitment to religious values. Between 54 per cent and 61 per cent of the men teachers (varying in the four states studied) stated that they attend religious services "regularly" or that they "always try to attend." Among women teachers declared church attendance was as high as 83 per cent. Furthermore, the vast majority perceived religious faith as relevant to their professional work. The author of the study notes that "if we add those who consider religion indispensable in teaching to those who feel religious belief to be a help, we find that a great majority of the teachers, three-fourths of them or more, consider religion to be a source of inspiration for teaching." [2]

Even among third-world elites who become secularized, however, it is most unlikely that traditional assumptions are totally eradicated. Basic attitudes and assumptions survive the early stages of the secularization process, at least the decline of con-

[1] Manning Nash, *The Golden Road to Modernity: Village Life in Contemporary Burma* (New York: John Wiley and Sons, Inc., 1965), p. 314.

[2] Aparecida Joly Gouveia, "Education and Development: Opinions of Secondary Schoolteachers," in S. M. Lipset and Aldo Solari, eds., *Elites in Latin America* (New York: Oxford University Press, 1967), pp. 484–513.

scious religiosity. In the future, largely secularized Hindu, Buddhist, and Muslim societies, which have not yet appeared in history, will still differ significantly from each other, as do the largely secularized Protestant and Catholic societies found in parts of the West today.

VALUES, STRUCTURES, AND BEHAVIOR

The question of the influence of religious values on political culture closely parallels Max Weber's inquiry into their effect on the development of economic life. In his famous work, *The Protestant Ethic and the Spirit of Capitalism,* Weber sought to explain why modern capitalism developed in western Europe and America and not elsewhere. His explanation was that a unique religious and ideological upheaval, the Protestant Reformation, had produced fundamentally new values which, particularly in their Calvinist form, had served to motivate and legitimate the efforts of the emerging capitalists in the following two centuries. In later research Weber extended his inquiry to the great non-Christian religions of Asia. His work generated a debate on the historical origins of capitalism which continues today, and the third world's quest for economic development has given new urgency to the fundamental question he asked.[3]

Here we are concerned with the impact of religious values on political culture. The concept of political culture has been criticized severely for its lack of precision, yet it points to a collective psychological and cultural reality which the political scientist cannot afford to ignore. Professor Sidney Verba's definition, quoted earlier, is that "the political culture of a society consists of the system of empirical beliefs, expressive symbols, and values which defines the situation in which political action takes place. It provides the subjective orientation to politics."[4]

[3] See S. N. Eisenstadt, ed., *The Protestant Ethic and Modernization: A Comparative View* (New York: Basic Books, Inc., 1968); and Robert N. Bellah, ed., *Religion and Progress in Modern Asia* (New York: The Free Press, 1965).

[4] Sidney Verba, "Comparative Political Culture," in Lucian Pye and Sidney Verba, eds., *Political Culture and Political Development* (Princeton: Princeton University Press, 1965), p. 513.

In a more recent definition Professors Almond and Powell emphasize the notion of propensities and also note the existence of subcultures within a general political culture: "In studying any political system, therefore, we need to know its underlying propensities as well as its actual performance over a given period of time. We refer to these propensities, or this psychological dimension of the political system, as the *political culture*. It consists of attitudes, beliefs, values, and skills which are current in an entire population, as well as those special propensities and patterns which may be found within separate parts of that population." [5]

The religious tradition of a society articulates values more explicitly than any other aspect of the society's general culture. However, the argument here is simply that religion is one among several important sources of attitudes and values contributing to political culture. Child rearing customs and family authority patterns begin to mold the child's attitudes toward his environment long before he can begin to learn the more abstract symbols of his culture. He is exposed to religious teaching at about the same age when school and other associations begin to influence his development. Secondary socialization is a complex process with many interacting factors. In the discussion below we shall try to suggest the outlines of political cultures informed by the basic values of the four major religions. In no sense, however, do we intend to suggest that religion constitutes the determining factor in the political culture of a given society. It must be seen as one important source among several of the values and attitudes of individuals and societies.

Clearly a society's values are not fixed and immutable. In particular, dysfunctional values may at first inhibit the operation of new structures introduced into a society, but in time they may be modified or replaced by values generated by the functioning of the new institutions themselves.[6] Thus authori-

[5] Gabriel A. Almond and G. Bingham Powell, Jr., *Comparative Politics: A Developmental Approach* (Boston: Little, Brown and Co., 1966), p. 23.

[6] This point has been made with respect to values and economic structures and is clearly applicable to political institutions as well. See S. M. Lipset, "Values, Education, and Entrepreneurship," in Lipset and Solari, eds., *op. cit.*, pp. 32–35.

tarian social values will definitely inhibit but will not invari-
ably prevent the development of a democratic political system.
Over time democratic structures tend to generate congruent
values. The postwar history of West Germany and Japan must
be seen, at least in part, in these terms.

Unique historical experiences may radically change a society's values. In our analysis below, we find traditional Catholicism to be conducive to a political culture dominated by
authoritarian and hierarchical values. But the mere identification of Mexico as predominantly Catholic is obviously insufficient to inform us about contemporary Mexican political
culture. However, a description of traditional Catholic values
will tell us a good deal about the kind of social and political
patterns the Mexican Revolution sought to destroy and the
reasons for the polity-dominance secularization which was
deemed necessary by the men of the Revolution.

Middle-class elites, especially in South and Southeast Asia,
the Middle East, and North Africa, have their own political
subcultures which differ markedly from the general political
cultures of their respective societies. Educated largely through
the medium of European languages and exposed to Western
political thought, experienced in the operation of Western administrative, legal, and political institutions, these elites may
have values which strongly support political structures im-
planted in an otherwise unfriendly cultural environment. In
some cases the development of elite political subcultures has
meant radical secularization and alienation from traditional
values. In other cases it has meant the compartmentalization
of life; the Madras lawyer is both an orthodox Brahman at
home and in his caste circle, and a highly competent professional in the office and in court where a quite different set of
values orients his behavior.

Religious values are being consciously redefined in the light
of what are regarded by the interpreters as more universal
values. The Vatican II document on freedom of religion,
Radhakrishnan's writings on social equality in Hinduism, and
the modernists' attacks on polygamy throughout the Muslim
world constitute conscious efforts to change both structures
and values. Our analysis of values relevant to political culture,

however, will largely ignore these reformulations, not because they are unimportant for they are not, but because the more traditional values are still far more characteristic of these societies as a whole.

To link formal, stated values with individual motivation and behavior is always difficult. The problem is compounded, however, when the values studied are ambiguous, even *a priori*, in their behavioral implications. Ideas of predestination, determinism, and fatalism, for example, can be found in all four religions. But writers have usually asserted that the Islamic variety has led to extreme resignation, passivity, and submissiveness. On the other hand, Weber found in the Calvinist version a powerful incentive to energetic work on the ground that the believer thus confirmed his place among the elect. Hindu and Buddhist notions of karma could logically lead to passivity and resignation. However, anthropological studies of Buddhist societies tend to refute this interpretation and instead suggest that the incentive to improve one's future karma through individual action is a more significant behavioral consequence.

Our selection of two clusters of values, from the many which may have political implications and effects, has been guided by the desire to minimize the ambiguity while focusing on the really crucial questions related to political culture, namely, attitudes toward authority and possible participation in the political system. As Professors Almond and Verba suggest, nonpolitical authority patterns to which the individual is exposed have a significant effect on his attitudes toward political authority. The individual tends to generalize from roles in family, school, or job to the performance of political roles; authoritarian or participatory expectations in the former are carried over into politics.[7] Religious authority patterns are too diffuse to be described in terms of the concept of "role." However, they derive from man's most fundamental assumptions about the nature of his world, the meaning of life, and right conduct. To a degree generally far greater than is found in school or

[7] Gabriel A. Almond and Sidney Verba, *The Civic Culture* (Princeton: Princeton University Press, 1963), pp. 323–330.

job, religious authority patterns are deeply rooted in the emotional aspects of man's nature.

Authoritarian religion strongly predisposes individuals and societies toward authoritarian political systems. The first cluster of values to investigate, therefore, concerns the place of authority in the four religions. Our second cluster concerns religious values relating to social structure. We must not overlook the fact that religions have not only implications but very explicit teachings regarding hierarchical or egalitarian social structure, and these are directly related to assumptions regarding political participation.

A comparative analysis of authority in the four religious systems is difficult because of their radically different total views of reality. Nevertheless, three points seem to be both inherently significant for all four systems and psychologically important in the formation of attitudes toward politics: (1) *dogmatic authority,* or the absoluteness of truth; (2) *directive authority,* or the comprehensiveness of regulations; and (3) *institutionalization of authority,* or the complexity and effectiveness of truth defining and rule enforcing structures.

Dogmatic authority concerns the nature of the truth claims made in a religious system that condition the individual to perceive the world in a particular way. The variation here is wide indeed, from unqualified assertions of absolute truth to an almost unlimited pluralism and relativism. Directive authority measures the extent to which the system articulates divine commands to regulate and guide human behavior. Here again the variation is wide, from systems which prescribe a minimal moral code to those which have elaborated comprehensive rules governing virtually all aspects of life. Both of these dimensions of authority, dogmatic and directive, are profoundly affected by the third, the extent of institutionalization of authority. That is, a system may be ranked high on the absoluteness of truth and the comprehensiveness of directives, but in the absence of strong institutionalization within the society — that is, authoritative structures to interpret and communicate the truth and to enforce the directives with visible sanctions — much of the authority of the system will remain diffuse. This is in fact the case with respect to one of the four systems being analyzed here.

It will be useful at this point to apply our analysis in summary form to the four religions. Figure VI.1 suggests some rough measure of the three dimensions of politically relevant religious authority.

Starting with this analysis of religious authority, the general hypotheses to be considered are as follows:

1. The authoritarian values of a religious system are a function of its degree of dogmatic authority, directive authority, and institutionalization of authority.
2. The higher the degree of religious authoritarianism, the stronger the authoritarian values in the political culture; the lower the degree of religious authoritarianism, the greater the congruence of the political culture with democratic political institutions.
3. The higher the degree of dogmatic authority in the religious system, the stronger the tendency toward an ideo-

FIGURE VI.1 *Religious Systems as Sources of Authoritarian Values*

	CATHOLICISM	ISLAM	HINDUISM	BUDDHISM
Dogmatic authority	3	3	0	1
Directive authority	3	3	3	0
Institutionalization of authority	3	1	1	0
Score — authoritarian values	9	7	4	1

Code: 3 — high
2 — medium
1 — low
0 — negligible

logical political culture; the lower the degree of dogmatic authority, the stronger the tendency toward a pragmatic political culture.

It is far easier to show authoritarian religion supporting authoritarian polity (proposition 2) than to show any significant influence of anti-authoritarian religion on polity, at least in the rather outstanding case of Buddhism. The correlation between high dogmatic authority and ideological political culture (proposition 3) is clear in the case of Catholicism and Islam, and the low dogmatic authority of Hinduism and Buddhism is related to pragmatic values in political culture.

As noted earlier, each religious system also contains certain explicit teachings regarding social structure that have a direct bearing on assumptions regarding the appropriate levels and extent of political participation. We can here add to the summary contained in Figure VI.1 the unelaborated statement that Hinduism and Catholicism have promoted hierarchical values, while Buddhism and Islam have on the whole promoted egalitarianism.

We can now proceed to examine the major values which each religion contributes to political culture. It must again be emphasized that we are here deliberately ignoring a large number of highly relevant variables which would have to be taken into account in the analysis of the political culture of any given society. However, by isolating the religious factor for comparative analysis some useful insights will be gained. We shall consider the four religions in the order found in Figure VI.1, from the most authoritarian to the least.

The argument consists of some generalizations concerning the politically relevant values articulated in the four religious systems, the systematic observations of social scientists and others, and some findings of survey research.[8] Further cross-cultural survey research which probes the various dimensions of religious values and political attitudes in the four culture

[8] See Frederick W. Frey, *Survey Research on Comparative Social Change: A Bibliography* (Cambridge, Mass.: MIT Press, 1969). Very few published studies throw light on the problem discussed in this chapter.

areas will be necessary for the systematic testing of our hypotheses.

CATHOLICISM:
AUTHORITARIAN-HIERARCHICAL VALUES

That the one Western religion among the four is the least conducive to an open, democratic political culture is remarkable. Present challenges to the principles of authority and hierarchy within the Catholic church are unprecedentedly strong and growing. Internal democratization since Vatican II, as a basic aspect of the *aggiornamento* of the church, has begun to bring about significant changes in structures and values. If traditional Catholicism is the least "democratic" of the four religions, it is also changing far more rapidly and coherently than the other three. But conservatives within the church still control the key positions, including the papacy under Pope Paul VI. The legacy of the past is not easily shaken off.

The church's dogmatic authority has insisted that it is the one true church, that it is the bearer of absolute truth, and that other doctrines cannot be tolerated since error has no rights. The directive authority claimed by traditional Catholicism left few areas of individual or social life untouched. The church has sought to control individual conscience and behavior on such varied questions as those relating to the sexual life of spouses, the education of children, and a wide range of cultural, social, economic, and political matters: the books which a Catholic can read or the films he can see, the union or other association he can join, and the political party he can vote for. The extreme institutionalization of this authority in the church structure, however, makes the Catholic church unique among the major world religions. The church is a hierarchical structure in which authority descends from an infallible pope through cardinals, archbishops, and bishops to the parish priest, who is called "Father" and who absolves the penitent of sins.

Careful observers of Latin American life have been virtually unanimous in seeing the church as a major source of the authoritarian values prevailing in politics. "Introducing education in the colonies and remaining to dominate it," Professor Blanksten writes, "the church has fostered heavily authoritarian thinking in the area." [9] Another political scientist, writing during the 1950's, alluded to the church's frequent alliances with political conservatism; this no longer generally occurs, but the more important attitudinal effect remains. "It is not simply that the Catholic Church is an authoritarian organization or that it has almost always been allied with conservative groups, movements, and individuals in Latin America. The indirect but more pervasive effect of the great influence of Catholicism has been to transfer a tendency toward acceptance of authority into other fields than the spiritual and ecclesiastical, especially into the field of politics. Thus, there is developed less of the sturdy attitude of questioning constituted political authority than would provide the most fertile soil in which to plant democracy." [10]

As noted earlier, religion constitutes just one of several major sources of values which influence political culture. One author, asserting that the "hierarchical, authoritarian, and absolutist" character of the church "conditions the individual more toward authoritarianism than toward democracy," points out that it is precisely the absence or weakness of democratically oriented social institutions in other areas of Latin American life which makes the influence of Catholicism so strong. "The authoritarian conditioning of the church would have a negligible effect on the development of anti-democratic sentiments if the majority of the people were exposed to democratic living in other important social institutions. Inasmuch as they are not, for the most part, the role of the church in the development of their political ideas is enhanced." [11]

[9] George I. Blanksten, "Latin America," in G. A. Almond and J. S. Coleman, eds., *The Politics of the Developing Areas* (Princeton: Princeton University Press, 1960), p. 487.

[10] Russell H. Fitzgibbon, "The Pathology of Democracy in Latin America: A Political Scientist's Point of View," in Ansher N. Christensen, ed., *The Evolution of Latin American Government* (New York: Henry Holt and Co., 1951), p. 274.

[11] William S. Stokes, "Catholicism and Democracy in Latin America," in Angel del Río, ed., *Responsible Freedom in the Americas* (Garden City, N.Y.: Doubleday and Co., 1955), p. 362.

It is important to remember that traditional Catholic doctrine explicitly prescribes a hierarchical structure for society. In the medieval view the clergy, rulers, and nobles functioned as God's lieutenants; in patriarchal fashion they protected the lower orders, which in turn owed them obedience. This basic model of society still informs part of Catholic social thought. In 1937 Pope Pius XI spoke of "a sane corporative system which respects the proper hierarchic structure of society." [12] And Pope Paul VI in a 1968 address to Colombian peasants could speak of brotherhood, but within a framework of "a hierarchical and organic order in the social make-up." [13] Within this traditional hierarchical scheme, political participation was clearly not a prerogative of the lower classes. A contemporary conservative *pensador* of Chile criticized the Christian Democrats for disregarding this principle: "They do not contemplate organizing suffrage upon a logical, hierarchical basis, but are content to rest it upon a foundation of equalitarianism. . . . Their ideology rests neither upon the glorious Aristotelian-Thomistic tradition, nor upon pontifical teachings." [14] The same writer summarized the values of traditional Catholic social and political thought when he wrote: "Only an authoritarian, honest, impersonal, and efficient regime, which does not represent the majority but rather the best, can instil in the masses a sense of obedience and implant in the social life the principles of order, hierarchy, and discipline, which are indispensable for attaining the common good and national progress." [15]

Papal encyclicals in the late nineteenth century explicitly rejected the basic tenets of democracy along with rationalism and liberalism. All three were condemned as opposed to the

[12] *Divini Redemptoris,* cited *ibid.,* p. 365.

[13] Consejo Episcopal Latinoamericano (CELAM), *La Iglesia en la Actual Transformación de América Latina a la Luz del Concilio* (Santiago, Chile: Ediciones Paulinas, 1969), vol. 2, p. 251.

[14] Jorge Hübner Gallo, *Los católicos en la política* (Santiago: Empresa Editora Zig-Zag, 1959), from a selection translated into English in Frederick B. Pike, ed., *The Conflict between Church and State in Latin America* (New York: Alfred A. Knopf, 1964), p. 199.

[15] *Ibid.,* p. 207.

principle of divine authority. Pope Leo XIII wrote in 1888: "For when man is once firmly persuaded that he is subject to no one, it follows that the efficient cause of the unity of civil society is not to be sought in any principle external to man, or superior to him, but simply in the free will of individuals; that the authority in the state comes from the people only; and that, just as every man's individual reason is his only rule of life, so the collective reason of the community should be the supreme guide in the management of public affairs. Hence, the doctrine of the supremacy of the greatest number, and that all right and duty reside in the majority. But from what has been said it is clear that all this is a contradiction to reason." [16]

Here again, this view must be balanced by reading the strongly democratic social encyclicals of Pope John XXIII, which represent the official Catholic position of the post-Vatican II church. The point, however, is that authoritarian values are deeply rooted in the Catholic tradition, in official pronouncements as well as in the general ethos; democracy is a recent and still unassimilated value, and the internal church structure has only begun to respond to the implications of the new idea. The basic impact of Catholicism on the political cultures of underdeveloped societies is still not too different from that suggested by Kingsley Davis a generation ago: "Catholicism attempts to control so many aspects of life, to encourage so much fixity of status and submission to authority, and to remain so independent of secular authority that it inevitably clashes with the liberalism, individualism, freedom, mobility, and sovereignty of the democratic nation." [17]

A Belgian Jesuit who has worked in Latin America for many years, and who is strongly committed to social, economic, and political modernization, frankly faced the problem of Catholicism's hierarchical and authoritarian values. According to his analysis the Catholic church, a "human-divine entity," expresses "the verticality of the divine authority" and is

[16] *Libertas Praestantissimum,* cited in Stokes, "Catholicism and Democracy in Latin America," in Río, *op. cit.,* pp. 374–375.

[17] Kingsley Davis, "Political Ambivalence in Latin America," in Christensen, *op. cit.,* p. 240.

"the maximum, infallible authority of the transmission of the gospel — the divine word — through tradition." The scheme of authority that characterizes Latin American social, economic, and political life is essentially vertical. In the political realm this has meant the rule of *caudillos* or dictators and the absence of mass political participation. "The cause . . . is that the Latin American tends to project a vertical scheme of authority that is valid and legitimate in the ethical and religious realm into the profane world." This view of authority has led to passive submission to the rule of oligarchies in social, economic, and political life. How, then, can modernization take place? Vekemans believes that a "cultural mutation" producing significant value change is possible without resort to totalitarian secularization.[18] Elsewhere in his writings he tentatively identifies the "cultural mutation" in Latin America with the Christian Democratic movement.

Catholicism's high dogmatic authority — the absoluteness of its truth — has encouraged strongly intolerant attitudes toward those who hold differing ideologies, undermining the democratic political system at one of its crucial points. As Seymour Martin Lipset has said: "Democracy requires a universalistic political belief system in the sense that it accepts various different ideologies as legitimate. And it might be assumed that religious value systems which are more universalistic, in the sense of placing less stress on being the only true church, will be more compatible with democracy than those which assume that they are the only truth. The latter belief, which is held much more strongly by the Catholic than by most other Christian churches, makes it difficult for the religious value system to help legitimate a political system which requires as part of its basic value system the belief that 'good' is served best through conflict among opposing beliefs." [19]

18 Roger E. Vekemans, "Economic Development, Social Change, and Cultural Mutation in Latin America," in W. V. D'Antonio and F. B. Pike, eds., *Religion, Revolution, and Reform* (New York: Praeger, 1964), pp. 136–137.

19 Seymour Martin Lipset, *Political Man* (Garden City, N.Y.: Doubleday and Co., 1963), p. 72.

Professor Fredrick B. Pike has suggested that the element of fanaticism frequently observed in Latin American politics is rooted in Catholic attitudes regarding the absoluteness of truth. Partly because of religious uniformity, Latin Americans have tended to think in terms of ultimates; they have not been conditioned by significant religious pluralism to accept the existence of differing views of reality. In the United States, on the other hand, religious diversity made the consideration of ultimates politically risky, and pragmatism became the basic approach to questions of policy early in the nation's history. The Latin American "pattern of dogmatic certitude regarding political issues" inherited from the colonial period still persists. "Even in their more secular modern society, many Latin Americans have apparently persisted in the belief that salvation, or at least self-respect, lies in an interior faith, in adherence if not to the traditional orthodox creed, then to ideals and immutable standards of some sort. Thus, it is better for one to be associated with a government that conforms fully to his ideas, or to be plotting the overthrow of one that does not, rather than to risk compromising ideas merely in order to bring about political stability." [20]

For the same psychological reasons, ideologies have played a significant role in Latin American politics. Political behavior has in fact often been characterized by extremely pragmatic and opportunistic maneuvers, in Latin America as elsewhere. But ideas and ideologies have also been regarded as intrinsically important. In Latin America as in Europe, highly ideological political cultures are associated with Catholicism. In both areas, conflicts directly involving the church have divided political forces since the early nineteenth century. In Latin America, the Conservative and Liberal parties which emerged in most countries after independence were, respectively, the Catholic and anticlerical parties. The pattern of ideological

[20] Frederick B. Pike, "Sources of Revolution: Their Impact on Freedom and Reform in Latin America," in Frederick B. Pike, ed., *Freedom and Reform in Latin America* (Notre Dame, Ind.: University of Notre Dame Press, 1959), p. 37.

politics was firmly established and was only intensified when Marxism replaced liberalism as the political heresy threatening the church.

In concluding this section on Catholicism, we must recognize the great potential significance of Christian Democracy in Latin America. In Chile particularly, this movement has a history of thirty years of serious ideological reformulation behind it. Christian Democracy repudiated political authoritarianism without challenging the theological and ecclesiastical authoritarianism associated with it. In articulating the values of individual freedom, egalitarianism, democracy, and pluralism, the movement anticipated Vatican II by a generation. Christian Democracy has conclusively shown that conscious value change is possible through a democratic political party. The only question, however, is how deeply this new Catholic ideology can penetrate and displace authoritarian values rooted in four centuries of Iberian Catholic tradition.

ISLAM:
AUTHORITARIAN-EGALITARIAN VALUES

Unquestionably a strong strain of authoritarianism which has supported authoritarian polities exists in the Islamic tradition. In Manfred Halpern's words: "In popular Islam, an unseen world demands continual propitiation; in orthodox Islam, the believer has been given rules to guide his entire conduct by a God so powerful that only submission is possible." Halpern argues that in fact the political culture informed by Islam is peculiarly open to Marxist appeals, for many Muslims are prepared to look for "a modern revelation as total in its concepts, emotional appeal, and the social control it exercises as was Islam in the past." [21] One might add that Islam's essential egalitarianism is another value it shares with Marxism. However, authoritarian-egalitarian values may support various types of regimes, and Nasser with his ideology of Arab socialism, which involves no rejection of Islamic theism, seems a more

---

[21] Manfred Halpern, *The Politics of Social Change in the Middle East and North Africa* (Princeton: Princeton University Press, 1963), p. 220.

likely pattern in the Middle East than a Marxist alternative. In any case, the prospect for democratic political institutions throughout the Muslim world does not seem too bright.

Dogmatic authority in Islam is very high. The truth is absolute, universal and unchanging; in orthodox theology the Qur'an is believed to be eternal, that is, the Word of God existed before it was communicated to the Prophet. Jews and Christians have valid but incomplete scriptures; the Qur'anic revelation is God's final and authoritative message to mankind.

Directive authority, the comprehensive set of rules by which men must order their lives, is found in the *shari'ah,* or sacred law. "Much more than a legal system properly speaking, the *shari'ah* is the comprehensive catalogue of God's commands and recommendations laid down for the guidance of men. How and what to eat, when to wash, what to wear, how and when to pray and fast — these and similar matters are treated on the same basis and with just as much meticulous concern as matters more strictly legal, such as marriage and divorce, or commercial transactions, or crime. Governing the whole range of man's relations with God and society, and in the absence of any organized Muslim church hierarchy, the *shari'ah* is incomparably the central institution of Islam." [22] This low ecclesiastical institutionalization of authority is what sharply distinguishes Islamic from Catholic authority patterns. While the *ulama* do interpret and apply the law, the mechanisms for its enforcement have always come from the political structures.

Authoritarian values are fostered by the Muslim understanding of the relationship between morality and law. God's command or decree in the Qur'an determines whether a given act is good or bad. "Nothing is either good or evil in itself, unless decreed to be so by Allah. Even murder would have been morally irrelevant if it were not for the fact that the Qur'an forbids it. Even now, it isn't innately immoral; it is just forbidden by Allah." [23] The shari'ah classifies all acts as manda-

[22] Richard H. Nolte, "The Rule of Law in the Arab Middle East," *The Muslim World,* vol. 48 (October 1958), pp. 295–296.

[23] Henry Siegman, "The State and the Individual in Sunni Islam," *ibid.,* vol. 54 (January 1964), p. 23.

tory, recommended, permissible, reprehensible, or forbidden. While the intricacies of jurisprudence are left to the ulama, this basic perception of the nature of human actions has profoundly influenced all Muslim life. In *Growing Up in an Egyptian Village* Hamid Ammar presents the following characterization: "Sanctity and sacred sanctions lie at the foundation of a great deal of human activities and behavior in the village; and ideally the sacred not only prevails over the profane but sanctions and to some extent directs it. According to the villagers, 'life on this earth is like a farm, the harvest of which will be reaped in the next world.' Social acts and value judgments are grouped into two main religious categories: *haram* (forbidden) and *halal* (allowed), two words with a distinctively religious flavor." [24] All acts are either forbidden or allowed *by Allah*.

Ethical considerations, then, do not concern motives and social consequences, but only obedience to the decrees of a sovereign God. The assumption is that what is forbidden or permitted is a matter of objective knowledge, since it is contained or implied in the Qur'an and Sunnah (traditions). While the ulama have been stripped of most of their judicial functions throughout the Muslim world, they are still sought by devout believers for advice on many questions outside the scope of modern law. Is it permitted or forbidden for a Muslim to listen to or own a radio? Permitted, said some Indonesian ulama in 1935. To photograph objects or persons with a camera? Forbidden. To pay premiums on an insurance policy? Forbidden.[25] And the process of issuing *fatwas* on such subjects continues today.[26] The assumptions underlying the process are strongly authoritarian.

[24] Hamid Ammar, *Growing up in an Egyptian Village* (London: Routledge and Kegan Paul, 1954), p. 73.

[25] Mochtar Naim, "The Nahdatul-Ulama Party, 1952–1955," unpublished M. A. thesis, McGill University, 1960, pp. 152–158.

[26] Some very interesting contemporary *fatwas* are found in "The Mufti," a regular feature of the English edition of *Minbar Al-Islam*, published by the Supreme Council for Islamic Affairs, Ministry of Waqfs, Cairo, United Arab Republic. For a *fatwa* finding it permissible for a Muslim to sell his blood to a blood bank see *ibid.*, vol. 2 (October 1962), no. 4, pp. 65–66.

In a cross-cultural study of authoritarianism and its correlates in Egypt and the United States, the respondents in Egypt included one hundred al-Azhar University students. Measuring authoritarianism by the F scale, the study again verified the higher average score in a culture known to possess more authoritarian characteristics. The mean score for American Protestant men was 55.8, compared to 68.2 for Egyptian Muslim men. However, the mean score for al-Azhar respondents, who are studying to become ulama, was still higher, 70.4. The highest relationship between authoritarianism and religious intolerance was found in this group. Positive and significant relationships between authoritarianism and family adherence to religious practice were found for all groups in both cultures, but here again the strongest relationship was for the al-Azhar theologians. In probing authoritarianism and personality correlates the author of this study suggests that "the authoritarian Muslim respondent in Egypt tends to be better adjusted according to this measure than either the Christian authoritarian in Egypt or the authoritarian in the United States. This fits in with the explanation that the Muslim authoritarian finds himself more in conformity with the Middle East culture whereas the U.S. authoritarian finds himself an alien in his culture." [27]

The authoritarian culture of the Middle East has been largely molded by Islam, which literally means submission. Submission to the will of Allah is expressed ritually five times a day in prayers during which the believer prostrates his whole body before the divine sovereign of the universe. Some scholars have found "a large measure of individualism" in Islam, in the sense that rewards and punishment will be meted out to men as individuals on the Day of Judgment.[28] While this is true — and parallel statements could be made for Catholicism, Hinduism, and Buddhism — the religious system as a whole is

[27] Levon H. Melikian, "Authoritarianism and its Correlates in the Egyptian Culture and in the United States," *Journal of Social Issues*, vol. 15 (1959), no. 3, p. 66.

[28] W. Montgomery Watt, *Islam and the Integration of Society* (London: Routledge and Kegan Paul, 1961), p. 11.

clearly not conducive to the development of individual ego strength and self-determination.

Even the egalitarianism of Islam is in part related to the fact of submission. According to Professor Najjar: "By nature men are unequal; they acquire their equality by submitting to God's will, and are thus reduced to the same level. Man is the slave of God, and as such he cannot claim any superiority. *Kulluna 'abidul-Allah* ('we are all God's slaves') is a current retort in Muslim countries to any display of superiority or exercise of discrimination." [29] Islamic egalitarianism, like that of primitive Christianity, did not extend to the rejection of the institution of slavery. And Islamic egalitarianism never extended to women. Nevertheless, the equality of believers is a value deeply embedded in Islam and one strongly favorable to the general processes of modernization. The Qur'an declares: "The believers are brothers." Over the long history of Islam, this was never understood to mean that all Muslims had an equal right to political participation. However, it still remains an ideal which can be given greater social, economic, and political content.

Authoritarian-egalitarian values are the most significant Islamic contributions to contemporary political cultures. Over the past hundred years considerable intellectual energy has been expended in attempting to prove or disprove the compatibility of Islam with democracy. Muslim interpreters attempting to establish this compatibility have been motivated by a sometimes confused mixture of apologetic and reformist considerations. Some have sought to prove the validity of Islam by showing that democratic ideas and institutions were an integral part of Islam from its inception. Others have sought to legitimize modern democracy and encourage Muslims to accept it by pointing to its alleged affinity to Islam. The major premise has often been unclear in such discussions. Furthermore, the argument often centered on largely irrelevant historical questions, such as the practice of *shura* (consultation) in connection with the appointment of the early caliphs. *Ijtihad*

[29] Fauzi M. Najjar, "Islam and Modern Democracy," *Review of Politics*, vol. 20 (April 1958), pp. 170–171.

(private judgment) was never understood as an open invitation to the Muslims to make their own laws. Modernist interpretations of ijtihad and *ijma* (consensus) as sources of law claimed them as a firm foundation for modern democracy, overlooking the fact that the consensus was that of the ulama on a point of legal interpretation. The concepts do not bear the least resemblance to any notion of popular sovereignty.[30]

While their interpretations were often strained and historically invalid, what was most important was not the modernists' arguments but their existence. The fact was that a considerable number of Western-educated Muslims found it possible to subscribe to liberal democratic values while remaining faithful to what they regarded as the essence of Islam. Their interpretations, even the farfetched ones, played a significant role in the Muslim encounter with modernity. However, they consistently underestimated the weight of tradition which, as we have suggested, has been and is strongly authoritarian.

While not as pronounced as in Catholicism, in Islam also high dogmatic authority has led to an ideological orientation toward politics. Islamic political parties, from Egypt and Sudan to Indonesia, have waged ideological *jihad* (holy war) against both liberal secularists and Marxists. In all of these countries there has been a moderate sector of Muslim opinion inclined toward accommodation of those holding opposing world views, but the most devout Muslims have generally been the least receptive to compromise. Since the truth has been so clearly revealed to man, categorical opposition to contradictory views is the only logical course for a true believer.

HINDUISM:
PLURALIST-AUTHORITARIAN-HIERARCHICAL VALUES

The continuing influence of religious values is noted in Professor Edward Shils's pioneering study of the Indian intellectual. He points out that not more than 10 per cent of his interviewees professed atheism or agnosticism and that many Hindu intel-

---

[30] H. A. R. Gibb, *Modern Trends in Islam* (Chicago: University of Chicago Press, 1947), pp. 10–11.

lectuals give expression to their religious consciousness through regular and in some cases elaborate ritual. "The religious indifference which is so widespread in the educated classes of the West has little counterpart among Indian intellectuals; even those without very intense religious sensibility speak in religious metaphors. The Hindu pantheon permeates their imagery in a manner evocative of the prominence of biblical imagery in writings of Victorian intellectuals in Britain and America. Moreover, the ecclesiastical amorphousness and doctrinal flexibility of Hinduism render easier the retention of Hindu affinities." [31] In the light of this continuing vitality of Hindu values and symbols, their impact on the political culture of the world's largest democracy is a matter of considerable importance.

The Hindu value system is the most complex of the four major religions. From the standpoint of political culture, its most important characteristics are the absence of revealed universal truth and an explicitly recognized pluralism in regard to beliefs and codes of conduct. While this pluralism has encouraged virtually unlimited speculation, it is closely related to the caste differences of a rigid social hierarchy. And within each caste unit, the individual's intellectual freedom is balanced by pervasive and strongly authoritarian prescriptions regarding social behavior. These interrelated elements merit closer examination.

We have scored dogmatic authority in Hinduism as 0; there is no absolute truth about which statements can be made. The philosophical concept of the Absolute is that it is totally without attributes. All of men's notions about reality are partial and limited by ignorance. There are no doctrinal norms, and a profusion of divergent religious ideas have evolved and coexisted peacefully. Pluralism in the realm of ideas has its ritual counterpart in polytheism and in the traditional Hindu view it was expected that the particular god a man worshipped would reflect his inherent capacities and prior conditioning.

The important connection between doctrinal pluralism and

---

[31] Edward Shils, *The Intellectual between Tradition and Modernity: The Indian Situation* (The Hague: Mouton and Co., 1961), p. 64.

the social hierarchy comes at this point, for it was also assumed that the individual's inherent capacities corresponded to his caste status. Professor W. Norman Brown has said: "Furthermore, the intellectual and spiritual, sometimes even the moral, endowments of a person at birth were regarded as a concomitant of his caste status. Hence a low caste person was expected to have a less sophisticated view of god, society, life, and morality than a high caste person. . . . So, too, standards of behavior were viewed as different. Normal conduct for a low caste man might be a sin for a Brahman. All this was understood to be in accord with cosmic law. It constituted an acceptance of relativity concerning human capacity and human behavior that is the basis of the Hindu tolerance mentioned above. There was no such thing as a single universal standard of duty." [32]

While caste inequality was perhaps the most important assumption underlying Hindu pluralism, relativism, and tolerance, it was not the only one. For even among Brahmans of equal status diametrically opposed doctrines emerged and there was no attempt to classify them as "lower" or "higher" conceptions of reality. There was, and is, a fundamental Hindu disinclination to regard any truth as absolute or ultimate, and this attitude, it can be safely predicted, will outlive the caste system. Professor Brown has also pointed to this aspect of the Hindu tradition of intellectual freedom: "Mutually contradictory doctrines have been allowed, and are still allowed, to stand side by side in argumentative and unreconciled, but not violently hostile, coexistence. There has been an amazing willingness to tolerate another's opinion on intellectual issues, though it may differ from one's own, on the generally accepted theory that no one of us has found the final word, knows the ultimate truth. Even the great teachers, to whom revelation was thought to have come by some mystic experience, were contradicted by other great teachers similarly venerated, and the followers of each let the followers of the others live and

[32] W. Norman Brown, *Man in the Universe: Some Continuities in Indian Thought* (Berkeley: University of California Press, 1966), pp. 12–13.

preach and worship for the most part unmolested." [33] While the Westerner may well grow weary of the modern Hindu apologist's incessant talk of Hindu tolerance, the basic fact is that Hinduism never generated the kind of fanatacism about belief systems which has characterized a considerable part of Christian and Islamic history.

While pluralism and relativism reflect Hinduism's negligible dogmatic authority, authoritarian values are associated with its high score on directive authority. In the high castes particularly, traditional Hindu religion confronts the individual with detailed regulations, and to the extent that he takes his *dharma* seriously, conditions him to conform rather than to exercise independent judgment. Interactions with members of other castes are carefully regulated to prevent ritual pollution and within the caste intricate rituals and taboos govern many acts, but especially those relating to dining. An anthropologist wrote: "Beliefs about ritual purity and ritual impurity form some of the most all-pervasive themes in Hindu culture. They are the basis of 'orthoprax' Brahmanism in that only a ritually pure individual may approach the higher gods. Brahmanic concepts concerning pollution relate the Indian system of social stratification to the Hindu religious system. . . . One of the important rationales for caste separatism (their refusal to intermarry, eat with one another, or touch one another) is that some castes arè more ritually pure than others, and that impurity may be transmitted from one caste to another through these acts." [34] Much like the Islamic shari'ah, the Hindu *dharmashastras* tended to develop comprehensive regulations of individual and social behavior.

The authoritarian and hierarchical values inculcated by Hindu religion were prominent in the world view articulated by Rajasthani villagers interviewed in 1950. "They knew without question that their life was only one of a long series of rebirths, that they must conform to right behavior in order to

[33] *Ibid.*, p. 42.

[34] Edward B. Harper, "Ritual Pollution as an Integrator of Caste and Religion," in Edward B. Harper, ed., *Religion in South Asia* (Seattle: University of Washington Press, 1964), p. 151.

advance their spiritual progress toward the desired aim of Release; and they knew that the hierarchy of castes and the gradations of sub-human life are a reflection of the soul's progress in working out its *karma*." [35] According to the author, a psychologist, the villager accepted the caste system, and his place within it, as part of the order of nature; his most prominent religious attitudes were "submission, resignation and obedience." In terms of observed social behavior, the villager was generally self-assured and at ease in formal interactions in which he could orient himself hierarchically, but emotionally insecure in informal situations for which no rules existed.[36] The authoritarian nature of Hindu socioreligious institutions emerges clearly from this study.

The Hindu institutionalization of authority was found chiefly in the functioning of caste councils, which had authority to punish offenders by fines and ultimately by excommunication, which meant social death. The councils, however, have been declining rapidly in recent decades and in many places have ceased to exist. For this reason Hinduism's institutionalization of authority has been scored as low in Figure VI.1. Informal social pressure, not institutionalized authority, is the most effective mechanism for the enforcement of caste conformity today.

Clearly, then, authoritarian and hierarchical values in the Hindu tradition are strong, and India's political culture, which is partly informed by them, is to that extent subversive of the democratic political institutions which are now functioning.[37] On the other hand are the Hindu traditions of intellectual freedom, pluralism, relativism, and tolerance. In the judgment of the present writer, these values, which are congruent with and reinforce a participant political system, have outweighed the former values in Indian political development thus far.

---

[35] G. Morris Carstairs, *The Twice-Born: A Study of a Community of High-Caste Hindus* (Bloomington: Indiana University Press, 1958), p. 145.
[36] *Ibid.*, p. 61.
[37] For a study strongly emphasizing the anti-democratic orientations in Hindu culture see A. B. Shah, *Planning for Democracy and Other Essays* (Bombay: Manaktalas, 1967), especially pp. 145–161.

Professor R. Bhaskaran has argued that the "receptive catholicism and pluralist tolerance" of the Indian national temper provided fertile ground for the transplanting of British liberalism in the nineteenth century. The liberal values of individuality, moderation, and compromise, in association with parliamentary democracy, were readily assimilated by the Hindu intelligentsia. "Intellectual freedom has never been feared or curtailed in our country, and a certain love of abstract reasoning is traditional in our schools. . . . The liberal tradition is therefore something congenial to the spirit of the country, something recognized as familiar and acceptable when encountered in the foreigner's schools." [38] The English-educated elite thus built their modern ideas of individualism and freedom on an older liberal tradition, native to the land.

Hindu values of pluralism and relativism have helped to create a pragmatic political culture. Bargaining and compromise have been far more characteristic of Indian politics since 1947 than rigid and doctrinaire positions. The political parties identified as Hindu are non-ideological. No Hindu ideology for the reconstruction of state and society has been articulated by any party; nothing even remotely resembles the ideological efforts of Muslim groups in Pakistan, Syria, or Egypt, or Christian Democrats in Latin America. But quite apart from the explicitly Hindu parties, more important is that Hindu culture in general is peculiarly unreceptive to pronouncements of absolute truth, whether religious or political. Ideological revelations of this nature may find a place for themselves in the Hindu *milieu,* but not on their own terms as universal and ultimate truths for everyone.

The pluralist, relativist, and hence non-ideological approach to politics promoted by Hindu values is well illustrated in Professor Bhaskaran's comments on India's foreign policy of nonalignment. "Yet, however distasteful it may be to the sophisticated architects and exponents of our foreign policy in its diurnal manifestations to consider its roots, it is the Hindu view of the ultimate truth that nourishes them. To hold that every nation

38 R. Bhaskaran, *Sociology of Politics: Tradition and Politics in India* (Bombay: Asia Publishing House, 1967), pp. 168–169.

has a right to go its own way and no nation has the right to wish that another may come to resemble it is to oppose 'colonialism' old or new. To concede and support the right of any people to determine and pursue its own way is to concede the possibility of varieties of valid *dharma* and the inherent validity of *svadharma* [one's own *dharma*]." In contrast to the ideological fervor generated by both sides in the cold war, the Hindu approach assumes "a divine ordering of the universe which permits endless variety and does not call for human exertion to extinguish difference and promote uniformity." [39]

The same basic outlook undermines all efforts to absolutize ideas and wage ideological wars on the domestic political scene. India's pragmatic political culture owes much to Hindu values. And if we are to take seriously Lipset's assumption, quoted earlier in the chapter, of an important relationship between a religion's low dogmatic authority and the viability of a democratic polity, Hinduism undoubtedly gives significant support to Indian democracy.

BUDDHISM:
INDIVIDUALIST-EGALITARIAN VALUES

Theravada Buddhism is the least authoritarian of the four major religions. Its dogmatic authority is scored as low. Buddhist doctrine is not pluralistic and relativistic as in the case of Hinduism, but it is still far from Catholic and Islamic notions of absolute revealed truth. The Buddha himself professed agnosticism on various important questions of metaphysics and simply expounded his teachings based on personal experience, inviting his followers not to accept them on his authority but to experiment with them and come to their own conclusions. Buddhism does not consign the followers of other doctrines to eternal hell, but assumes each individual's spiritual progress through many existences.

The directive authority of Buddhism is negligible, and this characteristic sharply distinguishes Buddhism from the other three religions. As Professor Nash pointed out in his study of

[39] *Ibid.*, pp. 92–93.

Upper Burma, "village Buddhism permits wide latitudes of behavior, and except for the minimal code of the five precepts, behavioral proscription and prescription are slight." [40] Nothing compares to the haram-halal (forbidden-permitted) orientation of the Muslim village, the caste and ritual purity regulations of the Hindu village, or the authority of the Catholic village priest. On the contrary, an impressive amount of anthropological evidence now attests to the individualism of the Thai or Burmese villager which is consciously related to Buddhist values. The late John F. Embree wrote of the "determined lack of regularity, discipline and regimentation" in Thai social life.[41] Subsequent scholarly studies have taken issue with the term he used to characterize it — "a loosely structured social system" — but there has been little disagreement over the basic facts.[42]

Not only has Buddhism *not* attempted extensive regulation of conduct, but it has provided a basic understanding of human existence which places the individual self at its center. Each individual is responsible for his own spiritual progress through the cycle of rebirth. The path to enlightenment is through individual accumulation of merit, a lonely enterprise. The extreme emphasis on the individual, a theme which runs through the Buddhist scriptures, is epitomized in the well-known verse from the Dhammapada:

> By oneself is evil done;
> By oneself one suffers;
> By oneself evil is left undone;
> By oneself one is purified.[43]

Even violation of the norms which do exist, such as a monk's partaking of a secret meal after noon, draws no rebuke. Ac-

40 Nash, *op. cit.,* p. 294.

41 John F. Embree, "Thailand — A Loosely Structured Social System," *American Anthropologist,* vol. 52 (April 1950), p. 182.

42 See especially Manning Nash *et al., Anthropological Studies in Theravada Buddhism* (New Haven: Yale University Southeast Asia Studies, 1966); and Hans-Dieter Evers, ed., *Loosely Structured Social Systems; Thailand in Comparative Perspective* (New Haven: Yale University Southeast Asia Studies, 1969).

43 *The Dhammapada,* trans. F. Max Müller (Delhi: Motilal Banarsidass, 1965), p. 46, chapter XII, verse 165.

cording to Michael Moerman, "there is neither an authority who requires conformity nor an expectation that conformity is appropriate," since all moral lapses are dealt with by the inexorable law of karma, and morality is up to the individual.[44] Another writer has referred to "the extreme tolerance the Thai show for deviant behavior, non-conformity, failure to live up to expectations, and the like." [45]

The institutionalization of authority in Buddhism is also negligible. While we have emphasized that Buddhism is a church system, and that the ecclesiastical organization of the Sangha has during certain periods been highly developed, the monastic order has never functioned as the regulator of lay conduct. In Nash's words: "The monk . . . is not the bearer of mystic lore; he is not the vehicle between a layman and divine mysteries, nor is he the shepherd of a flock, responsible for their morality, their link and hope of salvation. To a villager a *pongyi* [monk] is a Buddhist who has reached a level of understanding of the meaning of life that impels him to try to center his energies on salvation. The salvation the *pongyi* seeks is his own, for each person must be responsible for his own rebirth, his own depth of penetration into the Tipitaka [scriptures], his own extinction of self and false attachments." [46] In terms of the continuum of possible lay-clerical relations, the Buddhist monk stands at the opposite pole from the Catholic priest with his monopolistic control of the means of salvation, his authority to rebuke sin, impose penances, and absolve the penitent.

The egalitarianism of Buddhism is as marked as its individualism. Originating in part as a revolt against the Brahman-dominated caste hierarchy, Theravada Buddhism has continued to make for an egalitarian society. No hereditary status divisions nor rigid class systems appear in Burma, Thailand, Cambodia, or Laos, although Buddhism did accommodate itself to the Ceylonese caste system which developed under Hindu influ-

[44] Michael Moerman, "Ban Ping's Temple: The Center of a 'Loosely Structured' Society," in Nash *et al., op. cit.,* p. 154.

[45] Eliezer B. Ayal, "Value Systems and Economic Development in Japan and Thailand," *The Journal of Social Issues,* vol. 19 (January 1963), p. 47.

[46] Nash, *op. cit.,* p. 292.

ences. In the former countries the open and fluid nature of the social system permits extensive individual mobility. The Sangha itself is open to men of all socioeconomic backgrounds, and as a monk the son of the poorest peasant will receive the veneration of the powerful. Egalitarianism proceeds logically from the Buddhist emphasis on self-reliance and individual effort, and the social structure of Theravada societies is generally congruent with these values.

Sufficient anthropological and social psychological research has been reported to enable us to generalize about the great importance of individualist values and the pattern of highly individualistic behavior in these societies. That individualist value systems and behavior patterns are completely congruent with Buddhist teaching is perfectly clear, but the precise relationships which link them are complex and subtle. As Herbert P. Phillips has stated: "These formulations translate and function on the level of workaday behavior in an extremely subtle manner. Every time a Bang Chaner [a resident of the Thai village in which the research was done] is about to do something he does not ask himself whether it is in his own best moral interest. Similarly, every time he ignores another's expectations about how he will behave he does not justify his actions in terms of the Buddhist doctrine of enlightened self-interest. However, these formulations do impart a fundamental legitimacy to the pursuit of individualistic self-concern. More important, they establish — in a diffuse, unreflective, but nonetheless highly meaningful way — a definition of social reality that assumes the ultimate reference of every person's act is himself." [47]

The primary implications of the Buddhist values of individualism and egalitarianism for political culture are obvious. Buddhist authority patterns are highly incongruent with authoritarian political systems and supportive of systems which recognize a broad area of individual freedom. Buddhist values do not promote dogmatic ideological approaches to politics, and Buddhist politicians have in fact invoked the principle of

[47] Herbert P. Phillips, *Thai Peasant Personality: The Patterning of Interpersonal Behavior in the Village of Bang Chan* (Berkeley: University of California Press, 1965), p. 89.

the Middle Way as the spirit of compromise and mutual adjustment taught by Buddhism.[48]

Other facts, however, must be taken into account. For centuries the religion flourished under despotic rulers in all the
Theravada countries, and there was little evidence of conflict
between Buddhism and autocracy. General Ne Win's authoritarian regime replaced the system of parliamentary democracy
in Burma in 1962 with virtually no protest. Thailand has an
unbroken tradition of authoritarian government, the revolution of 1932 marking only the end of royal absolutism and the
beginning of a more unstable pattern of oligarchical rule. Only
in Ceylon has parliamentary democracy continued to function
without interruption; but the Ceylonese record, with the alter-
nation in office of two major parties (1956, 1965, and 1970), is
quite impressive in the context of the third world.

Hinduism, Islam, and Catholicism all contain important
elements of authoritarianism, as we have seen, and these have
served to reinforce traditional authoritarian polities. In the
Theravada Buddhist countries, on the other hand, anti-authoritarian religious values have coexisted with authoritarian governments in both the premodern and modern periods. Various
lines of explanation for this striking incongruity might be attempted. Most fundamental, of course, is the fact that in most
traditional societies autocratic rulers did not have totalitarian
aims and were content to allow the villages a large measure of
internal autonomy. Governmental authoritarianism for the
most part affected the individual subject only marginally and
indirectly. In any event the rural masses were understood to be
totally outside the possibility of political participation.

In the present disequilibrated situation in which the process
of politicization has drawn increasing numbers into the political process, it may well be that Buddhist individualism and
egalitarianism may intensify the psychological, and thereby the
political, problems generated by change. Thus, Lucian W.
Pye's study of Burmese politicians and civil servants suggests
that their individualism denies the possibility of lasting emotional ties and hence is productive of anxiety, suspicion, and

---

[48] Donald E. Smith, *Religion and Politics in Burma* (Princeton: Princeton University Press, 1965), pp. 310–311.

uncertainty about the intentions of others. "This Buddhist view seems to encourage the Burmese to feel that every person must follow his own particular ways, and that what others do is somehow determined by their natures. Consequently one cannot really feel any strong responsibility for the behavior of others, nor is there a need to criticize them." [49] Similarly, Pye suggests that a non-hierarchical social system may contribute to personal insecurity and the instability associated with political power struggles.[50]

Steven Piker suggests that the Thai peasant's individualism, and the "loosely structured" society in which he functions, do not lead to self-assured personality. There is rather "a pronounced ambivalence along the dimension of dependence-independence." [51] The Thai peasant acts like a rugged individualist but actually has little trust in his own abilities to face critical situations, and thus longs for the security of an authority on whom he can be dependent. Piker sees increased instability as changes in the coming decades aggravate the already existing psychological ambivalence.

These questions, hypotheses, and predictions will doubtless continue to be investigated and debated. The net effect of Buddhist individualism on the development of political culture cannot yet be gauged even approximately. Yet it would be surprising if a value so deeply engrained in Buddhist culture and behavior patterns would ultimately give way to simple authoritarian submission in the area of politics. Psychological insecurity and hence political instability will probably continue to characterize most transitional societies for the forseeable future. It is reasonable to expect that, to whatever extent religious values will exert influence, Buddhist individualism and egalitarianism, which are highly congruent with modernity, will in the long run cause less psychological insecurity than the inevitable undermining of traditional authoritarian and hierarchical values in other societies.

[49] Lucian W. Pye, *Politics, Personality, and Nation Building: Burma's Search for Identity* (New Haven: Yale University Press, 1962), p. 198.

[50] *Ibid.*, p. 146.

[51] Steven Piker, "Sources of Stability and Instability in Rural Thai Society," *Journal of Asian Studies*, vol. 27 (August 1968), p. 777.

CHAPTER VII

The Religious
Legitimation of Change

IT IS OUR ARGUMENT that, beginning with the disruption of traditional religiopolitical systems, the secularization of polities continues as a fundamental aspect of political development. However, interaction between now largely separate political and religious systems goes on. The question which concerns us in this chapter is the following: Can religion, which served to legitimize relatively static traditional structures (political, social, economic), be reinterpreted to provide positive ideological support and legitimacy to the modernizing task which is widely understood to be the prime responsibility of the political system? Can reformulated religion become an effective ally of a state committed to extensive socioeconomic change?

To pose the question in this way is to reject the still common notion of religion as a completely static and inert complex of beliefs and structures which can only be a massive obstacle to change. Clearly, profound changes have been taking place within all four religious systems over the past hundred years, the tempo of change has accelerated markedly in the past two decades, and the prospect is for nothing but more radical change in the future. This change is not necessarily self-generated within the religious system; on the contrary, the "modernization of religion" is above all a response to external pressures — ideological, political, social, and economic. However, this fact in no way diminishes the significance of the religious redefinition nor its potential role in the immediate future.

If a religious world view characterizes the vast majority of the people of the third world, changes in the ideas and values associated with that world view may have a profound impact on motivation and behavior. Before examining the content of the major religious ideological reformulations, the organizational context in which the redefinition has been taking place will be analyzed. The question of the effectiveness of the new ideas in changing behavior is closely related to this context.

THE ORGANIZATIONAL CONTEXT
OF IDEOLOGICAL REFORMULATION

Throughout this study, religious ideational and religious organizational factors have been identified as two major sets of intervening variables in seeking to explain diverse patterns of political development. The interaction of these two sets of variables is nowhere more evident than in the analysis of religious ideological reformulation in the third world.

Assuming that a traditional religious concept has been redefined in order to give it a modernist content or that a traditional idea has been used in order to legitimize a modernizing secular ideology, four major questions will be asked concerning the organizational context of the new interpretation. First, how many relatively autonomous interpreters (individuals and groups) have been involved, and what has been the extent of their ideological interaction? Our hypothesis is that the larger the number of interpreters and the greater the extent of their ideological interaction, the broader the consensus the new doctrine will achieve.

That is, a *multilateral process* of ideological reformulation is more likely to maximize acceptance than an isolated individual effort. As we shall see, some of the doctrinal reformulations, while impressive in their intellectual content, have in fact been produced by a few individuals writing their pamphlets in a virtual vacuum. The new vision proclaimed by these prophets goes unheeded and has little impact beyond a small segment of the elite.

Second, what religious authority does the new interpretation bear? In the more organizationally developed ecclesiastical systems, the voice of Pope, prelate, or council is indeed a divine voice, and for many of the laity this authority will not be questioned. In the less hierarchical structures, the voices of clergy or episcopate will be respected, but essentially regarded as the opinions of devout and honorable men. In a completely non-hierarchical system, authority does not reside in any ecclesiastical office, but may be found in impersonal sources such as sacred books; here new interpretations are always possible, but no formal mechanisms exist for establishing them as accepted doctrine.

In the third place we must ask: What is the nature of the communications network by which the new ideas might become known and accepted by the masses? An organizationally centralized religious system has regular channels of communication: indoctrination classes, sermons, publications, radio programs, films, and so on. New ideas which receive the hierarchical stamp of approval are quickly transmitted throughout the system. In the absence of such a hierarchy, the new ideas may be communicated only informally and intermittently, unless some other centralized organization, such as the government, assumes the communications function. In the Muslim world, governments have frequently been the most active promoters of modernist versions of Islam. This role is perfectly in keeping with Islamic tradition, but it is also necessitated in part by the organizational looseness of the religious system.

Last, to what extent are the new ideas associated with action programs, movements which go beyond the realm of ideas? The *Sarvodaya* ideology of Vinoba Bhave, which can well be regarded as a kind of Hindu socialism, derives much of its intellectual and moral force from precisely this connection between ideas and action. When the Catholic hierarchy of Chile interprets social justice in terms of agrarian reform, this is noteworthy; but when it goes on to distribute church lands to the peasants, the reformulated Catholic social doctrine must obviously be taken more seriously.

The most effective ideological reformulations, then, would

be those which (1) evolve out of extensive multilateral ideological interaction, (2) are authenticated by established ecclesiastical authority, (3) are transmitted by a well-organized communications network, and (4) are associated with meaningful action programs.

We must now identify the principal kinds of interpreters and communicators of religious ideologies of change. Certain of these have been prominently associated with all four major religious systems while the rest have appeared less uniformly. Table VII.1 gives some idea of distribution.

1. *Individuals*. Individual thinkers, working outside any formal organization, have made significant contributions to ideological reformulation. These intellectuals, both clerical and lay, academics, lawyers, journalists, and politicians, present their ideas in articles, pamphlets, and books. There is a considerable amount of such activity going on, but most of the individual interpreters remain obscure unless their ideas attract the favorable attention of one of the collectivities mentioned below. One Buddhist interpreter whose ideas have had a considerable impact on the Western-educated elite in Ceylon is D. C. Vijayavardhana, author of *The Revolt in the Temple* (1953). Among other things, this book makes a strong case for the ideological affinity of Buddhism to democracy and socialism.

2. *Religious research centers*. Relatively autonomous research organizations sometimes engage in pioneering efforts at doctrinal redefinition. In Latin America, Jesuit research institutes have made an important contribution, and more will be said later about the *Centro Bellarmino* in Santiago, Chile. The relatively autonomous nature of such research organizations is important. Despite Catholicism's tradition of doctrinal conformity, the Jesuit institutes do in fact function with a fair degree of independence from the hierarchy.

In the Muslim world the threat to independent religious redefinition comes from quite a different quarter, namely, government. Some of the major centers, such as the Central Institute of Islamic Research in Pakistan, are governmental agencies which follow a carefully prescribed ideological line. When the

TABLE VII.1 *Interpreters and Communicators of Religious Ideologies of Change*

	Hinduism	Buddhism	Islam	Catholicism
I. Individuals [a]	Rammohan Roy, Dayananda Saraswati, Vivekananda, M. K. Gandhi, Vinoba Bhave, S. Radhakrishnan	Anagarika Dharmapala, *D. C. Vijeyavardhana*, Walpola Rahula (Ceylon); U Nu (Burma)	Muhammad Abduh, Rashid Rida (Egypt); *Amir Ali*, Sayyid Ahmad Khan, *Muhammad Iqbal* (India)	Alceu Amoroso Lima (Brazil); Alberto Hurtado (Chile)
II. Religious research centers	Ramakrishna Mission Institute of Culture (Calcutta)	International Institute for Advanced Buddhistic Studies (Burma)	Institute of Islamic Research, Institute of Islamic Culture (Pakistan)	Center of Cultural Research and Documentation (CIDOC) in Cuernavaca, Mexico; Centro Bellarmino (Chile); Centers of Social Research and Action (CIAS) in various countries; Centro Dom Vital (Brazil)
III. Ecclesiastical authorities			Formerly, the rector and Council of Leading Ulama of al-Azhar — now completely dominated by the government	The popes, Vatican Council II, national episcopates, CELAM (Latin American Bishops' Council)
IV. Religious sects	Brahmo Samaj (Rammohan Roy); Arya Samaj (Dayananda Saraswati); Ramakrishna Mission			
V. Lay movements and organizations	Sarvodaya movement (Vinoba Bhave and J. P. Narayan)	Young Men's Buddhist Association (Burma and Ceylon); Maha Bodhi Society (India, Burma, Ceylon); All-Ceylon Buddhist Congress	Muhammadiyah (Indonesia)	Numerous Catholic Action-related groups: Catholic university students (especially in Chile and Brazil), Catholic labor unions, and others
VI. Political parties			Muslim League (Pakistan); Masjumi (Indonesia)	Christian Democratic Party in most Latin American countries
VII. Governments		Burmese government under U Nu, Ceylon governments under the two Bandaranaikes	Pakistan government's official agency, Council on Islamic Ideology	Christian Democratic government of Frei in Chile

[a] Many of the outstanding individuals did in fact lead movements or form organizations to promote their new ideas; others functioned within institutions already established. The names of the most important individual interpreters who functioned without institutional support are italicized.

government of Pakistan created the institute in 1960, it explained that its purpose was, first, "to define Islam in terms of its fundamentals in a rational and liberal manner and to emphasize, among others, the basic Islamic ideals of universal brotherhood, tolerance, and social justice," and second, "to interpret the teachings of Islam in such a way as to bring out its dynamic character in the context of the intellectual and scientific progress of the modern world."[1] Similarly, contemporary research emanating from the Nasser regime–dominated al-Azhar university will surprise no one by its emphasis on Islamic socialism. Such research organizations cannot be classified under the present heading but are simply the agencies of government, which constitutes a separate category discussed below.

3. *Ecclesiastical authorities.* Formal, authoritative restatements of doctrine dealing with social change are, of course, most prominently associated with the Catholic church. Pope John XXIII's social encyclicals, the documents of Vatican Council II, and Pope Paul VI's *Populorum Progressio* ("On the Development of Peoples") are notable examples. However, the national episcopates have made major statements of a quite independent nature, some of them in decided contradiction to the spirit if not the letter of papal pronouncements. Thus Pope Paul's *Humanae Vitae* ("Of Human Life") in 1968 reaffirmed the traditional Catholic teaching which condemns artificial contraception. However, 120 French bishops issued a declaration that the use of artificial methods of birth control "is not always guilty," and other national episcopates followed suit.[2] Such open conflicts unquestionably tend to weaken the teaching authority of the church. However, for the present at least, this formal ecclesiastical authority is still a major support for reformulated social doctrine.

4. *Religious sects.* In the nineteenth century, various Hindu

[1] Cited in Donald E. Smith, "Emerging Patterns of Religion and Politics," in D. E. Smith, ed., *South Asian Politics and Religion* (Princeton, N.J.: Princeton University Press, 1966), pp. 32–33.

[2] *New York Times,* November 9, 1968. The full text of the pastoral note, in English translation, is given here.

sects produced important new concepts of society. Dayananda Saraswati, founder of the Arya Samaj, fearlessly denounced what he regarded as the evils of Hindu society and called for a return to the pure religion of the ancient Vedas. He rejected such religiously sanctioned institutions as caste, child marriage, and the subjection of women to men. The Arya Samaj and other reformist sectarian movements played a major role in the renascence of Hinduism, and their reaffirmation of the essential spiritual values of India (as they interpreted them) constituted an important source of emerging Indian nationalism. Contemporary Hindu interpreters owe much to them.

5. *Lay movements and organizations.* All four major religious systems contain lay groups which have contributed to the process of ideological reformulation. In recent decades especially, much of the modernist religious thought has emanated from groups of laymen. In the cases of Hinduism, Buddhism, and Islam this is largely attributable to the rise of a new, Western-educated middle class which largely usurped the prerogatives of clerical groups as the intellectual elites of their respective societies. In Latin America of the 1930's, Catholic university students were able to engage in ideological dialogue with a relative freedom largely denied their clerical advisers. In the early 1960's, some of the most radical Catholic statements on the subject of revolutionary change came from these groups in Brazil.

6. *Political parties.* Ideological political parties of religious orientation are related to both Islam and Catholicism, and the party itself must be regarded as a significant source of religious redefinition. Party manifestos must be drafted and the political relevance of religious ideology constantly reexamined and redefined. As new issues arise, the religious ideology must be interpreted to deal with them. Within both Islamic and Catholic parties, for example, the concern for economic development has emerged only during the past two decades and has necessitated a serious search for the theological and philosophical undergirding for programs of change.

7. *Governments.* As already indicated, a significant part of the ideological redefinition in the Muslim world is being done

by government-sponsored research institutes. Governments controlled by political parties of religious ideology, such as the Christian Democratic government of Eduardo Frei in Chile, are ipso facto also involved in the process of ideological reformulation. In Burma, the U Nu government sought to promote ideas of Buddhist socialism. U Nu asserted in 1959 that "the reason why an average Buddhist concerns himself not with the final release from *samsara* ["endless rebirths"] but with the acquisition of property is to be found in the economic system that prevails in the world." [3] While governments have impressive resources to bring to the task of religious reinterpretation and communication, the new ideas fail to have the ring of authenticity for many, and their capacity to generate new forms and directions of mass action has usually been disappointing.

In Table VII.1 some of the important religious interpreters have been identified, using these seven categories. The distribution reveals the very different patterns of organizational context in the doctrinal reformulation of the four major religions.

It was suggested earlier that a process of multilateral ideological interaction tends to broaden and deepen acceptance of the resultant doctrine of change. This kind of multilateral interaction could be documented at great length in examining the evolution of Christian Democratic ideology in Chile over the past thirty years. A brief sketch of the major actors and events in this process follows.[4]

As early as 1910, a Jesuit priest in Santiago, Father Fernando Vives, interested himself in the application of the social teachings of *Rerum Novarum,* and in the twenties and thirties he and other Jesuits gathered around them a group of young Catholic laymen of progressive views. Father Alberto Hurtado, the most influential of the later Jesuit leaders, became national assistant to Catholic Action and worked closely with Catholic

[3] Cited in Donald E. Smith, *Religion and Politics in Burma* (Princeton, N.J.: Princeton University Press, 1965), pp. 132–133.

[4] The following discussion is based largely on Thomas G. Sanders' excellent newsletter, "The Centro Bellarmino," Institute of Current World Affairs, November 23, 1967.

university students. Father Hurtado insisted that the Conservative Party was not *the* party of the church and thus encouraged the young Catholics who broke with the Conservatives in 1938 to form the Falange Nacional, the forerunner of the Christian Democratic Party.

Shortly before his death in 1952, Father Hurtado conceived the idea of the Centro Bellarmino, a center in which the Jesuits would serve the Latin American church by rethinking its relationship to social, economic and political issues. He founded a journal, *Mensaje* ("Message"), which quickly became a leading Catholic publication. In 1957 Father Roger Vekemans, a Belgian sociologist, founded CIAS (Center of Research and Social Action) which was later united with *Mensaje* to form the Centro Bellarmino. The center now has eighteen associates, a number of them with Ph.D.'s in the social sciences, and has exerted an enormous intellectual influence on the hierarchy, the Christian Democratic Party, and since 1964, on the Frei government. In Professor Sanders' words: "The Centro Bellarmino appeared on the scene with a wealth of talent precisely at the time when it became possible for the church to change and when the Christian Democratic Party made the jump from an insignificant also-ran to a competitor for national leadership." [5]

But it was not simply the brain trust constituted by the Centro Bellarmino; it was the ideological interaction of over thirty years in which clergy and laity were both involved which made Christian Democracy a convincing ideology. Many of the present-day leaders of the party worked with Father Hurtado and other Jesuits in Catholic Action in the 1940's. Eduardo Frei and various others wrote books on the social and political thought of Maritain. Jacques Chonchol (a major ideologist of the party), Gabriel Valdés, William Thayer, Sergio Ossa, and Radomiro Tomic — all members of the Frei government — contributed articles to *Mensaje* during the politically unpromising decade of the 1950's.

The crucial year in the evolution of Christian Democratic

[5] *Ibid.,* p. 3.

ideology was 1962. In September, the Chilean bishops issued a famous pastoral letter on "Social and Political Duty in the Present Hour" in which they called for a "profound and rapid renovation" of the country's socioeconomic structures, while also condemning Marxism in harsh terms.[6] In December, a special issue of *Mensaje* was devoted to "The Revolution in Latin America."[7] The *Mensaje* editorial went beyond the bishops' perception of an option between Christian and Marxist sponsorship of rapid change; the revolution was already under way, largely because of Marxist inspiration, and the Christian's task was to humanize it, to defend the sacred character of the human person.[8] In the 1964 presidential-election campaign, Frei and the Christian Democratic Party proclaimed as their program "Revolution in Liberty."

The multilateral nature of this ideological interaction in Chile is portrayed diagrammatically in Figure VII.1. The question may well be asked: Why has Christian Democracy not had a greater impact elsewhere in Latin America, given the strong Catholic cultural traditions of the area and the presumed appeal of an ideology based on Catholic teaching? Part of the answer lies in this thirty-year process of ideological formulation in Chile. A significant similar process has not taken place elsewhere in Latin America, and without it, the ideas and symbols have not come to life.

We have argued that, in coming to grips with contemporary problems, a high degree of ecclesiastical organization in a religious system enables the leadership to reinterpret doctrines and communicate new ideas more coherently and effectively. However, it is also true that the more complex the ecclesiastical structure, the greater will be the strains and conflicts produced by major ideological changes. On the basis of research in Chile and elsewhere, David E. Mutchler suggests that the conflicts *within* the Latin American church have been the most prominent result of the ideological interaction with

[6] *El Deber Social y Político en la Hora Presente* (Santiago: Secretariado General del Episcopado de Chile, 1962), p. 24.

[7] No. 115, December 1962.

[8] For a detailed analysis of shifts in the ideological stance of *Mensaje*, see Hector Borrat, "La Revolución de Mensaje," *Cristianismo y Sociedad*, vol. 3, no. 7 (Montevideo, 1965), pp. 26–36.

FIGURE VII.1   *Ideological Interaction in Chile*

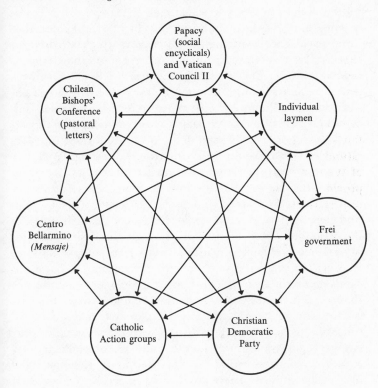

the modern world, even to the serious weakening of the hierarchical system.[9] The divisive tendencies to which he points must be taken seriously. Nevertheless, it seems likely that the essential church structure will survive by making necessary adjustments. The Asian religions at present are characterized by considerably less internal conflict, but this does not bode well for the future. It points only to the absence of structures within which creative tensions can develop, structures which make possible an integrated systemic response. This is especially true of Hinduism and Islam.

9 David E. Mutchler, "Adaptations of the Roman Catholic Church to Latin American Development: The Meaning of Internal Church Conflict," *Social Research,* vol. 36 (Summer 1969), pp. 231–252.

Having analyzed the organizational context of ideological reformulation, we must now examine the content of the new formulations. The remainder of this chapter is divided into three parts, each containing a discussion which attempts to capture the assumptions, intent, and spirit of the doctrinal redefinitions. (1) *Toward a neo-religious society*. The basic assumption here remains the traditional one that the patterns of social organization are properly determined by religious concepts and structures; nevertheless, within that framework, certain changes are possible and desirable and reformist interpretations elaborate the direction and extent of change. A cluster of Western ideas associated with nineteenth-century liberalism provides the major external influence upon these reformist interpretations. (2) *Toward a religiosocialist society*. The assumption here is that socialist ideology, broadly defined, provides the basic guidelines for the structure of the desired society; nevertheless, religion provides an important supporting and legitimating role within the new interpretation. (3) *Toward a secular-pluralist society*. This body of religious thought makes the assertion in different forms that religion, apart from its relationship to general ethical principles and individual ethical action, is largely irrelevant to society; there are no distinctively religious "answers" to the problems of contemporary society. Secular ideological "answers" fall under the same judgment. The ends of society are defined in terms of consensual humanist values, and the means are pragmatic.

These three religious redefinitions which legitimate change should not be interpreted as "stages" in the strict sense of the word. All of the relevant data cannot fit into three neat chronological stages. However, in a general way one can say that the interaction of traditional religion with nineteenth-century liberalism continued right up to the Second World War (1); that, thereafter, religious interpretation increasingly concerned itself with coming to terms in a positive way with socialism (2); and that even while this was taking place, one significant group of interpreters moved in the direction of secularism-pluralism (3). The consideration of religion as a proto-ideology in the legitimation of traditional systems and of its gradual displacement by secular ideologies as secularization proceeded adds a significant historical dimension often overlooked by those engaged in the decline-of-ideology debate. Some comments on this point will be made at the conclusion of this chapter.

TOWARD A NEO-RELIGIOUS SOCIETY

The religious legitimation of change in the nineteenth century, as we have observed, did not attack the fundamental assumptions of the religious framework of society. It was assumed that religious concepts and structures would continue to order society, but that internal reforms could be instituted without undermining the religious legitimacy of the system as a whole. Reformist interpretations centered on four quite different problems in the four major religions, depending on systemic characteristics and particular historical situations. Compared with the other three, Buddhism faced no serious problems of adjustment to liberalism, and while the Buddhist modernists urged a more positive view of material values and a clearer statement of the relevance of Buddhism to a changing society, there was no real crisis. On the other hand, critical issues were faced by Hindu interpreters in dealing with caste, by Muslim reformulators of the law, and by Catholic authorities in the redefinition of economic justice.

Restructured Hindu Caste System. The historical, philosophical, scriptural, ritual, and legal connections between Hindu religion and caste were so powerful that, with few exceptions, even radical reformers found it difficult to repudiate the caste concept altogether. The general line of approach was to argue that the original system of the four varnas expounded in the Vedas, while divinely ordained, was also a rational division of labor based on inherent differences in capacity. This original concept was still religiously and socially valid, but the accretions of the centuries had resulted in the vast proliferation of caste groups, irrational social rigidity, gross inequalities, and above all the curse of untouchability. The Hindu interpreters, therefore, called for the elimination of these unwholesome accretions and a restructured caste system closer to the original scriptural norm.

From the early nineteenth century on, however, the new

interpreters were consciously engaged in responding to the challenges presented by Christianity and Western civilization. Whether the response was defensive and imitative or defiant and aggressive, the new formulations stressed individual freedom and equality and sought to find a basis for these social ideals within Hinduism, without abandoning the caste idea. Swami Dayananda Saraswati sought to provide a measure of social mobility based on individual merit. In his major work published in 1908 he wrote: "At present he deserves to be a Brahman who has acquired the best knowledge and character, and an ignorant person is fit to be classed as a Shudra." [10]

Another Hindu reformer, Swami Vivekananda, sought to detach caste from its traditional meaning as a hierarchy of social groups and interpreted it solely in terms of occupational specialization. "Caste is a natural order. I can perform one duty in social life, and you another; you can govern a country, and I can mend a pair of old shoes, but there is no reason why you are greater than I, for can you mend my shoes? Can I govern the country?" According to Vivekananda, the natural caste order which could never be eliminated did not include the notion of differing rights, privileges, and sanctity. Furthermore, he found a positive basis for human equality in Hindu metaphysics. "If you teach Vedanta to the fisherman, he will say, I am as good a man as you, I am a fisherman, you are a philosopher, but I have the same God in me as you have in you. And that is what we want, no privileges for any one, equal chances for all; let everyone be taught that the Divine is within, and every one will work out his own salvation." [11]

Like his predecessors in the long line of Hindu religious reformers, Gandhi was unwilling to reject the notion of caste altogether, although his views moved slowly in that direction over the years. Early in his public career he declined to condemn orthodox prohibitions on intercaste dining, despite their well-known and potent rationale of ritual pollution. At one

[10] Cited in Roland W. Scott, *Social Ethics in Modern Hinduism* (Calcutta: Y.M.C.A. Publishing House, 1953), p. 162.

[11] W. Theodore de Bary, *Sources of Indian Tradition* (New York: Columbia University Press, 1958), p. 649.

point he was willing to permit the law of karma to take care of the inequities of this life, for in their next existences the unworthy Brahman and the saintly Shudra would receive their just deserts. Gandhi fought a life-long battle against untouchability based on fervent moral conviction, but his general views on caste were unclear and self-contradictory. He struggled hard at one point to produce a rationalized theory of caste.[12] Gandhi's final conclusion was that caste was an institution the origin of which he did not know; however, he regarded it as irrelevant to his own spiritual quest for truth. This gradual desacralization of the caste concept in Gandhi's thought is indicative of its very considerable survival power within the Hindu tradition.

Reformist concepts of a restructured caste system provided a certain religious legitimacy to changes which were already being brought about by essentially nonreligious forces, including Western education, legal and administrative systems based on equality before the law, a largely secular social-reform movement, Indian nationalism, and so on. The role of the religious interpreters was thus a secondary one of rationalization; they were responding to, not motivating, change. Furthermore, much of their effort was not so much concerned with social change as with the intellectual defense of Hinduism. By finding the social values of freedom and equality within their own Hindu tradition, they sought to strengthen it against the onslaughts of Christianity and the West. This apologetic function, with all of its ambiguous but mostly negative consequences for the cause of significant social change, was also most prominent in the reinterpretation of Islam. If Asian religion already contained the values of modernity, the announcement of this fact would probably produce more complacency than change.

Modernism in Islamic Law. The concept of shari'ah in traditional Islam, like that of caste in Hinduism, provided the basic framework within which the reformist interpreters had to

---

[12] Scott, *op. cit.,* pp. 156, 170, 180. See Dennis Dalton, "The Gandhian View of Caste, and Caste after Gandhi," in Philip Mason, ed., *India and Ceylon: Unity and Diversity* (New York: Oxford University Press, 1967), pp. 159–181.

function. The religious legitimation of change in the Muslim world was largely the effort to justify in Islamic terms modifications in rules of law. The desired changes in these rules clearly reflected Western liberal notions of rationality, utilitarianism, and individualism. Associated with the great names of Muhammad Abduh and Rashid Rida at al-Azhar, the modernist movement sent impulses of reform throughout the Islamic world, from Morocco to Indonesia. But the reformists did not challenge the basic classical assumption that true law is the command of a sovereign God who has revealed his will to man in the Qur'an.

Muhammad Abduh (1849–1905), an *alim* who rose to become Grand Mufti of Egypt, was also in touch with European intellectual trends. He learned French, lived for brief periods in Paris and Geneva, and greatly admired Herbert Spencer whom he visited in England. Abduh responded to the intellectual challenge of the West by attempting to incorporate in Islam a more dynamic outlook, an acceptance of modern sciences (including the social sciences), an emphasis on reason in the interpretation of revelation, and considerations of social utility in the redefinition of law. In order to accomplish these objectives, he severely limited the orthodox sources of Islamic law. The Qur'an, in effect, became the sole major source of doctrine and law; Abduh rejected most of the Sunnah (Traditions of the Prophet) as later inventions, and ijma (the consensus of the Community, in practice, of the ulama) had no validity since it had simply paralyzed the process of interpretation centuries ago. As Professor Safran noted: "The unanimity he would accept was that of universal reason, which after the Qur'an was to him the main source of doctrine." [13] Abduh was convinced that reason could not ultimately be in contradiction to the Qur'anic revelation. In the exercise of reason, social utility, or whatever demonstrably promoted human well-being, would be the guiding principle.

Muhammad Rashid Rida (d. 1935) was Abduh's disciple and

---

[13] Nadav Safran, *Egypt in Search of Political Community* (Cambridge, Mass.: Harvard University Press, 1961), p. 65.

continued his work of Islamic redefinition. However, while Abduh's ideological attacks were directed mostly at the traditionalist ulama, whom he regarded as the main obstacle to reform, Rida increasingly saw the secular-minded, Westernized nationalists as the chief threat to a revitalized Islam in Egypt. Conscious of the dangers inherent in Abduh's position, Rida retreated from his teacher's rationalism, restored ijma and Sunnah as authentic sources of law, and generally became more conservative. He wanted the interpretation of law to be progressive and emphasized the importance of the public interest in legal interpretation, but this was to be done within a fairly rigid framework which recognized divine sovereignty as traditionally understood. He laid great emphasis on the classical doctrine of the caliphate and finally concluded that without the restoration of this institution, there could be no integral application of the shari'ah, understood in its own terms.

The modernists' legitimation of change has indeed played a role in the reform of law in the Muslim world, but not the intended role. The intent was to reestablish a viable Islamic sociopolitical order built on classical ideological assumptions but flexible enough to adjust to changing conditions. The modernization of law which has taken place has proceeded by fits and starts, without an overall rationale, but under massive Western influence. Particular rules of the shari'ah have been discarded altogether or radically overhauled. In some cases legislative assemblies have eclectically fashioned rules of law from among the four classical schools of jurisprudence. But in all cases it has been a secular, not a religious, process. The secular modernizers have invoked the names of Abduh and Rida in order to reassure the faithful that the changes are religiously valid; they have ignored the fundamental assumptions of the reformists. In Professor Kerr's words: "The shift from traditional Islamic piety and acceptance of what was presumed to be a divinely ordained social order to the new ethos of 'social engineering' — from the idea of divine voluntarism to that of human voluntarism — is symbolized, if not exactly explained, in the failure of the Islamic reformist of Muhammad Abduh's and Rashid Rida's generations to establish a middle ground." [14] The radical and rapid social change which has occurred has not been theologically related, much less directed, and in this process Islam has become largely subservient to nationalism.

The "Social Question" in Catholicism. Our argument is that the late nineteenth- and early twentieth-century interpreters sought to legitimize change without undermining the basic idea of a religious sociopolitical order. The Hindu caste system could be restructured to accommodate the idea of equality, but it was religiously important not to repudiate the principle of caste itself. Islamic law could be reinterpreted by reason in response to changing social needs, but one could not reject the fundamental doctrine that law is a divine command made known by revelation. The Roman Catholic analogue was that the changes produced by industrialization would necessitate new institutions to operate within the socioeconomic order, but the church still stood as the divine authority in the midst of human society with power to direct, guide, and judge all temporal institutions.

Catholicism had to respond to the intellectual challenges of liberalism and rationalism several decades before Hinduism and Islam. The French Revolution which shattered the *ancien régime* with its traditional union of altar and throne left the church no choice, and Catholicism had to come to terms with the principles of liberty, equality, and fraternity as best it could. As we shall see, the hierarchical church repudiated the liberal Catholic movement which attempted to respond positively to accommodate and incorporate these principles, and the decisive ideological reconciliation did not come until Vatican Council II. The European center of the church also meant that Catholicism was forced to respond to the challenges of industrialization and Marxist socialism almost a century before this became a serious ideological problem for the Asian religions.

The French priest Lamennais, ably supported by Montalem-

14 Malcolm H. Kerr, *Islamic Reform: The Political and Legal Theories of Muhammad Abduh and Rashid Rida* (Berkeley: University of California Press, 1966), p. 223.

bert and Lacordaire, began in the 1830's his campaign to convince the hierarchy that the church should support democratic revolutionary movements, universal suffrage, freedom of speech and press, religious toleration, and separation of church and state. "The church, he insisted, had everything to gain by the overthrow of the traditional political powers which held her, as they held the People, in thrall. The natural alliance was that between *Le Pape* and *Le Peuple;* the unnatural alliance, which had cost the church so dear and had perverted her principles, was between *Le Pape* and *Le Roi.*" True religion, he asserted, could only flourish in "a free church in a free state." [15] The Vatican harshly rejected his arguments *in toto,* with ideas which later found expression in the *Syllabus of Errors* (1864). This encyclical concluded with the pronouncement that it was an error to say that "the Roman Pontiff can and should reconcile himself with, and accommodate himself to progress, liberalism, and modern civilization." [16]

The "social question," as it became known in Catholic writings, concerned the plight of the working class in an industrialized society cut off from the paternalistic norms which had operated in predominantly agrarian societies. The social question became an issue as the Marxist analysis of this problem became increasingly influential and as socialist parties emerged to press for a revolutionary solution. Pope Leo XIII's great encyclical *Rerum Novarum* (1891) marked the beginning of the modern development of the church's social doctrine. The pontiff condemned the exploitation of the working class by a small group of powerful capitalists, legitimized trade unions organized to protect the workers' interests and state legislation directed toward the same end. He also attempted to define the just wage.

In *Rerum Novarum* the hierarchical church addressed itself to the problem of economic justice, a peculiarly modern problem, without having come to terms with the broad framework

[15] E. E. Y. Hales, *The Catholic Church in the Modern World* (Garden City, N.Y.: Doubleday & Co., 1960), pp. 91, 127.
[16] Anne Fremantle, ed., *The Papal Encyclicals in their Historical Context* (New York: G. P. Putnam's Sons, 1956), p. 152.

of modern society itself. While upholding the natural-law right of private property, and thus condemning Marxism, the Pope could equally reject capitalism, for this phenomenon was based on laissez-faire individualism and liberalism which already stood condemned on other grounds. *Rerum Novarum,* although impressive on its own terms, was not an expression of Catholic self-criticism; it was the condemnation of institutions which had been spawned by a series of disastrous developments since the disruption of medieval Catholic society. Protestantism, rationalism, democracy, liberalism, secularism, capitalism, and Marxism were all mutations of this illegitimate brood.

Catholicism had to deal with the modern world as a complex of alien, threatening values, almost in the same way that it appeared to nineteenth-century Hinduism and Islam. Unlike the two Asian religions, within which self-criticism and reform (however halting and ineffectual) was attempted, the official Catholic response was one of dogmatic assertiveness. While condemning all that had gone wrong in Western society over the past four centuries, and thus acknowledging that many aspects of life were beyond her effective control, the church nevertheless retained the medieval assumption that she could speak with full, divine authority on virtually the whole range of political, social, and economic questions. The church, in other words, carried the assumption of monolithic authority into an increasingly pluralist age.

Because the basic medieval assumptions were never seriously reexamined, they did not lie far beneath the surface even when the church addressed itself in "modern" terms to "modern" problems. Thus, as E. E. Y. Hales pointed out, a decade after *Rerum Novarum* Leo XIII asserted that Christian Democracy "must insist that the right to have and to hold be kept inviolate; it must maintain such distinction between classes as properly belongs to a well-ordered state; in short, it must assert that human society should have that form and character which its divine Author has imposed upon it." [17] Despite such limita-

---

[17] *Ibid.,* p. 206. The quotation is from *Graves de Communi* (1901).

tions, Leo XIII initiated a line of creative ideological reformulation which has produced impressive results, as we have already noted in the case of Chile.

TOWARD A RELIGIOSOCIALIST SOCIETY

By the end of World War II, it was clear that the neo-religious society, whether in its Hindu, Islamic, or Catholic form, was destined to remain an unrealized ideal, victim of a process of secularization so universal and so multifaceted that little escaped its force. As secular liberalism provided the cluster of ideas which challenged traditional societies in the earlier period, the dominant idea which has symbolized change since 1945 is socialism. Socialism does not qualify or modify a religious framework of society but provides the framework itself — the basic ideas and assumptions. Religion is now clearly the handmaiden to the secular ideology, even in the thought of the exponents of the new religiosocialist vision. Religion supports and legitimizes, but socialism sets the goals and decides the means of society. Given the high degree of religiosity in most parts of the third world, religion is believed to provide an important linkage of meaning between socialist government and illiterate peasant. But the auxiliary, and temporary, role of religion cannot be doubted.

Ideologies of change have been developed which link each of the four major religions to some concept of socialism. We shall examine them briefly.

Sarvodaya: Hindu Socialism. The Sarvodaya movement emerged in 1951, three years after the assassination of Gandhi, led by his close disciple, the saintly Vinoba Bhave. Gandhi's nonviolent *satyagraha* campaigns had played a significant although not decisive role in the political struggle for independence. It was left to Vinoba to develop and apply Gandhian principles to the urgent new problems of socioeconomic change which became salient with the achievement of political freedom. The term *sarvodaya* (literally, "welfare of all") was coined by Gandhi himself, and has come to mean "an ideal social order based upon nonviolence and envisaged in terms of harmonious, casteless, classless society with equal opportunity for all." [18] In Vinoba's words, the problem was how to achieve this "social revolution" desired by the Mahatma.

The movement inaugurated in 1951 was in direct response to Communist terrorism against wealthy landlords in Hyderabad State. Vinoba began his campaign by appealing to landowners to deed away part of their holdings for distribution to the landless. Framing his moral appeal in Hindu religious language, Vinoba called for *bhoodan yajna* ("land-gift sacrifice") and explained that while formerly land was dedicated to deities in the temples, in the changed circumstances it should be given to the landless. As his movement rapidly spread to other states, over five million acres — including several thousand villages — were offered for redistribution. The impressive moral fervor of the campaign, however, was not matched by an efficient organization for distribution of the land and technical and financial aid for the new peasant landlords. As a consequence, much of the land has remained undistributed. The Sarvodaya movement, in fact, has evidenced distrust of organization of all kinds, and especially that of the state. Following Gandhian principles, the formulated aim is a stateless society composed of a network of self-sufficient village communities. The communitarian emphasis in Sarvodaya is strong.

In an address in 1957, Vinoba Bhave compared the Sarvodaya and Communist ideologies and found striking similarities in basic objectives. He referred to Marx as a *Mahamuni* ("great sage") whose ideas had changed the thinking of innumerable people throughout the world. The Communists believe that the *Satya Yuga* ("golden age") will come in the future with the withering away of the state. But the Sarvodaya worker is convinced that the nonviolent stateless society can begin in the present and can be ushered in without violence. But nonviolence is not to be understood as support for the status quo; social revolution is the order of the day, and the only question

[18] Joan V. Bondurant, "The Nonconventional Political Leader in India," in Richard L. Park and Irene Tinker, eds., *Leadership and Political Institutions in India* (Princeton, N.J.: Princeton University Press, 1959), p. 284.

concerns the means of its unfolding. "If this work of nonviolence and Sarvodaya has no effect, then you will have to take
to Communism. Such is the nearness between the two ideologies. . . . Communism believes in violence but there can be
no doubt that it is generated by compassion. This is a strange
paradox. There is inspiration from compassion but at the same
time there is faith in violence." [19]

Evidence that the ideological appeal of Sarvodaya is capable
of making inroads on the Marxist position itself is provided by
the case of Jayaprakash Narayan. Narayan was an important
Marxist leader in the early 1930's who gradually moved away
from the class-struggle concept and the belief that the individual's life was determined by his environment. The democratic-
socialist position, however, proved to be but a halfway house as
Narayan became increasingly impressed by Gandhi's argument
that the new social order could not be brought about by the
manipulation of laws and institutions, but only by a profound
change in the moral and social values of men. Widely regarded
in the early 1950's as a likely successor to Nehru as prime minister, Narayan renounced politics in 1954 to devote himself to
the Sarvodaya movement.[20]

While Sarvodaya, as a social philosophy and as a movement,
has been embraced by Indians of various religious beliefs, including atheism, it is clearly rooted in Hindu religious and
philosophical traditions. It is, in short, the peculiarly Hindu
version of socialism. Any objective analysis of the Sarvodaya
program over the past two decades would have to conclude
that its direct impact on Indian society as a whole has been
slight. However, it has undoubtedly popularized and reinforced
the general notions of equality (the casteless, classless society)

19 de Bary, *op. cit.*, p. 928. See Joan V. Bondurant and Margaret W.
Fisher, "The Concept of Change in Hindu, Socialist, and Neo-Gandhian
Thought," in Donald E. Smith, ed., *South Asian Politics and Religion*
(Princeton, N.J.: Princeton University Press, 1966), pp. 235–248. See also
the same authors' *Indian Approaches to a Socialist Society* (Berkeley,
Calif.: Indian Press Digests Monograph Series, University of California,
1956).

20 See Bimla Prasad, ed., *Socialism, Sarvodaya and Democracy* (New
York: Asia Publishing House, 1964).

which the government and other agencies have been seeking to propagate. Its greatest contribution has been made not as a program of reform, but as one ideological influence in the legitimation of change.

Buddhist Approaches to Socialism. In Burma and Ceylon there has been considerable debate over the compatibility of Buddhism and socialism, but no distinctively Buddhist development of socialist thought. That is, although there are many Buddhist socialists, there has been no Buddhist version of socialism. As we have already noted in an earlier chapter, one Burmese cabinet minister asserted in 1951 that Buddhism and Marxism were complementary because they functioned in two completely separate spheres of life.[21]

Buddhist socialists have emphasized the ideological affinities of the two belief systems in their atheism and scientific view of causality. Marx's condemnation of religion as the opiate of the people was in fact antedated by the Buddha's rejection of Brahmanical ritualism and priestcraft, Marx's vision of a classless society by the Buddha's rejection of the caste hierarchy and the admission of men from all castes into the Sangha. The monastic order is in fact an embryonic socialist society, for in this classless community, every member is equal and there is no private property. "Communism, in its orthodox theoretical form, is thus not at all inconsistent with the communism of the original Sangha. . . . There are many Buddhists who are convinced that there is much more in common between Buddhism and communism than between Buddhism and capitalism. The Buddhists, therefore, should avoid an indiscriminate condemnation of communism, which would compel many, especially of the younger generation, to feel that they must choose between Buddhism and communism." [22]

Considerable ingenuity has been evidenced on occasion in the effort to make a stronger and more meaningful connection between Buddhism and socialism. Thus U Nu argued in 1959

[21] See above, p. 21.
[22] D. C. Vijayavardhana, *The Revolt in the Temple* (Colombo, Ceylon: Sinha Publications, 1953), p. 597.

that a socialist society was necessary for the masses to achieve the ultimate spiritual goal. This goal was Nirvana, which could only be attained through the serious discipline of meditation. The present capitalist society militates against this ideal by stimulating the acquisitive instincts of man, and its materialist values discourage even the monks who renounce the world to seek spiritual liberation. Capitalist materialism ignores the Buddhist doctrine of the impermanence of all things. U Nu declared that "the reason why an average Buddhist concerns himself not with the final release from *samsara* ["endless rebirths"] but with the acquisition of property is to be found in the economic system that prevails in the world." [23] A socialist society, however, would eliminate gross inequalities, discourage the acquisitive instinct, and provide sufficient leisure for the common man to practice meditation. Socialism would thus serve the interests of Buddhist spirituality.

In the early 1940's in Ceylon a small group of Buddhist monks became strong supporters of the Marxist group, Lanka Sama Samaj Party (LSSP). In attempting to reach the masses, the Western-educated Marxists naturally had to come to grips with the Sinhalese language. They used the term *sama-sama-jaya*, (literally, "equal society") as the translation of "socialism." While the Marxists probably did not realize it, the term was deeply rooted in Buddhist concepts and had a familiar ring to it for the monks. The Reverend Walpola Rahula, an early LSSP follower and an eminent scholar of Buddhism, wrote in 1946: "The task of the monk is to work for the good and happiness of the common man and not for the sake of the interests of a couple of individuals. . . . I do not know what Marxism or Leninism is . . . or whether the Soviet system of government is black or white. . . . But I do know what is meant by Samasamajaya and this I know from what is found

---

[23] Quoted in Richard Butwell, "The Four Failures of U Nu's Second Premiership," *Asian Survey*, vol. 2 (March 1962), p. 8. For extended treatments of this subject see E. Sarkisyanz, *Buddhist Backgrounds of the Burmese Revolution* (The Hague: Martinus Nijhoff, 1965); and Donald E. Smith, *Religion and Politics in Burma*.

in the Buddhist texts. . . . The foundation of a society without distinctions of caste or status, giving equal opportunities to all were first laid by the Buddha and not by Marx." [24]

Although significant similarities could be found between general socialist ideals and Buddhist concepts, most monks and laymen found much in orthodox Marxism which was reprehensible: the doctrine of class struggle, the advocacy of violent revolution, the denial of spiritual values, and the basic tenets of economic determinism. All of these seemed completely contrary to the Buddha's gentle humanism, individualism, and teachings on nonviolence, to say nothing of his doctrines of rebirth and Nirvana.[25]

It is quite clear that the Buddhist tradition has within it ideational elements which can be used to legitimate change in the direction of democratic socialism or modernity in general. However, as noted earlier, there has been no development of a coherent doctrine of socialism coming from within the Sangha itself. Much of the writing on this subject has been motivated by one of two considerations: (1) apologetic, the effort to prove that Buddhism is valid because it contains these modern elements, or (2) propagandistic, the effort to give ideological support to a party or government which proclaims socialist ideals. Though the latter may be of some use in the legitimation of governmental programs of change, it is doubtful that the process has succeeded in affecting the motivation of many people.

Islamic Socialism. One of the early efforts to construct a theory of Islamic socialism is contained in an essay written by Jamal al-Din al-Afghani in the 1890's. Like many later interpreters, Afghani emphasized the Qur'anic notion of sharing wealth, the institution of *zakat* ("an annual levy collected by the state for distribution to the poor"), and the prohibition of *riba* ("interest-taking"). He criticized Western socialism as es-

---

[24] *Samasamajaya,* February 7, 1946. Cited in K. N. Jayatilleke, "Buddhism and Marxism in Ceylon Politics" (paper delivered at the XXVII International Congress of Orientalists, Ann Arbor, Michigan, August 1967).

[25] For a summary of Buddhist critiques of communism see Ernst Benz, *Buddhism or Communism: Which Holds the Future of Asia?* (Garden City, N.Y.: Doubleday & Company, 1965), pp. 217–234.

sentially negative, the reaction to gross inequality and unjust laws, whereas Islamic socialism grew out of the positive provisions for equality designed by "God the Great Legislator." Afghani concluded: "Any socialism which is at variance with Islamic socialism in spirit and in fundamentals must end up in bloodshed. . . . Glib talk of socialism may be a catchword which will benefit some, but it is a good word misused. To repeat, Islamic socialism is truth itself. . . ." [26]

Much of the writing on Islamic socialism has been motivated by apologetic considerations, the desire to convince the reader that all valid modern ideas were already present in the Qur'an. Most of this writing has therefore been theoretically superficial and has tended to legitimize, not change, tradition. The distortions of history engendered by such efforts have been extreme. For example: "The holy prophet of Islam was the greatest socialist the world has ever known. He did not like to call his followers his disciples, but called them *ashab* which means 'comrades'." [27]

In addition to the stock references to "zakat" and "riba" in treatments of Islamic socialism, various writers have developed a distinctive doctrine of *jihad*. Originally understood primarily as a holy war against infidels to extend the domains of Islam, the basic meaning of jihad is "dynamic, aggressive action for what is right." The Indian Muslim Sindhi found in this concept the basis for Islamic socialist revolution. While jihad need not be violent, it could take the form of a revolutionary war to bring about radical social change. [28] The great significance of the concept is that it is an authentic imperative to bring about change, one deeply embedded in the Islamic tradition. However, it is still difficult to apply the concept persuasively to internal socioeconomic structures. It is far easier for the Pakistani ulama to declare jihad against India on the Kashmir question (or their Egyptian counterparts to do so against

26 S. A. Hanna, "Al-Afghani: A Pioneer of Islamic Socialism," *Muslim World*, vol. 57 (January 1967), pp. 28, 32.

27 Cited in Wilfred Cantwell Smith, *Modern Islam in India: A Social Analysis* (Lahore: Ripon Printing Press, 1947), p. 105.

28 Aziz Ahmad, *Islamic Modernism in India and Pakistan, 1857–1964* (London: Oxford University Press, 1967), pp. 198–99.

Israel) than to call for serious structural changes within Muslim societies.

As the Sinhalese translation of "socialism," sama-samajaya, elicited a strong, positive response from monks steeped in the Buddhist texts, the Arabic term *ishtirakiyyah* ("socialism") has powerful emotional overtones in Arab Muslim culture. As Professors Gardner and Hanna point out, the root word and its derivatives "carry in our time a richness of meaning that fits them admirably as vehicles or symbols for the central socialist value which dominates the new societies emerging in the Arab world." [29] The authors present a translation of excerpts from a book by Dr. Mustafa al-Siba'i entitled *The Socialism of Islam* (Cairo, 1960), which is considered to be "a major statement of ideology for Egyptian socialism." Siba'i squarely faces the critics who see socialism as nothing but a passing ideological fad and therefore decry the talk of Islamic socialism which links the eternal truth to an ephemeral theory. "I have chosen the term Islamic socialism, although I am fully aware of all that is being said by such people, because I do not believe that socialism is a passing fashion. It represents rather a human tendency which finds clear expression in the teaching of the prophets and in the work of reformers from earliest times. The people of today, and especially the undeveloped nations, are trying to achieve it in order to rid themselves of social injustice and atrocious class inequality which is derogatory to human dignity. The essence of socialism is not nationalization, or expropriation of capital, or the limiting of ownership, or progressive taxation. All these things are but means, and are seen by its advocates as the right way of reaching the goal which is socialism." What socialism really aims at is the elimination of capitalist exploitation of the masses and the creation of a society based on social equality and substantial economic equality. According to the author, "Islam clearly had these same goals in mind when legislating, and so legislated as to guarantee its

[29] G. H. Gardner and S. A. Hanna, "Islamic Socialism," *Muslim World*, vol. 56 (April 1966), pp. 72, 73, 75–76, 84–85. See also Malcolm H. Kerr, "Islam and Arab Socialism," *ibid.*, vol. 56 (October 1966), pp. 276–281.

realization in the best possible form." Islamic socialism emerges, then, not out of specific institutions such as zakat, but out of the common goals of social justice found in Islam and socialism.

Siba'i seeks to establish the ideological uniqueness of Islamic socialism. "Islam's answer to communism here is that Islam has a clear-cut socialist system which differs from communism, socialism, and capitalism. Islam thus does not fight communism in all its socialistic aspects, neither does it follow it in all its tendencies." Specifically, Islamic socialism rejects communism's materialist philosophy, doctrine of class war, view of private ownership of property, and ideas on religion and morality. "Islamic socialism springs from the people's conscience and is part of their faith."

Although Siba'i's case for the existence of a totally distinctive ideological position may well be questioned, there is perhaps a greater possibility for meaningful dialogue and the creative ideological interaction of Islam with socialism than with any other imported ideology of change. Socialism appeals to the Muslim's sense of the reality of the community, to his feeling that there must be a "right" blueprint for society, to his conviction that social justice is rooted in transcendent values. Unlike the individualism of the earlier Western liberalism, socialism coalesces easily with some important Islamic attitudes. As pointed out earlier, however, there is always the danger that the recognition of such affinities will lead to more complacency than change. The Muslim intellectual may find so much emotional satisfaction in the idea that Islam is socialistic that he will be undisturbed by the gross poverty, disease, illiteracy, and inequality around him.

Christian Democracy: Catholic Socialism. We have already outlined the process of multilateral interaction by which Christian Democratic ideology has evolved in Chile. In considering the content of this ideology one notes the claim, if only to reject it, that Christian Democracy represents a distinct, unique, and self-contained political philosophy, an ideological position to be sharply distinguished not only from both capitalism and Marxism, but also from democratic socialism. Although Christian Democracy indeed has its own philosophical history rooted in the social encyclicals and nurtured by Neo-Thomism, in contemporary Latin America it is best described as a Catholic version of democratic socialism.

The straining to establish a distinctive ideological identity is well illustrated by a book written by Jaime Castillo Velasco, president of the Chilean Christian Democratic Party, entitled *The Sources of Christian Democracy*. In his analysis there are three major sources: Christian philosophy, the social problems of the modern age, and contemporary Catholicism. Although the author alludes to the nineteenth-century conflict between Marxism and capitalism as the occasion for Leo XIII's condemnation of both, he does not see Christian Democracy as part of that complex process out of which ideological syntheses emerged. He is rather intent on establishing the unique religious source of his ideology. He concludes: "Christian Democracy is, in the final analysis, the fruit of an attitude which has issued from traditional Catholicism in which a path was opened through the emphasis on certain values. . . . The best that is in it is of pure Christian and Catholic origin, but certainly it is not the whole of historic Catholicism nor of doctrinal Catholicism, nor does it in any way pretend to represent these two things. Let us conclude, then, by compressing all this in a formula: Christian Democracy is a politics of Christian inspiration." [30]

The ideological distinctives of Christian Democracy, it is claimed, lie in two major areas: its emphasis on the Christian understanding of man (usually formulated in terms of Maritain's "integral humanism") and a social and economic theory of communitarianism. Christian humanism is clearly different from both Marxist and liberal secularist views of man, and this has been a constant theme. Eduardo Frei wrote in a work published in 1952: "He who has a systematic and firm interpretation of the origin and destiny of man can later derive from it his concepts of social organization and the limits of the

---

[30] Jaime Castillo Velasco, *Las Fuentes de la Democracia Cristiana* (Santiago, Chile: Editorial del Pacífico, 1968), p. 105.

state, and have a sense of history. He who lacks this interpretation will be the changing plaything of events." [31] The impact of Maritain's thought is pervasive in Chilean Christian Democratic circles and nowhere more evident than in such discussions of the nature of man.

The proposed communitarian economic system is based on a critique of capitalist notions of private property. In one of the most influential ideological writings on this subject, the authors devote over thirty pages to demonstrating that the early Church Fathers, Saint Thomas Aquinas, and the modern social encyclicals all reject the notion of private property as sacred and inviolable.[32] Communitarian theory, however, also rejects the typical socialist alternative of making the state the major or sole owner of capital and the means of production. Their vision of the communitarian society is of a highly pluralistic economy in which individual enterprises are owned and managed by the workers who supply the labor.[33] The practical problems involved in implementing such a plan in present-day Chile are formidable, and in 1969, after four years in power, the Christian Democrats had still made no serious effort in that direction.

Confronted with this fact in an interview, Radomiro Tomic, widely regarded as Frei's successor, admitted that as a matter of fact Christian Democrats were still confused over the *theory* of communitarianism, to say nothing of implementation. He argued that the thirty years of Christian Democracy was too short a time for the elaboration of a full-blown theory and program. Nevertheless, the history of this period had confirmed the basic contention that neither capitalism nor Marxism was capable of providing valid answers for man in our time and, concretely, for the people of Chile. Tomic held that

31 Foreword to Marcelo Martínez Candia, *Ni Marxismo ni Liberalismo: Social-Cristianismo* (Santiago, Chile: Editorial del Pacífico, 1952), p. 8.

32 Julio Silva Solar and Jacques Chonchol, *El Desarrollo de la Nueva Sociedad en América Latina* (Santiago, Chile: Editorial Universitaria, S. A., 1965), pp. 42–73.

33 Father Mario Zañartu, S.J., of the Centro Bellarmino, has specialized in communitarian economic theory. See his "Hacia una Empresa Comunitaria," *Mensaje,* no. 152 (September 1966).

the elaboration of a communitarian program was indeed a most urgent task facing his party.[34]

The concern with theoretical distinctives, even when these seem to have little practical meaning, is of course a reflection of the highly ideological orientation of the Chilean political culture. The Christian Democrats speak of "neither capitalism nor Marxism" almost in a nineteenth-century view of ideological polarity, and largely ignore the broad tradition of democratic socialism which combines representative government, individual freedom, and extensive state regulation of the economy. Their basic ideas, however, are best understood as part of this broad tradition.[35] And fortunately, Eduardo Frei's government has proceeded with its sound programs of agrarian reform, expansion of the educational system, construction of public housing, and others without awaiting ideological clarifications.

As we conclude this section on the four religious versions of socialism (Hindu, Buddhist, Islamic, and Catholic) the decidedly secondary role of the religious legitimation becomes apparent. Although sincere believers may be convinced that their socialist ideas were derived directly from the social values of their respective religious traditions, the overpowering fact is that today, throughout the third world, secular socialism in some form represents the basic value consensus of the modernizing elites, and religion has had to come to terms with it. Indeed, in some cases socialism may be legitimizing religion more effectively than religion is legitimizing socialism.

TOWARD A SECULAR-PLURALIST SOCIETY

At the same time that religious ideas are being interpreted to support a socialist theory of society, other currents of religious thought vigorously deny the ultimacy of all societal structures, whether associated with religious doctrine or secular

[34] *Prisma,* July 1968, p. 17.
[35] This is recognized by the left wing of the party. "Theoretically, then, it can be said that it [communitarianism] is a variety of socialism. A communitarian socialism, different from state socialism. . . ." Silva and Chonchol, *op. cit.,* p. 74.

ideology. These theological currents see in religiously sanctioned socialism the same idolatry that was found in religiously sanctioned nationalism or capitalism. The temptation, in this view, is always to sacralize the relative and make it an absolute. In various ways, the religious interpretations to be discussed here legitimize social change by rejecting all closed world views and by developing an attitude of complete openness to the future. In its extreme form this can become a denial of any relevance of religion to society. In other forms it suggests that in a secular-pluralist society, religiously motivated individuals and groups may have a prophetic role to play and may in fact help to articulate universal humanist values. But this legitimation of change offers no religious or religio-ideological blueprint for future society. The only guideline offered is a humanism which, drawn from the most diverse sources, has become a consensual value for contemporary man. Implicitly or explicitly, this approach uses pragmatic criteria in evaluating all socioeconomic institutions. Man is indeed the measure of all things, and ideological orthodoxies (religious or political) are becoming increasingly irrelevant.

Spiritualization of Religion. Religion is defined in such a way as to make individual spiritual experience its very essence. The social, economic, political, and even ecclesiastical institutions historically associated with particular religions have little or nothing to do with their essence. This emphasis, of course, represents a very old tradition of mysticism in all the major religions. In medieval times Hindu *bhakti* ("devotion") sects ignored caste, Sufi saints overlooked the shari'ah, and Catholic mystics dispensed with priestly intermediaries. The renewal of this emphasis among contemporary Hindu and Muslim interpreters, however, has new dimensions. The denial of a place to social institutions within the new definition of religion both facilitates radical social reform and defends religion at the point of its greatest vulnerability to Western attack.

Dr. S. Radhakrishnan, the leading exponent of Neo-Hinduism, writes that the whole meaning of religion is spiritual experience, not belief or conduct. Spiritual self-realization is described in these words: "When the individual withdraws his soul from all outward events, gathers himself together inwardly and strives with concentration, there breaks upon him an experience, secret, strange, and wondrous, which quickens within him, lays hold on him, and becomes his very being. Even if God be an idea and has no reality apart from one's ideation, that which frames the idea of God and strives to realize it is itself divine." [36] Radhakrishnan writes that for all schools of Indian thought, Buddhist as well as Hindu, "belief and conduct, rites and ceremonies, authorities and dogma, are assigned a place subordinate to the art of conscious self-discovery and contact with the divine." [37] Hinduism teaches a humanism which is derived from this spiritual consciousness and potentiality of man. The caste system, although useful and beneficent in the past, must now be condemned because in its present form it denies the dignity of man and the preciousness of human life. "The right of every human soul to enter into the full spiritual heritage of the race must be recognized." [38] Spiritual experience is thus the essence of Hindu religion, and the spiritual nature of man the basis of a humanism by which social institutions are judged.

The spiritualization of religion in the Islamic context is well illustrated by the thought of A. A. A. Fyzee, a Shia scholar who is resolutely committed to the separation of law from religion. Religion must be defined in terms of spiritual experience: "While its rules, its ritual and its trappings can be of general application in a community, the inner core of belief is exclusively personal." [39] And again: "Religion is unchangeable in its innermost kernel — the love of God for his own sake is sung by Sufis and mystics throughout the world." [40] The problem for Islam, according to Fyzee, is that the term *shari'ah* embraces both religion and law. Thus the unchangeable, innermost kernel of religion is linked to law, which by its very

[36] S. Radhakrishnan, *Eastern Religions and Western Thought* (London: Oxford University Press, 1940), p. 22.

[37] *Ibid.*, p. 21.

[38] *Ibid.*, p. 378.

[39] Asaf A. A. Fyzee, *A Modern Approach to Islam* (Bombay: Asia Publishing House, 1963), p. 86.

[40] *Ibid.*, p. 87.

nature is relative to time and place. Laws must change and do change as human societies evolve. Fyzee's radical solution is simply that the two things must be separated; the "inner life of the spirit" must be separated from "the outward forms of social behavior," however un-Islamic this prescription might appear.

Fyzee makes it quite clear that modern humanist values provide the criteria by which laws are to be judged, and their relationship to Islamic legal norms is essentially irrelevant. "It is becoming increasingly clear that something good and legal may be entirely outside the rules of *shari'ah,* just as, surprisingly enough, some rules which are unjust and indefensible may be within the orbit of acts permitted by the *shari'ah.*" [41] Fyzee cites in particular the law of divorce now applied to Muslims in India. The spiritualization of religion will leave society without a religious blueprint, but this will only be recognition of the fact that the old blueprint has long since ceased to bear any meaningful relationship to social reality.

Legitimation of Temporal Autonomy. While the Hindu and Muslim interpreters approximate the idea of a secular-pluralist society by indirection and implication, as an inference drawn from their emphasis on the spiritual nature of religion, Catholic thinkers are engaged in developing an explicit and positive doctrine of the autonomy of the temporal. With the encyclicals of Pope John XXIII, the documents of Vatican Council II, and the work of various commentators, there has emerged quite clearly a new notion of the church's role in the world, strongly at variance with the dominant assumptions behind Rerum Novarum.

The starting point for much of the discussion is the following statement in Vatican II's "Pastoral Constitution on the Church in the Modern World" (*Gaudium et Spes*): "If by the autonomy of earthly affairs we mean that created things and societies themselves enjoy their own laws and values which must be gradually deciphered, put to use, and regulated by men, then it is entirely right to demand that autonomy. Such is

41 *Ibid.,* p. 62.

not merely required by modern man, but harmonizes also with the will of the Creator." [42] This principle is specifically applied to scientific research, and the section concludes with the admonition that temporal autonomy should not be interpreted to mean that created things be used by man without reference to their Creator. Nevertheless, the quoted text clearly states that "*societies* themselves enjoy their own laws and values." This emphasis is consistent with the rest of the document, which speaks of "*dialogue* between the church and the world," of the church's desire to serve mankind "without always having at hand the solution to particular problems." [43] As has been pointed out, the documents of Vatican II do not refer to "the social doctrine" of the church, presumably because this expression tends to connote a comprehensive and overarching theory of society, the church's blueprint *for* society.[44] The layman is warned not to expect solutions to complicated temporal problems from the clergy, for this is not their mission. Furthermore, it should not be assumed that there is only one valid Christian view of a particular problem: "It happens rather frequently, and legitimately so, that with equal sincerity some of the faithful will disagree with others on a given matter." [45] In short, the pluralism of the modern world is recognized, and the church does not claim to have all the answers.

The point at which the church opens its dialogue with the modern world is in a common concern for man. "For the human person deserves to be preserved; human society deserves to be renewed. Hence the pivotal point of our total presentation will be man himself, whole and entire, body and soul, heart and conscience, mind and will." [46] Chapter I in *Gaudium et Spes* is entitled "The Dignity of the Human Person," and

[42] Walter M. Abbott, ed., *The Documents of Vatican II* (New York: The America Press, 1966), sect. 36, p. 233.

[43] *Ibid.*, sects. 40 and 33 respectively. (Italics mine)

[44] Pierre Bigo, "Autonomía de lo Temporal," *Mensaje*, no. 153 (October 1966), p. 562.

[45] *Gaudium et Spes*, sect. 43.

[46] *Ibid.*, sect. 3.

although there is an extensive exposition of the Christian view of man, this is preceded by a simple but eloquent statement of the virtually universal consensus on humanist values. "According to the almost unanimous opinion of believers and unbelievers alike, all things on earth should be related to man as their center and crown." [47] The church's concern for man leads to concern with a wide range of social, economic, and political problems, but this concern is primarily expressed not through authoritative pronouncements on specific issues but through the responses of the individual Christian conscience.

In the exposition of Father Pierre Bigo, the church has jurisdiction over the social, but no jurisdiction over society. The church's jurisdiction over the social is based on the fact that the gospel changes all existence, but the church has no jurisdiction over society because its mission is not to rule the temporal order. The church "only intervenes in temporal things through the conscience of the citizen." [48] The "mediation of conscience" means that the church acknowledges the freedom of the layman to make his own decisions in temporal matters. Thus the church affirms both the autonomy of the temporal and its commitment to the struggle for human dignity. As Bigo puts it, John XXIII was both the Pope of the great social encyclicals and the Pope of dialogue with an autonomous modern society.

Religion and Revolution. A most serious engagement of religious thinking with the problems of change and development has been taking place within Latin American Catholicism over the past decade. Unlike Christian Democracy in Chile, which with the Frei government suggests to some a "new Christendom," revolutionary Catholic thought in Colombia, Brazil and elsewhere is based on a radical idea of pluralism. To the late Father Camilo Torres and his followers, the notion of a "Catholic society" had no validity whatsoever. The essence of Christianity was love for man; Colombia's socioeconomic struc-

47 *Ibid.*, sect. 12.
48 Pierre Bigo, "Fronteras de Dos Ciudades," *Mensaje*, no. 142, September 1965, p. 490.

tures were oppressive and dehumanizing, and cooperation with Marxists and other revolutionaries committed to a more just society was necessary.

Camilo Torres, a scion of an influential aristocratic family, entered the priesthood, studied sociology at the University of Louvain, and returned to Colombia committed to a program of radical social change. His convictions regarding the Christian imperative for structural change led him into a United Front with Communists and other Marxists in an unsuccessful effort to unite all revolutionary elements, into conflict with the church hierarchy which resulted in his leaving the priesthood, and later into the Army of National Liberation, a guerrilla movement operating in the mountains. He met death in 1966 in his first armed encounter with government troops. However, Camilo Torres's life of selfless dedication to the cause of the masses has become a powerful symbol throughout Latin America.[49] And in his own Colombia — the traditionalist Catholic country *par excellence* — three years after his death, a group of young priests was calling for an "opening toward Marxism." [50]

The themes of humanism, pluralism, and revolution were so interwoven in Torres's thought that it is impossible to analyze any one of them in isolation. He started with the basic proposition that "the basis of Catholicism is love of neighbor." [51] For such love to be true it must be effective, but it is clear that as interpreted in the past — in terms of paternalistic charity — this teaching has completely failed to solve the problems of the ma-

[49] The first book-length biography of Torres to appear in English is German Guzman, *Camilo Torres* (New York: Sheed and Ward, 1969). For a very useful bibliography and a collection of articles on Torres, mostly in Spanish, see Alejandro del Corro, ed., *Colombia, Camilo Torres: Un Símbolo Controvertido* (Cuernavaca, Mexico: Centro Intercultural de Documentación, dossier no. 12, 1967).

[50] See *Visión* (Mexico City), May 6, 1969, p. 11 and the article by Alberto Lleras, "La Iglesia de protesta," p. 17.

[51] Camilo Torres, "Mensaje a los Cristianos," in *Camilo Torres* (Cuernavaca, Mexico: Centro Intercultural de Documentación, sondeos no. 5, 1966), p. 325. This is a collection of Torres's writings over the last ten years of his life. For an English translation of this collection see Camilo Torres, *Revolutionary Writings* (New York: Herder and Herder, 1969).

terial misery of the majority. Because a privileged minority re-
fuses to sacrifice its privileges, it is necessary to take power away
from the oligarchy and give it to the poor majority. "This,
done rapidly, is the essence of a revolution." Torres thus
brought the Christian teaching directly to the center of the
struggle for change. In a letter to the cardinal archbishop of
Bogotá in 1965 Torres asserted: "I am concerned for all those
who consider the doctrine of the church a beacon of progress
and feel that they would exist only on the margin of history, if
they cannot participate in the fundamental socioeconomic
changes which humanity needs in order to accomplish, even in
part, the supreme precept of charity." [52]

Torres emphasized pluralism as a fundamental characteristic
of present-day society. Concretely, ideological pluralism is evidenced by the existence of Marxism in societies dominated by
other world views. Torres did not gloss over profound philosophical differences. "Communism has a philosophical system
which is incompatible with Christianity, although in its socioeconomic aspirations the majority of its postulates do not
conflict with the Christian faith." [53] Led to a program of revolution by his Christian humanism, Torres finds among the
Communists some of the same revolutionary ideals. "I have
said that I am a revolutionary as a Colombian, as a sociologist,
as a Christian, as a priest. I consider that the Communist Party
has authentically revolutionary elements and, therefore, I
cannot be anti-Communist as a Colombian, as a sociologist, as
a Christian, or as a priest." [54] Torres declared that he would
never join the Communist ranks but that he was ready to
fight with them for the seizure of power by the people.

But Torres's United Front was not based simply on a common revolutionary program. Transcending the ideological differences was a common moral commitment — the commitment
to man. Universal humanist values underlay the various calls
for revolutionary change. The humanist principle of "love thy

[52] Guzman, *op. cit.*, p. 129. This letter and related correspondence is re-
produced in this source.
[53] *Camilo Torres, op. cit.*, sondeos no. 5, p. 269.
[54] *Ibid.*, p. 329.

neighbor" which Torres saw at the heart of Christianity had in fact become the undisputed central value of the modern world, a value subscribed to by Christians and anti-Christians alike. "In a pluralist world the uniting in action for the good of men is a union on a presumably Christian base." [55] He then quoted the words of Pope John XXIII in *Pacem in Terris:* "It must be borne in mind, furthermore, that neither can false philosophical teachings regarding the nature, origin and destiny of the universe and of man, be identified with historical movements that have economic, social, cultural, or political ends, not even when these movements have originated from those teachings and have drawn and still draw inspiration therefrom. Because the teachings, once they are drawn up and defined, remain always the same, while the movements, working on historical situations in constant evolution, cannot but be influenced by these latter and cannot avoid, therefore, being subject to changes, even of a profound nature. Besides, who can deny that those movements, in so far as they conform to the dictates of right reason and are interpreters of the lawful aspirations of the human person, contain elements that are positive and deserving of approval? It can happen, then, that a drawing nearer together or a meeting for the attainment of some practical end, which was formerly deemed inopportune or unproductive, might now or in the future be considered opportune and useful." [56]

Camilo Torres failed on many counts, and his failures have been analyzed in great detail in the voluminous commentaries on his death. He was naïve politically in accepting uncritically the altruistic motives professed by his leftist collaborators, and he vastly underestimated the difficulties of achieving leftist unity. More importantly, he dismissed out of hand, without even a trial, the possibility of building by constitutional means a mass party which could win elections. His thought on the relationship of violence to social change and to human values was simplistic. Nevertheless, when all the failures and ambigu-

[55] *Ibid.,* p. 206.

[56] Anne Fremantle, ed., *The Papal Encyclicals in their Historical Context* (New York: Mentor-Omega Books, 1963), p. 423.

ities are recognized, the question still remains for many Latin American churchmen: Was not Camilo *ultimately* right in insisting that an authentic humanism makes revolution necessary?

A rapidly growing body of literature is seriously examining the "theology of revolution," and the conclusions of the Catholic radicals make Eduardo Frei's "Revolution in Liberty" appear mild and almost innocuous by comparison.[57] Dom Helder Cámara, archbishop of Recife, Brazil, and a leading spokesman of the progressive wing of the church, argues that Latin America's present unjust social structure is in itself a form of violence, that what is urgently needed is a structural revolution, and that the use of violence to achieve it cannot be ruled out. "I respect those who, in conscience, feel themselves obliged to opt for violence, not the too easy violence of the drawing-room guerrilla fighters, but of those who have proved their sincerity by the sacrifice of their lives. It seems to me that the memory of Camilo Torres and of Che Guevara merits as much respect as that of the pastor Martin Luther King." [58]

Emerging Consensus: Humanist Ends, Pragmatic Means. It is clear that the thought of contemporary religious interpreters is coming to terms with what was referred to in Chapter I as "valuational-functional pluralism." There is increasing recognition of pluralism in the sphere of values and belief systems and acceptance of the relative autonomy of various spheres of human existence. For the religions of Indic origin, Hinduism and Buddhism, valuational pluralism presented few problems, but there were serious difficulties in adjusting Hinduism to the notion of a secular society. For the Semitic religions, Islam and Catholicism, adjustment to both facets of pluralism necessitated reformulations of a fairly radical kind.

In coming to grips with pluralism, however, the interpreters

---

57 See, for example, Bernardo Castro Villagrana, *et al., La Iglesia, el subdesarrollo y la Revolución* ["The Church, Underdevelopment and Revolution"] (Mexico: Editorial Nuestro Tiempo, 1968).

58 Dom Helder Cámara, "La Violencia: Opción Unica?," *Informaciones católicas internacionales* (May 12, 1968), p. 7. For a collection of the Archbishop's writings in English translation, see Helder Camara, *The Church and Colonialism: The Betrayal of the Third World* (Denville, N.J.: Dimension Books, 1969).

have rediscovered man. In so doing the Indic religions were at a considerable disadvantage, since it was necessary somehow to disengage man from the nonhuman orders (animals and gods) involved in the same cycle of rebirth. The Semitic religions had perhaps a stronger metaphysical base for the development of humanism, but the traditional view of a theocentric universe presented other difficulties. Indeed, it still comes as something of a shock to read in an authoritative Catholic document, *Guadium et Spes,* that "all things on earth should be related to man as their center and crown."

Whatever the difficulties, the religious interpreters have rediscovered man. A cynic might remark that with the existence of the gods so much in doubt these days, the theologians have done well to anchor religion to a less-questioned reality. If humanism is indeed the meaning of religion, the relevance of the latter will presumably be safe from attack for some time to come. If humanism is the true meaning of religion, however, it will be increasingly difficult to sustain distinctive doctrines and rituals.

Like religious belief systems, rigid political ideologies are being eroded by the contemporary processes of secularization. A spirit of relativism casts doubt on the doctrinal distinctives of all orthodoxies, and in practice Catholic Christian Democrats form stable and effective coalition governments with Social Democrats of Marxist background. But the decline of ideology is not simply the loss of faith. Consciously or unconsciously, it has been an evolutionary process by which many have come to the simple view that the only important normative concept in politics is the well-being of man. Humanist values constitute the only valid ends, and the appropriate means must be discovered pragmatically.

The new articulators of this humanism-pragmatism have little patience with those who would supplement the two-point creed with additional "fundamentals." The democrat's emphasis on procedural consensus is questioned because it ignores the vast socioeconomic inequalities which in most parts of the world deny any meaningful participation and power to the masses. Thus by emphasizing procedures the democrat loses sight of man and, in effect, constructs a system which excludes the majority of men. The new pragmatism with respect to means implies openness to all paths which can lead to a better life for man; violent revolution, as we have seen, is not excluded.

Orthodox Marxism is also questioned because its preoccupation with the class struggle within a rigid historical determinism blinds it to the needs and aspirations of individual men. Communism's willingness to disregard the claims of whole generations of individuals in order to prosecute class warfare seems to many a denial of humanism. And at the same time the Marxist's dogmatic insistence that peaceful methods cannot effect any significant change go contrary to the pragmatism of the emerging consensus.

Most fundamental, in both the Communist and capitalist worlds, it has been the pragmatic search for ways to achieve economic goals which has undermined rigid ideologies. On one hand, decentralization in production and distribution and the use of various profit incentives within the Communist world; on the other, the rapid expansion of welfare-state functions and state regulation of the economy in the capitalist world. In the contemporary world, economic systems are measured by economic and not ideological norms.

All the topics considered in this chapter may be seen as points in a process of ideological change which moves from valuational particularism to valuational universalism. Without suggesting rigid, automatic, or irreversible stages, it is broadly true that religious, ideological, and universalist values, in this order, have oriented Western man's thinking about society. In Figure VII.2 we attempt to identify some major points in this process. Throughout the third world today, the majority of men still perceive their social environment through traditional religious lenses, and all subsequent stages are represented on the contemporary scene. The entire process has two aspects: negatively, the decline of closed world views and the general relativization of thought as a part of *secularization;* positively, as the process exposes the fundamental concern for man, it may be described as *value universalization.*

FIGURE VII.2   *Process of Religioideological Change*

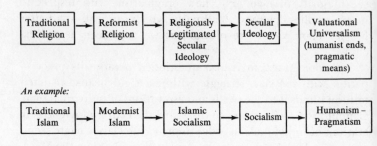

An example:

In Figure VII.2 we have used Islam to illustrate the process: there are individual Muslims whose thinking over the past forty years has moved from traditional Islam through all of the intermediary steps to humanism-pragmatism. Such is the telescoping of the intellectual processes which are a part of modernization in the third world. Modernist Islam emerged from the interaction of traditional religion and Western liberalism; the basic assumptions, however, remained Islamic. Part of the failure of liberalism may be attributed to the fact that it did not constitute a coherent ideology. As socialism began to exert an important influence on intellectuals, serious efforts were made to interpret it in Islamic terms. These efforts tended for the moment to obscure the fact that socialist ideology was a more universal theory than Islam, that, whether accepted or rejected, it spoke relevantly to the problems of all contemporary societies. Islam's universalist vision, like that of Christianity, was in reality capable of concrete realization only by a minority of mankind. The auxiliary role of Islam could be quietly dropped; socialist ideology could stand on its own, at least until it became subject to erosion by relativism.

There are many Muslim intellectuals who have skipped the two socialist stages; their ideological pilgrimage has proceeded from Islamic modernism to secular humanism-pragmatism. Once one has determined that the true meaning of "Islamic society" is "just society," one can forget entirely the shari'ah and other historical embodiments of the idea of justice. In fact, if social justice is indeed the main idea, it is no longer necessary to speak of Islam at all. The purely cultural aspects of Islam may continue to be cherished, but its sociopolitical ideas are no longer relevant. Though secularization has condemned these *ideas* to oblivion, Islamic humanism has made its contribution to the universalization of *values*.

CHAPTER VIII

Religious Systems
and Political Development

THE MAIN ARGUMENTS of this book have centered on four religiopolitical processes: the secularization of polities, the role
of religion in politicization, the influence of religion on political culture, and the formulation of religious ideologies of social change. At numerous points the discussion revealed that a
particular phenomenon cannot be understood as accidental
but as stemming from systemic characteristics of the religion in
question. In this concluding chapter the focus will be on an
examination of the relationships between political development and the four major religions in "whole system" terms.

"HISTORICAL ACCIDENTS"
AND RELIGIOUS SYSTEMS

Many facts having to do with religion are quite unrelated to
religious systemic characteristics. The precise form which the
four religiopolitical processes take in a given society must be
viewed as essentially the result of the interaction of religious
systemic characteristics with a unique complex of elements of
historical particularity. The systemic characteristics of Theravada Buddhism, for example, set the parameters of what responses to its environment are possible and probable. In

Burma and Ceylon this response has included the emergence of political monks as a significant force; in Thailand this has not taken place. The explanation is not that monks in Thailand are inherently less politically inclined than elsewhere but that historical circumstances have been vastly different. The traditional pattern of subservience of Sangha to king was never disrupted by foreign rule, nor was the association of monks with anti-imperialist nationalism ever necessary. Nevertheless, the systemic characteristics which made political monks possible in Burma and Ceylon are also present in the Sangha of Thailand, and this phenomenon may well appear in the future.

Several of the key nonsystemic, historical factors have already been touched on, but it will be useful to set them forth explicitly. First, the patterns of diffusion of the major religions are a basic consideration. In some countries the pattern includes very sizable religious minorities. Thus in pre-1947 India one-fourth of the population was Muslim, and political events revolved around this religious pluralism rather than the systemic characteristics of either Hinduism or Islam. Other countries have experienced successive waves of religious expansion. Indonesia, for example, or at least Java and Bali, came first under pervasive Hindu influence, and the process of conversion to Islam was substantially completed only in the seventeenth century, Bali remaining Hindu to this day. Hindu and syncretist cultural and religious elements remain important throughout Indonesia and have had a significant influence on the political culture of the country.

The second basic set of historical factors concerns the patterns of imperialism — which Western power established its rule, whether it followed a policy of direct or indirect rule, the nature of the institutions (legal, administrative, political, educational) which it established, and in particular, the religious policies it evolved over time. When considering the secularization of polities, for example, we must contrast the British official policy of religious neutrality in India, which was clearly enunciated by the end of the eighteenth century, with the Spanish Catholic pattern of union of church and state which was established in the Philippines and continued until the islands' annexation by the United States in 1898, after which the American principle of separation was imposed.

Thirdly, there are many unique historical events and figures for which we have no truly adequate explanation. The most careful study of Gandhi's life up to the age of forty-five would not have enabled one to predict his enormous impact on India after 1914. Father Camilo Torres, the religious revolutionary, was a Colombian, but an analysis of objective conditions would not lead us to regard the emergence of this kind of leader as more likely in Colombia than in any one of a half-dozen other countries of Latin America. Elements of historical uniqueness abound and continue to defy adequate explanation, to say nothing of prediction.

The notion of system, however, asserts that not all is unpredictable uniqueness, that there are patterns and regularities of interaction which suggest probabilities for the future. It is in this modest sense that the term "religious systems" is used.

The problem, of course, is to find analytic categories which make sense of as many of the data as possible. As previously stated, ideas and structures must be examined in interaction at every point of the analysis, and this rule will be followed here. We shall make use of two distinctions which appear to be fundamental.

First, the historical-ahistorical distinction — one which has long been familiar to students of religion. Historical religions perceive human history as real and even central, for it is the stage on which the divine breaks through to man. Particular historical events are crucial acts of revelation, but all of human history has meaning since there is a divine plan leading to its culmination. History has a beginning and an end, and individual salvation is dependent on what has been revealed in history. It is clear that the concept of revelation *in an objective sense,* as contrasted with individual mystical communion with the divine, is closely tied to the notion of history, and some writers have preferred to speak of such faiths as theistic religions of revelation. Also closely related is the notion that these religions are dogmatic, not in the pejorative sense of this word, but in the sense that great emphasis is placed on propositional truth, or dogma. Truth revealed objectively in history is the same for everyone and therefore absolute.

Ahistorical religions perceive human history as irrelevant to the spiritual quest, although the guidance of religious leaders of the past or present may be useful. History has no divine purpose, no beginning, no end, and may be cyclical in nature. Individual salvation or self-realization is the whole point of the spiritual quest, and historical events bear no significant relationship to the process. The human self-realizational center of the system permits a wide diversity in statements about the nature of the divine, so that theism, pantheism, atheism, and so on, may all be accommodated as valid.

The second major distinction is the structural one introduced in the first chapter, the church-organic distinction. Church religions emphasize as essential and central a particular structure, ecclesia or sangha, an assembly separate from both government and society. A church may dominate government and society or may easily be dominated by government, but its separate identity, in theory and in organizational structure, is clear-cut.

Organic religions, on the other hand, tend to define their collective expression in terms of the structure of an entire society. Sacral law and sacral social structure are of the essence of organic religions. Religion is largely equated with society, and distinct ecclesiastical organizations, to the extent that they exist, are secondary. As the genius of church religions makes for a natural development toward greater complexity in ecclesiastical organization, the genius of organic religions makes ecclesiastical structures secondary at best and ultimately nonessential.

The terms "historical" and "ahistorical" have of course frequently been used to characterize the Judeo-Christian-Islamic (or Semitic) and the Hindu-Buddhist (or Indic) religious streams respectively. The distinction thus not only points to fundamental differences in assumptions and ideas but is sustained by clear-cut differences in historical origin and development. The church-organic distinction, on the other hand, separates Theravada Buddhism and Catholicism from Hinduism

FIGURE VIII. 1 *Analysis of Religious Systems*

Analysis of Ideas

	Ahistorical	Historical
Organic	HINDUISM	ISLAM
Church	BUDDHISM	CATHOLICISM

Analysis of Structures

and Islam, thus cutting across the two streams of historical development. The simple model which results from the joining of the two dimensions is found in Figure VIII.1. This model ignores a myriad of facts about each of these four religions; it does not take into account the considerable diversity within a major religion from one society to another. However, like all such analytic schemes, it seeks to identify the major factors which have the greatest explanatory power. We shall now proceed to test it by reference to the four religiopolitical processes which have been considered: the secularization of polities, the involvement of religion in politicization, the influence of religion on political culture, and the formulation of religious ideologies of change. Our analysis will relate each of the four religious systems to these four sets of religiopolitical interactions.[1]

HINDUISM: AHISTORICAL-ORGANIC SYSTEM

The ahistorical character of Hinduism has often been noted by writers. One of Hinduism's major unifying factors and systemic characteristics amidst a bewildering array of sects and

[1] The four religions will be examined in the same order in which they appear in Chapter II, in which more detailed descriptive material is found. The processes dealt with in Chapters IV, V, VI, and VII will be discussed only briefly, as the object here is to relate them to the analysis of religious systems.

philosophies is precisely the assumption that no objective historical events constitute the revelation of truth for everyone, that the spiritual quest for liberation from the wheel of rebirth, or self-realization through absorption in the Absolute, can be successfully pursued by many diverse paths. Truth for one man may constitute the grossest error (or ignorance) for another, yet the validity of all paths is recognized; caste status, individual capacities, and inclinations determine the choice. History is cyclical, but more fundamentally it is *maya* or "illusion," and modern neo-Hindu interpreters such as Radhakrishnan have struggled valiantly but with limited success to make it meaningful.

The organic character of Hinduism stands in seeming contradiction to part of what has just been said, yet the empirical reality is abundantly clear. The collective expression of Hinduism is not an ecclesiastical structure but an entire society which is organized according to divine prescriptions. The classical concept of varnashrama-dharma, a divinely ordained caste order, tells us much about how Hindu society actually evolved, even though certain varna categories became unclear and were for the most part replaced by *jatis* ("subcastes") as the effective unit of society. The hierarchical nature of the system, with the Brahmans at the apex, continued and in many ways became more rigid as jatis proliferated. The ancient dharmashastras, comprehensive religiolegal codes, formalized inequalities based on varna, and certain of these inequalities were enforced in the Indian courts of law until after independence.

The ahistorical aspect of Hinduism thus promoted completely unrestricted speculation in matters of philosophy and religion and unlimited freedom in the development of new cults and sects. Simultaneously the organic nature of the system resulted in a divinely ordained social structure with detailed regulations which severely restricted the individual in social interactions. These are the two major facts of the Hindu religious system. The contradictions implicit in these two facts were never fully resolved. From the philosophical standpoint, caste regulations along with the whole of society and the phenomenal world were at a lower level of reality, and ultimately maya; the Absolute had nothing to do with caste distinctions or for that matter the existence of individuals. In practice, one who left society to become a *sannyasi* ("wandering holy man") in pursuit of *moksha,* or "salvation," automatically stepped outside the entire caste structure. Historically, the religious seer whose free speculations led him to reject caste distinctions usually started a sectarian movement which in time became an endogamous social unit—in effect, a new caste.

With these few statements of a general nature on the Hindu religious system, we must now proceed to our analysis of the religiopolitical processes which interest us. Unlike our discussion of the other three religious systems, we must here draw primarily on the political experience of a single country, India. Out of the hundreds of Hindu kingdoms which existed on the subcontinent before 1947, Nepal alone remains, although isolated until very recently from many of the historical forces which are associated with political development.

Secularization of Polities. Polity-separation secularization involves the separation of the polity from religious ideologies and ecclesiastical structures. In India this phenomenon has been related to various nonsystemic, historical factors, including the British policy of religious neutrality, Western secular ideologies, and the influence of the large Muslim minority. Hinduism's ahistorical character, however, with its tolerant and relativistic approach to religious differences, constitutes one significant influence on India's effort since independence to build a secular state.

 The organic nature of Hinduism implies that polity-separation secularization does not touch the essential core of the religious system. Far more significant is polity-expansion secularization, the process by which the state extends its effective jurisdiction to perform regulatory and service functions which were formerly performed by religious structures. In India, frontal attacks by the state on untouchability and the caste system in general, and the secularization of Hindu law (a process which has now gone very far), have been at the center of polity expansion. It is obvious that many nonsystemic factors have converged in order to motivate and effectuate these changes. The net effect of this process of polity-expansion secularization has been to disrupt the Hindu religious system most radically and indeed to place its very survival in question. Hinduism's organic character was the basic point when the anthropologist M. N. Srinivas wrote: "If and when caste disappears, Hinduism will also disappear." [2]

No Hindu society has experienced polity-dominance secularization, a revolutionary form of secularization in which the state moves into the purely religious sphere (private belief, worship) in order to destroy or radically alter religion. This fact is closely related to the question of anticlericalism, which is discussed briefly in the following paragraphs.

Role of Religion in Politicization. Seventy-five per cent of the religious element in Indian politics may be explained in terms of the nonsystemic factor of religious pluralism. The communal problem, as it has long been known, has primarily involved conflict between the Hindu and Muslim communities, but serious problems have also arisen involving the Christian and Sikh communities. Most of the basic conflicts have involved the political and economic interests of the different communities (or their respective leaders), and religious symbols have primarily served to represent and sanctify group interests. The political phenomena generated by these conflicts have included savage communal riots, separatist movements (the Muslim demand for Pakistan, the Sikh demand for a separate state in the Punjab), and communal political parties.

The so-called Hindu parties, the Hindu Mahasabha and Jana Sangh, are communal parties, not the proponents of a Hindu blueprint for society. The Hindu Mahasabha became significant, and the Rashtriya Swayamsevak Sangh (RSS) came into existence, in the 1920's during a period of intense Hindu-Muslim conflict; the post-independence Jana Sangh, based on RSS organizational support, continues to feed on anti-Muslim sentiment and communal tensions. The only significant theoretical statement of these groups has involved a definition of

[2] M. N. Srinivas, "A Note on Sanskritization and Westernization," *Far Eastern Quarterly,* vol. 15 (1956), p. 495.

the Hindu nation — again, religion as group identity not belief system.

Closely related to Hinduism's organic character, which has relegated the development of ecclesiastical organization to a minor position, is the insignificance, one could almost say absence, of clericalism in Indian politics. At this point the contrast with many other countries of the third world is striking. On a few occasions *sadhus* (holy men) demonstrated in front of parliament for a law banning cow slaughter, but these few incidents and the politically marginal nature of the issue only serve to underline our basic point.

The near absence of clericalism has had its counterpart in the relative insignificance of anticlericalism. Anti-Brahman movements have developed, and among them the Dravidian movement in the Tamil-speaking areas of South India has been very important. At one stage the Dravidian movement took the traditional priestly function of the Brahman seriously and developed an ideology which was not only anti-Brahman but anti-Hinduism, antireligion, and atheist. The antireligious emphasis quickly faded, however, since the real point of the movement was opposition to a caste which had secured a disproportionately large share of political, social, economic, and educational benefits available in the society. The fact that Brahmans had *traditionally* been priests (by 1947 only a small minority of them were priests by actual profession) became increasingly irrelevant.

Hinduism's organic character manifested in the caste structure has led to the significant political phenomenon of caste associations playing a direct role in politics, supporting their own candidates in elections, maneuvering for representation in state government cabinets, and functioning as interest groups of some importance in the legislative process. This development runs closely parallel to the above-mentioned pattern of communal politics based on the existence of various religious communities.

The undeveloped nature of Hindu ecclesiastical organization and the consequent near absence of clericalism also means that laymen speak for Hindu interests in Indian politics. The

Hindu political parties mentioned earlier, Hindu interest groups such as the RSS and the Arya Samaj (although this originated as a religious sect), are almost entirely organizations of laymen. It is no accident that the most influential religious figure in Indian politics since 1919, a Mahatma ("Great Soul") with uncanny political instincts, was the lawyer trained in England, M. K. Gandhi.

Religious Values and Political Culture. The impact of Hinduism on India's political culture is complex; the major inputs have been pluralist, authoritarian, and hierarchical values. Pluralism is related to the assumption of differences and inequality in the caste hierarchy, but perhaps more importantly to ahistorical Hinduism's assumption that ultimate truth is forever beyond man's grasp, and that therefore an infinite number of contradictory doctrines might be regarded as valid. This relativism has contributed to the nonideological orientation of Indian political culture.

The Hindu parties' communal orientation stems from conflict with the Muslims, but their nonideological stance must also be seen as a function of Hinduism's systemic characteristic as an ahistorical religion. Without a concept of history as meaningful, and without fixed points held to be objectively true, how does one go about constructing a convincing ideology from the Hindu tradition? Where do ideas such as "justice" come from, when the Absolute is without attributes? One can build a philosophy but not an *ideology* of relativism. One could only turn to Hinduism's organic characteristic. A holy man, the Jagadguru Shankarcharya of Puri, did precisely this and, to the consternation of all, announced in 1969 that the blueprint was *varnashrama-dharma,* including the practice of untouchability prohibited by the Indian constitution a generation ago.[3]

Indian political life in general has been remarkably nonideological and pragmatic in nature. There are numerous nonsystemic factors which help to account for this, such as the dominance of the middle-of-the-road Congress Party until

[3] *New York Times,* April 10, 1969.

1967, Nehru's own moderate socialism which evolved slowly from a fairly strong Marxist orientation in the 1930's, and the dynamics of compromise in a democratic political system. Note must also be taken, however, of the prevalence of attitudes and indeed a general atmosphere of pluralism, relativism, and tolerance in the realm of *ideas* which is clearly related to the ahistorical systemic character of Hinduism. India's nonideological and pragmatic political culture owes much to the Hindu world view.

The political culture also contains strongly authoritarian and anti-egalitarian traits. Hinduism's authoritarianism is not derived from dogmatic authority, as we have noted, but from its extensive directive authority, the tendency to impose comprehensive rules to regulate life. The high-caste Hindu, that is, has been strongly conditioned by his religion to conform in behavior. Many of the rules which govern his conduct, both within his caste and in inter-caste relations, concern notions of ritual purity. These regulations are closely related to hierarchical values, the assumption that outside of one's subcaste one can meet only superiors or inferiors, but never equals.

Formulation of Religious Ideologies of Change. To restate the question which was asked in Chapter VII: Can religious systems give ideological support to developing political systems committed to far-reaching socioeconomic change? The answer with respect to Hinduism vis-à-vis Indian development is a clear negative. This is what one would expect from our model and is abundantly clear from empirical evidence.

Hinduism's organic character provides no ecclesiastical structures or procedures by which doctrines can be authoritatively reinterpreted. There are no formal communication networks by which new ideas can be articulated, debated, and finally adopted. There is no Hindu counterpart to the Islamic fatwa or the Catholic encyclical. The reinterpretation of Hindu social doctrine, therefore, has been primarily the work of individuals, and furthermore, of laymen. Although Swami Dayananda Saraswati and Swami Vivekananda in the nineteenth century stand as important exceptions, the generalization is still valid, from the retired civil servant Rammohan Roy who began his work in 1814 up to Gandhi and S. Radhakrishnan in our time.

The Sarvodaya movement, while it makès use of Hindu religious symbols in articulating its message (especially in the person of the saintly Vinoba Bhave), is based on a neo-Gandhian social philosophy stressing social equality, the dignity of labor, village communitarianism, and opposition to industrialization. These ideas, mostly derived from Western sources, as Gandhi frankly stated, have been dressed in Hindu garb. But Sarvodaya has no connection at all with what goes on in Hindu temples, festivals, and other religious institutions. There are no local Hindu youth groups connected with the temples engaged in the study of Sarvodaya philosophy and program, in the way that Catholic Action groups participated in the development of Christian Democratic ideology.

Hinduism's organic character has also meant that the religious interpreters have had to expend vast amounts of intellectual energy in dealing with the question of caste. Any statement of socioeconomic change in the direction of modernization had to start here. Precisely because varnashrama-dharma was so integral a part of Hinduism, it could not be ignored or summarily rejected. This has remained true up to the present day. So the new egalitarian interpretations had to radically reform Hindu religion itself first. Only after the substantial elimination of caste inequality from Hindu social life (obviously still a long way off) could religious resources be directed seriously to other problems of socioeconomic change. Drastic modernizing changes would have to be brought about in Hindu society before it would begin to resemble, say, the typical Theravada Buddhist society as it is today.

The implications of Hinduism's ahistorical character for the formulation of ideologies have already been touched on. If pluralism and relativism in ideas make for a pragmatic political culture (which most Western political scientists would hold to be an asset), they also produce poor raw materials for ideologies. In the absence of anything resembling a prophetic tradition, in the Old Testament or Qur'anic sense of a messenger from God denouncing the evils of society, Hinduism has tolerated the most extreme ideas and practices as long as it was claimed that they had religious sanction. Moral judgments on society were few and far between. Thus the abolition of *sati* ("widow-burning") had to await the coming of the philosophically naïve British who *knew* that this practice contravened the Sixth Commandment and hence was wrong. Moral judgments on society, and a concept of human history as both real and meaningful, are of the essence in the matter of ideological formulation. The development of a convincing Hindu ideology of change to motivate, inspire, and guide the process of modernization in India has clearly not happened yet and seems unlikely in the future.

BUDDHISM: AHISTORICAL-CHURCH SYSTEM

The ahistorical character of Theravada Buddhism stemmed naturally from Hindu religious and philosophical tenets, the wheel of rebirth, the law of karma, a cyclical notion of history encompassing countless aeons. Though Gautama was a historical figure of the sixth century B.C., as the Buddha he was soon relegated to a position of being one among the 550 Buddhas who had preceded him and the many who would follow, in the countless worlds which are eternally created and destroyed. Although the historical Gautama rejected all suggestions that he was more than a man who had attained enlightenment and professed agnosticism regarding the existence of divine beings, an elaborate Buddhist cosmology was soon developed which peopled the universe with many supernatural Bodhisattvas and gods of various ranks, in addition to the reigning Buddha. Although this process was carried much further in Mahayana Buddhism, the Theravada school of southern Asia was deeply affected by it.

Even though the Buddha believed that he had discovered spiritual laws of universal validity and hence sent his monk-followers out into the world to preach the Dharma to all men, his approach was experimental and nonauthoritarian. He explicitly warned against acceptance of the doctrine on his authority and simply invited men to experiment with it and come to their own conclusions. The Buddha's message was one of individual liberation or salvation, a gospel of self-realization. The remarkable expansion of Buddhism throughout most of Asia was achieved without the use of coercive means, and local non-Buddhist cults were easily accommodated within the system.

Theravada Buddhism's systemic character as a church religion was clear from its inception. The Sangha, or monastic order, was founded by the Buddha himself and soon demonstrated considerable capacity for ecclesiastical organization, in the holding of the early great councils, in the elaboration of the Vinaya or code of monastic discipline, in the standardization of the extensive canon of scriptures, in the development of large monasteries, and later, in the evolution of society-wide ecclesiastical hierarchies. Whereas the organic religions developed legal codes for the regulation of entire societies, Buddhism elaborated in the Vinaya, consisting of many volumes, a detailed code for the internal life of the Sangha. The centrality of the Sangha is proclaimed daily by the devout layman in the formula of refuge in the Three Jewels: "I take refuge in the Buddha, I take refuge in the Dharma, I take refuge in the Sangha." Many sophisticated, Western-educated laymen in Burma and Ceylon react with near horror to the thought of a Sangha-less Buddhism.

Secularization of Polities. Polity-separation secularization has had a more drastic disruptive effect on Theravada Buddhism than on the other three systems. For the two organic systems, of course, the reason is clear; their centers did not rest in ecclesiastical organizations, and the severance of these from governments hence had relatively little effect. Catholicism had a more highly developed and complex structure and adjusted quickly to the autonomy which had been forced upon it. The Buddhist church structure, although capable of considerable internal organizational development, was heavily dependent on the king for patronage, the *enforcement* of the discipline prescribed for monks in the Vinaya, and the appointment of the clerical hierarchy in the traditional Buddhist religiopolitical system. The refusal of the British to assume these functions in Ceylon and Burma led to serious disruption, lack of discipline, demoralization, and the decline of the monastic order. In Thai-

land, on the other hand, where the traditional system remained relatively intact, the Sangha remained disciplined and
prospered.

Polity-expansion secularization, on the other hand, had few
adverse effects. As a religion of individual salvation centered
in the Sangha, there was no Buddhist law or sacral social order
to be secularized by the state. Traditional education, it is true,
was centered in the monasteries, and this function was gradually usurped by the polity. However, the state expanded its
educational system largely because the monastic schools failed
to make even modest changes in their curriculum, and the
issue produced no real conflict. Monastic landlordism in Ceylon,
of course, constituted a more serious problem, and in this case
the conservative leadership of the Sangha hierarchy has thus
far succeeded in warding off land reforms which would affect
its interests.

There has been no case of polity-dominance secularization in
a Theravada Buddhist country. In fact, as we shall see, there
has been very little anticlericalism of any kind. Revolutionary
secularization, of course, has been and continues to be an important aspect of Communist Chinese policy in Tibet. But the
Lamaist church there had achieved a measure of socioeconomic-
political power unknown in the history of Theravada Buddhism.

Role of Religion in Politicization. Stemming from its character as a church system, Buddhism's most prominent relationships in the political process have involved the monks as
political actors. Buddhism's ahistorical character suggests that
this involvement has not been ideologically motivated. As a
religion of individual salvation Buddhism provides no ideas
to motivate the political monk and many ideas to discourage
him. As one committed to the quest for Nirvana through a
process of study and meditation designed to eliminate desire,
the serious monk could only regard the passion and struggle
for power which characterize politics as a snare and a delusion.
It was, after all, precisely to avoid such temptations that he
had left the layman's life in society to enter the Sangha. The

Vinaya, furthermore, explicitly rebukes unrestrained monks who are always meddling in the king's affairs.

The nonideological motivation of the monks' intervention in politics is revealed by other facts. After the Mahayana Buddhist monks in South Vietnam had overthrown their third government, Western correspondents pressed the Venerable Tri Quang and his colleagues for a statement of what they were after. The extremely vague replies made it clear that the monks had no blueprint for society; the more important fact, which might have been obscured by circumstances at that time, is that *Buddhism* has no blueprint for society.

Nonsystemic, historical factors go far in explaining the motives for the monks' political intervention. The Sangha constitutes a traditional elite which fell on very hard times with the advent of foreign rule. From a position of high prestige in which the monks, the most learned and respected men in society, instructed princes and advised kings, they fell to a position in which they were increasingly regarded as irrelevant to society by both the foreign rulers and the new Westernized middle class which together usurped their traditional prerogatives. Nostalgia for the traditional past, enmity toward those who have destroyed it, and dreams of its restoration have motivated their politics. Most of their political activity has been oppositional, against foreign rulers in Burma, a Westernized elite in Ceylon, a Catholic dictator in South Vietnam, or others who have been identified as "enemies of Buddhism."

There have been, and continue to be, prominent individual monk-politicians. Associations of monks, such as the United Monks Front in Ceylon, and many such groups in Burma, have played a powerful role. The political importance of these voluntary associations of monks, in contrast to formal Sangha hierarchies, is related to the latter's serious decline under Western rule. Ecclesiastical hierarchies disintegrated completely in Burma and in parts of Ceylon. The traditional Sangha hierarchy remains strong only in Thailand, Cambodia, and Laos, but part of the traditional relationship has been strict monastic discipline and obedience to the king, so it has not become an overt political actor in any independent way in these countries.

The prestige of the yellow robe is still so high in Theravada countries that anticlericalism is a virtually unknown political phenomenon. The assassination of S. W. R. D. Bandaranaike by a monk in 1959, the result of a conspiracy led by another monk, produced only temporary expressions of resentment against monks in general and a flurry of newspaper articles calling for reform of the Sangha. These reforms were recommended in an official commission report but never implemented.

Although the political role of the monks has been a prominent one, the activities of Buddhist laymen have been equally important. Prime Minister U Nu assumed the role of the traditional Burmese king as patron and protector of Buddhism; whatever his motives, this image proved to be politically useful for a considerable period of time. Western-educated laymen formed voluntary associations such as the All-Ceylon Buddhist Congress, which had a significant influence on the 1956 elections.

Related to Buddhism's ahistorical character is the absence of significant political parties which have claimed a Buddhist identity and ideology. Religiopolitical movements of Buddhist resurgence in both Burma and Ceylon were superimposed on essentially secular parties (the AFPFL and the SLFP respectively).

Although not as prominent as on the Indian subcontinent, the nonsystemic factor of religious pluralism in the Theravada countries has led to the politics of communal conflict on occasion: Buddhist-Muslim (Burma and Thailand), Buddhist-Hindu (Ceylon), and Buddhist-Catholic (Ceylon, and Mahayana Buddhist South Vietnam).

Religious Values and Political Culture. Of the four major religions, Buddhism is unquestionably the least authoritarian. As an ahistorical religion it is low in dogmatic authority, making no claim to ultimate truth and assuming that other religious paths may be relatively valid for their followers, since progress toward Nirvana takes place over many existences.

Buddhism's directive authority is almost nil so far as the lay-man is concerned, prescribing only the minimal moral code found in the Five Precepts. The relatively high potential for ecclesiastical organization in the Sangha has never been di-rected to the creation of mechanisms for the supervision and control of the laity. Not only is Buddhism low in terms of authoritarian values; it contains a strong positive emphasis on individualism and self-reliance. Closely related to individual-ism is the Buddhist value of egalitarianism. There are no caste or rigid class divisions in Burma, Thailand, Laos, and Cam-bodia; some anthropologists have referred to these as "loosely structured social systems," explicitly relating this generaliza-tion, *inter alia,* to Buddhist values.

The religious contributions of nonauthoritarian, individual-ist, and egalitarian values to political culture would seem to predispose Buddhist societies toward open, participant politi-cal systems. Historically, however, traditional Buddhist mon-archies have been as autocratic as their Hindu, Muslim, and Catholic counterparts supported by more authoritarian reli-gious values. Nonauthoritarian religious values alone, obvi-ously, are incapable of *creating* democratic political structures. In the absence of other crucial factors, democracy does not develop or survive. Since 1962 Burma has been under military rule, despite a vigorous and relatively stable period of parlia-mentary democracy under U Nu's leadership. Only in Ceylon have the Western institutions continued to function fairly well, with transfers of power between the two major parties in 1956, 1965, and 1970.

Ahistorical Buddhism does predispose a society toward a nonideological, pragmatic kind of political orientation. Even authoritarian governments have been able to arouse very little serious interest in ideological formulations, as General Ne Win found in attempting to promote the "Burmese path to social-ism" as the country's new ideology.

Formulation of Religious Ideologies of Change. While ef-forts have been made to develop the social egalitarianism of Buddhism into a socialist doctrine of economic change and development, the ahistorical, monastic and self-realizational qualities of Buddhism have constituted major obstacles. Theravada Buddhism's major concern, structurally, has not been society but Sangha. Economic development, clearly, is not a likely path to the individual's achievement of Nirvana.

Efforts have been made, especially in Thailand, to mobilize villagers for the tasks of community development through use of the Buddhist notion of merit. For the layman, the acquisition of merit is indeed progress on the path toward eventual Nirvana, and merit making deeds have traditionally included the feeding of monks, building of pagodas, and the like. With declarations by the abbot of a local monastery that the building of a road would earn merit for those participating in the project, an important religious source of motivation could be tapped. The limits of this device, however, soon became evident. Regardless of what the monks said (often at the prompting of government officers), the villagers believed that work on a road leading to a pagoda was more meritorious than work on roads leading elsewhere, and no one believed that merit could be earned by building factories.[4] The artificial manipulation of the idea of merit points up the inherent difficulties in articulating a Buddhist doctrine of socioeconomic development which makes such development a *religious* good in its own right.

The weakness of Buddhist ideas on social reconstruction is evidenced by the kind of changes introduced after the victory of forces of Buddhist religious resurgence in Ceylon and Burma in the elections of 1956 and 1960 respectively. Apart from the increased political influence of the Sangha (by far the most important consequence), the Buddhist programs (1) made *poya* days holidays in place of Sunday, (2) prohibited or restricted the use of alcoholic beverages, and (3) provided for the teaching of Buddhist scriptures in schools and prisons.

The absence of a relevant social ethic has been a matter of profound concern to Western-educated Buddhist laymen. To this end C. D. S. Siriwardane wrote: "If Buddhism is to survive

[4] See the very interesting monograph by Neils J. A. Mulder, *Monks, Merit and Motivation* (Delcalb, Ill.: Center for Southeast Asian Studies, Northern Illinois University, 1969).

it must take its place in society and its principles must influence the changes that are going on. Yet it is clear that within the last century or two Buddhism has contributed little to the social changes that have gone on around us. . . . Buddhism . . . must cease to be purely a monastic religion, and it must provide the solutions for the questions that interest people today." [5] Despite this timely warning, little attention has been given to the development of a positive Buddhist doctrine of social change. The major international journals of Buddhism, including those edited by laymen, are mainly devoted to the detailed exposition of classical Buddhist concepts relating to the path of individual salvation. And a venerable Thai monk told the World Fellowship of Buddhists: "What we need to do is create interest in what is known as the heart of Buddhism; that is, working directly toward the elimination of each individual's defilements. . . . Preaching morality for the benefit of society and the state . . . is less meaningful than self-practice and individual endeavor." [6]

ISLAM: HISTORICAL-ORGANIC SYSTEM

As we move from the two ahistorical religious systems to Islam, the contrast could not be greater. Whereas the Hindu and Buddhist scriptures speak of gods and Bodhisattvas traversing thousands of worlds and millions of years, the Qur'an records Allah's self-revelation to mankind in history. It is a progressive revelation, in which Abraham, Moses, and Jesus prepare the way for the Prophet of Islam. The message calls individuals to faith and obedience as the way of salvation, but obedience means the building of an Islamic social order on earth and in time (history). On the final Day of Judgment men will be held accountable for their deeds, that is, for their acts of participation in history. The historical consciousness of medieval Muslims in India, as elsewhere, produced a succession

5 C. D. S. Siriwardane, cited in Donald E. Smith, ed., *South Asian Politics and Religion* (Princeton, N.J.: Princeton University Press, 1966), p. 509.
6 Bhikkhu Buddhadasa, "The Right Approach to Dhamma," *The Middle Way*, vol. 41 (London, 1967), p. 147.

of major historical works utterly without parallel in the Hindu-Buddhist tradition.

The organic character of Islam is equally clear. The Muslim calendar dates history from a political fact, the establishment of the Islamic community at Madina. The Prophet was not only the leader in prayers but judge under the divine law, commander of the army, and supreme leader of the community in all things political. Early Islam was a thoroughly integrated religiopolitical unity. Islamic law developed to cover the total life of individual and community. Diametrically opposed in concept and tendency to the creation of the Buddhist Sangha, the collective expression of Islam was an entire society.

A clerical group, the ulama, did emerge, not as a separate religious organization, but largely as a function of this organic structure of Islam. The ulama were the learned men who studied and applied the sources (Qur'an and Traditions) of Islamic law. As Muslim society became more complex their interpretations of the law and its application to new situations became very important. Because this legal function was primary, the ulama were closely related to the ruler (caliph, later sultan or king), who in fact by his appointments created whatever ecclesiastical hierarchy developed, from the Shaykh-al-Islam or Grand Mufti down to the judges or other law officers in local courts.

In a preceding section of this chapter we noted the unresolved contradictions between the ahistorical and the organic characteristics of the Hindu system. No such contradictions exist in the historical-organic Islamic system. The word of God which is revealed, which breaks into human history through the Prophet, is precisely the sacred law by which man's total society is to be ordered. This fundamental conviction was expressed by a learned divine in his note of dissent on proposals to change Muslim family law in Pakistan. Opposing recommendations to restrict polygamy and introduce other reforms, he thundered: "In Islam the provisions of the Holy Qur'an and the Sunnah, be they in the form of basic principles or individual laws, are authoritative and final for all occasions

and for all epochs between the time of revelation and doomsday." [7]

   Secularization of Polities. Polity-expansion secularization has
both eroded and attacked frontally the Islamic organic system
in the crucial area of law. The jurisdiction of the shari'ah, or
Islamic law, has been contracting steadily since the early nineteenth century, and this process has accelerated in the twentieth. Islamic criminal law was modified, then replaced, by
Western penal codes in various parts of the Muslim world.
The shari'ah was abolished in its entirety in Turkey in 1926,
but in most Muslim countries it still survives in the law of marriage, divorce, and succession. Almost everywhere, however,
impulses of social reform have compelled its modification, especially in the restriction or abolition of polygamy. An equally
important motive, however, has been the drive to create modern legislative states with authority over the whole range of
social relations within their borders. Thus the 1955 law which
abolished the separate shari'ah courts in Egypt was explained
by an official memorandum in the following terms: "The rules
of public law require that the sovereignty of the state be complete and absolute in the interior, and that all those who live
in it, without distinction of nationality, be subject to the laws
of the country, to its courts, and to a single juridical jurisdiction. . . ." [8]

   Polity-separation secularization has been of relatively little
significance in the Muslim countries. The decisions to delete
the provision that the religion of the state is Islam from the
constitutions of Turkey or the United Arab Republic did not
effect any important structural changes. There was, however,
in these and other cases, a certain symbolic and ideological
significance, a declaration of the aspiration for modernity with
all of its implications of secularism. Then too, such decisions
constituted a clear repudiation of any claims of the ulama to
participation in the guidance of the respective republics.

[7] *Gazette of Pakistan, Extraordinary*, August 30, 1956, p. 1567.
[8] Cited in Nadav Safran, "The Abolition of the Shar'i Courts in Egypt,
Part I," *The Muslim World*, vol. 48 (1958), p. 21.

Wherever the nonsystemic factor of religious pluralism is important, polity-separation secularization naturally takes on greater meaning in terms of the religious minorities' support of the political system. Thus, Ayub Khan's decision after the 1958 coup to delete the word "Islamic" from the official name of the Republic of Pakistan had some positive significance for the sizable Hindu minority, although this was probably not an important consideration for Ayub.

Polity-dominance secularization formed part of Kemal's Turkish Revolution, with the abolition of the mystical orders, the mandatory use of Turkish in Islamic ritual, and the abolition of the traditional mosque school. Despite a sustained ideological hostility to Islamic traditionalism, however, the regime later found it necessary to moderate its religious policies. More recently, Muslim leaders committed to rapid modernization, like Nasser in Egypt or Bourguiba in Tunisia, have found it expedient to affirm their personal faith vigorously while pressing for basic changes in Islam. The strategy of overt opposition to religion, it would appear, entails unacceptable political risks and in particular seriously weakens the legitimacy of a regime. Whereas many have admired Ataturk, few have dared to emulate him.

Role of Religion in Politicization. Throughout the Muslim world, laymen have assumed much of the role of representing Islam in contemporary politics, One such person, M. A. Jinnah, who was not devout personally, functioned as a spokesman for the Indian Muslim community in a situation of communal conflict. Mohammed Natsir of Indonesia, on the other hand, was seriously concerned with the development of a modernist Islamic ideology and program. The most dynamic Islamic movement today is the fundamentalist Muslim Brotherhood, founded by a layman, Hasan al-Banna. The Brotherhood has functioned as an interest group and also as a political party where local circumstances have permitted.

Islamic political parties, with predominantly lay leadership, have been important in the Muslim world. As stated before, there have been no Hindu ideological parties (only communal ones) and no Theravada Buddhist parties of any description.

The existence of the Islamic parties is clearly related to Islam's historical-organic systemic character. There is an authoritative revelation, and it concerns man's total society. The ideological preoccupation of the Islamic parties has divided them into traditionalist and modernizing groups, with much of the inspiration for the latter deriving from Muhammad Abduh's modernist movement in Egypt early in this century. The Islamic parties, both traditionalist and modernizing, have frequently come into conflict with Communist parties, from North Africa to Indonesia, and the ideological element in this conflict has been most pronounced.

As has been pointed out, the organic character of Islam meant that the ulama were relegated to an instrumental role, although an important one, vis-à-vis the sacred law and the traditional ruler, and hence they did not experience the kind of autonomous internal ecclesiastical development found in church systems. Nevertheless, their role in the politics of developing Muslim states has been more significant than our basic model would suggest. Their political influence has been declining steadily since the beginning of this century but is still a force to be reckoned with. The most highly developed and autonomous ulama hierarchy was that found in the al-Azhar mosque-university of Cairo, but the Nasser regime has reduced it to a docile legitimizer of his policies. The most politically vital ulama groups today are voluntary associations, and some of them have been organized by Islamic political parties.

Religious Values and Political Culture. Both the historical and the organic aspects of Islam have given rise to strongly authoritarian values. The dogmatic authority of Islam is high, with its assertions of revealed absolute truth. Its directive authority is equally high, with comprehensive rules to govern the life of the believer. These have tended to condition the Muslim to unquestioning faith and blind obedience, and it is only the absence of a high institutionalization of authority (effective truth-defining and rule-enforcing structures) which mitigates the authoritarianism of the system. Strongly authoritarian Islamic values have profoundly influenced Muslim political culture and predisposed these societies to the acceptance of authoritarian government. Islam has also articulated strongly egalitarian values, which should be more favorable to the development of participant political systems. Egalitarianism in worship, however, has not had an important effect on assumptions regarding political participation.

Islam's high dogmatic authority is associated with an important ideological orientation in Muslim political culture Unlike the Buddhist monks, the ulama have been ideologically motivated — strongly so — in their interventions in politics The ulama, like the monks, are a side-tracked and resentful traditional elite, but their perception of the situation has been ideologically oriented. They have been very vocal on issues relating to the shari'ah, to Islam as the state religion, to Western cultural influences, and especially to the Marxist challenge to Islamic ideology. Prior to the 1955 elections in Indonesia, the ulama of the Masjumi Party issued a fatwa in which they declared that "communist-Marxist ideology and teachings are not only in total conflict with the teachings and law of Islam, but . . . also constitute a dire threat to religion in general and threaten the security of the Republic of Indonesia which is based on a belief in One God." [9] They went on to pronounce, on their own authority, the excommunication from Islam of all those who might accept the communist ideology or join the Indonesian Communist Party.

This generally ideological political culture, however, has been significantly moderated in some cases by other influences. In Indonesia, for example, notwithstanding the vehement dogmatism of the fatwa quoted above, Hindu syncretism has been at work producing much more pragmatic political expressions.[10] Sukarno's pragmatic political style reflected more of his Balinese Hindu mother's tradition than it did the Islam of *jihad* and the Day of Judgment. Nasser's political style, on the other hand, is more akin to Islamic fundamentalism.

[9] Cited in Boyd R. Compton, "Muslim Radicalism: The Anti-Communist Front," *American Universities Field Staff* newsletter, March 5, 1955, p. 7.
[10] See the very interesting monograph by Benedict R. Anderson, *Mythology and the Tolerance of the Javanese* (Ithaca: Cornell University Modern Indonesia Project, 1965).

Formulation of Religious Ideologies of Change. Like the interpreters of the other great organic religious system, Hinduism, the advocates of a modernist Islam have had to struggle very hard to extricate what they regard as the essence of the religion from the structural forms by which it has regulated society. But to separate Islam from law is as difficult as to separate Hinduism from caste. In both cases the state has been more effective than religious reinterpretations in separating the two. Broadly speaking, polity-expansion secularization may also be regarded as a process by which the organic religious systems have been radically redefined. The theories still remain fuzzy, but the facts of the historical process are quite clear.

As an organic system Islam lacks the kind of coherent ecclesiastical organization which could redefine its social doctrine in a methodical way, but as a historical system Islam is not lacking in inspiration and basic perspectives for developing an ideology of social change. For the Islamic message makes one thing unmistakably clear: God is involved in human history as a participant, and social justice on earth is one of His major purposes. Islamic socialism may be the ideological formula which can gather up and articulate this concern for social justice in a relevant fashion. Certainly socialism with its emphasis on equality combined with social solidarity fits in with basic Islamic assumptions far better than the old liberalism did. But it is still too early to say; Islamic socialism may turn out to be little more than a slogan in which a politically weak Islam and an imported socialism trade legitimacy for relevancy.

Quite apart from formal ideologies, Muslim writers find in the Qur'an clear evidence that God wills man's active participation in the task of economic development. The earth is God's gift to man; man's purpose on earth is, first, to worship God and, second, "to cultivate the earth and to establish various and magnificent civilizations, with a full exploitation of the riches of the earth for man's prosperity and happiness. . . . Constructive work, in the light of modern science, is not confined to agriculture or architecture only; it also means the full exploitation of the mineral wealth and the expansion of industry." [11] Although this interpretation contains a new emphasis, it is certainly in keeping with basic Islamic notions, which have never denigrated the material aspects of man's life on earth.

CATHOLICISM: HISTORICAL-CHURCH SYSTEM

Christianity had its origins in the life and teachings of Jesus, who gathered a small band of disciples and went about proclaiming the Kingdom of God. What appeared at first as simply another Jewish sect became a separate religion when, after the crucifixion, the disciples and the Apostle Paul developed a theology which posited the cross and resurrection of Jesus as unique historical events in which God revealed himself to man, superceding and at the same time fulfilling all previous revelations in history.

The notion of church, ecclesia or assembly, was equally clear in primitive Christianity. As a small and persecuted minority in the Roman Empire, the church could not be other than totally distinct from government and society. The Christian church rapidly developed its internal ecclesiastical structure, with organized local congregations led by clergy (teachers, preachers, and, as the sacramental system developed, priests), an ecclesiastical hierarchy of bishops and Pope, and canon law for the regulation of internal church matters.

Developments in medieval Catholicism tended to obscure both the historical and the church characteristics. The dynamic biblical notion of God working and revealing himself in history was largely forgotten after Aquinas adopted Aristotelian categories to express the Christian faith. The resulting world view emphasized a static universe ruled by immutable natural law and a static hierarchical society regulated by sacral social and political institutions.

Medieval Catholicism thus developed strong organic tendencies toward the identification of religion with society. But there are two important qualifications to this statement. First, whatever the church's political pretensions or success in securing

[11] Al Bahay Al Kholi, "On Property and Ownership between God and Man," *Minbar Al-Islam* (English ed., Cairo, January 1962), pp. 25–26.

political power, it remained structurally and organizationally completely separate from the state. Second, no matter how extensive the church's regulatory powers over society became, these could be cut off completely without destroying, or even causing major damage to, the church's essential structure. The important implications of these two facts are that in modern times the Catholic church can be separated from the state, stripped of its societal regulatory functions, but still emerge structurally intact. This is precisely what distinguishes it from the organic religious systems, Hinduism and Islam.

Secularization of Polities. Polity-separation secularization has occurred in half of the Latin American republics. Because of the Spanish colonial pattern of governmental appointment of bishops and archbishops, which was continued by the new republics after 1810, separation of church and state has in fact meant a much greater freedom and autonomy for the church itself. Nevertheless, official Catholic doctrine steadfastly opposed separation until Vatican Council II. Pope Leo XIII declared in his 1885 encyclical "On the Christian Constitution of States": "There must, accordingly, exist between these two powers [church and state] a certain orderly connection, which may be compared to the union of the soul and body in man." [12] He shrewdly noted the fact that such arrangements benefited the state itself by establishing its legitimacy: "The ruling powers are invested with a sacredness more than human," and the subject's obedience "is not the servitude of man to man, but submission to the will of God, exercising His sovereignty through the medium of men." [13]

With such unequivocal official doctrine, church hierarchies everywhere opposed separation. The archbishop of Santiago in 1923 condemned the proposal for church-state separation in Chile as signifying "a public and solemn denial of God, a true and terrible national apostasy." [14] Two years later, however, he

---

[12] Etienne Gilson, ed., *The Church Speaks to the Modern World: The Social Teachings of Leo XIII* (Garden City, N.Y.: Image Books, Doubleday and Co., 1954), p. 168.

[13] *Ibid.*, p. 169.

[14] *La Revista Católica* (Santiago), May 5, 1923, p. 643.

found it possible to accept the fact, if not the principle, of separation. Of the four major religious systems, Catholicism has offered by far the greatest resistance to all forms of secularization.

Polity-expansion secularization has involved a sweeping curtailment of the church's socioeconomic power: the nationalization of extensive land holdings, the secularization of education, the abolition of clerical control over marriage, and so on. This process was begun by the nineteenth-century Liberals, many of whom were inspired by positivist philosophy and ideological anticlericalism.

Polity-dominance secularization in the Mexican Revolution involved violent assaults on all manifestations of Catholic religion — private faith and the celebration of mass were attacked along with church landlordism and clericalism in politics. At its most extreme, school teachers were compelled to profess and propagate atheism, since the consciences of children had to be liberated from "religious prejudice and fanaticism." An official memorandum published in 1935 presented the nature of the larger conflict in these terms: "The stand taken by the Catholic clergy, and its seditious, visionary, and unpatriotic activities, induce it to believe that it will thereby achieve the restoration of inordinate power like that wielded by it in the past, and it fails to take into account . . . the modern state, which no longer circumscribes its functions to the creation of law, but on the contrary extends its action much farther and embraces all matters connected with economic, political, and cultural administration and which has set for itself as one of its specific objects, the extirpation of fanaticism. This is why in the Mexican State the men of the Revolution cannot allow the people to remain sunk in ignorance and sloth. . . ." [15]

Role of Religion in Politicization. As the most highly developed church system, the Catholic Church has the organizational means for effective political intervention and has in fact been a significant political factor from colonial days to the

[15] Emilio Portes Gil, *The Conflict between the Civil Power and the Clergy* (Mexico City: Ministry of Foreign Affairs, 1935), pp. 4–5. Portes Gil was attorney general of the Republic.

present. Unlike the Hindu, Buddhist, and Muslim experience, in which indigenous clerical hierarchies were gravely weakened under Western imperialism, the Catholic ecclesiastical structure in Latin America was an integral part of the Spanish and Portuguese imperial systems and enjoyed extensive state patronage and support, as well as considerable control. With independence from Spain and the emergence of the new republics, the church was able in some cases to enlarge its political role.

Among the four religious systems, only the Catholic ecclesiastical hierarchies (bishops and archbishops), organized on a national basis, have played and continue to play an important political role. A national episcopate is able to command considerable political resources in the lower clergy, and through them the laity, from one end to the other of a country. In the organic religions, Hinduism and Islam, laymen have tended to become the political spokesmen for religion by default, that is, because of the weakness of clerical organization. In Catholicism, on the other hand, the ecclesiastical hierarchy (from the Pope down) deliberately created lay organizations to function under clerical control in the sphere of public affairs. The Catholic Action movement owed its origin in 1930 to the recognition by the hierarchy that the increasingly democratic *assumptions* of public life made the masses (that is, the laity) a key factor in terms of influence on society. The Catholic laity were a largely untapped political resource which had to be organized. As late as 1951 Pius XII spoke of Catholic Action as "an instrument in the hands of the hierarchy." [16] The relative autonomy of Catholic lay interest groups is a very recent development and was not legitimized theologically until Vatican II.

Christian Democratic political parties in various Latin American countries had their origins in the Conservative Party, the traditional Catholic elite party which dates from the early years of independence. The Conservative Party subscribed to a highly theological and traditionalist ideology which saw as its task the preservation of a static, hierarchical, and sacral social

---

[16] Quoted in Gianfranco Poggi, *Catholic Action in Italy* (Stanford: Stanford University Press, 1967), p. 65.

order, in which church and state constituted the two major pillars. Nascent Christian Democracy found this ideology incompatible with the social encyclicals beginning with Rerum Novarum (1891), which responded to the problems of industrial society with trenchant criticisms of laissez-faire economic policies and strong demands for the protection of workers.

Christian Democratic parties have been no less ideological in their basic orientation than the old Conservatives, but they have stressed the universal values found in Christian humanism, especially as interpreted by Maritain, and have insisted that this concept of man implies an unbridgeable gulf between them and Marxist parties. The left wing of the Partido Demócrata Cristiano in Chile, however, has pressed for a more pragmatic approach, pointing out that there is a considerable area of agreement with Socialists and Communists on matters of program. The outcome of this struggle within the Chilean PDC will be of great importance.

Eduardo Frei and others have vigorously asserted the independence of the PDC from the church hierarchy and the nonconfessional nature of the party's political objectives. "Christian Democracy has never endeavored to implement a policy of church privileges, let alone to impose religious belief or to establish Catholicism as the official state doctrine. . . . We have spent our life maintaining that no party has the right to proclaim itself the Catholic party, to assume the representation of the Church, or to take itself to be the only 'orthodox' vessel for those Catholics who are active in public life. . . . We are not concerned with creating a state that is 'decoratively Christian,' full of ostentation and religious emblems, like some that are at present in existence, but a state that is Christian in essence." [17]

Anticlericalism, chiefly related to the secularization conflicts already discussed, has been a prominent political phenomenon in Latin America in the past but has declined greatly in recent decades. One reason for this is that the Marxists, traditional

[17] Cited in Ernst Halperin, *Nationalism and Communism in Chile* (Cambridge, Mass.: M.I.T. Press, 1965), pp. 202–03.

enemies of the Catholic Church, have found unexpected allies within that structure, in politically left-wing priests such as Father Camilo Torres whose revolutionary ideas led him to an early death as a guerrilla. The left wing in the lower clergy has frequently found itself in conflict with conservative bishops, in Colombia, Brazil, Argentina, and other countries.

Religious Values and Political Culture. Of the four religious systems, traditional Catholicism has generated the most strongly authoritarian values. As a historical system, its dogmatic authority is high and has been characterized by unqualified and exclusive claims of absolute truth. Its directive authority has been expressed in the extensive regulation of the laity in personal, social, cultural, economic, and political spheres of life. Catholicism's high institutionalization of authority in a hierarchical church structure has been a major component in the authoritarianism of the system. An infallible Pope proclaims ultimate truth in matters of faith and morals at the top of the hierarchy, and at the bottom a village priest hears confessions, imposes penances, and forgives sins. The hierarchical principle was also explicitly applied to society as a whole, as we have noted, in a patriarchal order which relegated the lower classes to a role of obedience to their natural superiors.

Catholic religious authoritarianism has unquestionably conditioned Latin Americans to the acceptance of and submission to authoritarian governments led by *caudillos* or oligarchies. Authoritarian values in the religious sphere have been reinforced by authoritarian values in family, school, and economic structures, and the net effect has been a political culture highly incongruent with the formal political institutions of representative democracy which Latin Americans have been unsuccessfully attempting to operate since the early decades of the nineteenth century. The rise of Christian Democracy, noted above, is an important phenomenon based on radically different values, but its influence has thus far been significant only in a few countries. Supported by the internal democratization of the church, which has now begun, Christian Democracy may in the future play a major role in the restructuring of Latin American value systems. For the present, however, traditional authoritarian and hierarchical values are still dominant in Latin American political cultures.

Catholicism's high dogmatic authority has tended to produce an ideological political culture in which political differences are related to transcendent, ultimate principles. Bargaining and compromise are rendered difficult, for they involve a betrayal of the truth which is regarded (in its respective versions) as objectively known and absolute. These basic attitudes persist among many Latin American politicians, including those who have long since lost all faith in Catholic dogma.

Formulation of Religious Ideologies of Change. Catholicism, as a historical-church religious system, would appear to have the necessary organizational and ideational resources for the formulation of an ideology of change. However, until Vatican II, the dynamic biblical notion of God working through historical change lay, not rejected but forgotten, beneath a massive theological superstructure formed of static Aristotelian essences. And the organizational genius of the Catholic church was devoted to preserving this conservative world view by an imposing array of bureaucratic devices. Thus it was not simply a widely held Catholic view but the *motu proprio* of a Pope, pronounced in 1903, that it was "in conformity with the order established by God that there should be in human society, princes and subjects, patrons and proletariat, rich and poor, learned and ignorant, nobles and plebeians." And seven years later the same Pius X pointed out that Christians "should maintain that distinction of classes which is proper to a well-constituted city, and should seek, for human society, the character that God, its author, has given it." [18]

Still, it was again the organizational genius of Catholicism which enabled Vatican II to happen, although it came late in the day, long after *individual* Hindu and Muslim interpreters had sought to relate their respective faiths more positively to the modern world. But the Hindu or Islamic counterpart to Vatican II is still inconceivable.

[18] Both of these quotations are found in Thomas F. O'Dea, *The Catholic Crisis* (Boston: Beacon Press, 1968), p. 78.

The recovery of the dynamic biblical view of history was one of the great achievements of the council, expressed most clearly in the remarkable pastoral constitution "On the Church in the Modern World." In O'Dea's words: "The document is deeply committed to eschewing a narrow moralism and an ahistorical ontologism, and to seeking to comprehend the significance of 'man's total vocation' as it is to be observed in our day." [19]

The new emphasis on history in contemporary Catholic thought has strengthened the hand of Christian Democratic ideologists within Latin American Catholicism. It has also laid the groundwork for significant Catholic-Marxist dialogue, and as we have seen in the case of Brazil, Catholic-Marxist collaboration. Regardless of particular ideological developments, the important fact is that Catholicism is beginning to relate itself meaningfully and positively to the developmental process. The 1967 encyclical of Pope Paul VI, *On the Development of Peoples,* although a disappointing document in several respects, calls attention to the dimensions and urgency of the task. In their 1962 pastoral letter the Chilean bishops declared: "Love of neighbor implies a serious responsibility for economic development. . . . This is not a shameful concentration on the material aspect of life but a response to the situation of underdevelopment in which we find ourselves. We do not hesitate to speak of a true 'spirituality of economic development.' " [20] The extent to which these new religious ideas can inspire, motivate, and direct individual and collective action should not be overestimated. Nevertheless, the doctrinal restatement in itself is significant and has at the very least created new attitudes of openness to the developmental process.

19 *Ibid.,* p. 114.
20 *El Deber Social y Político en la Hora Presente* (Santiago: Secretariado General del Episcopado de Chile, 1962), pp. 16, 18.

Index

8-102